THE LIMITS
OF CORPORATE POWER

Existing Constraints on the
Exercise of Corporate Discretion

Ira M. Millstein
Salem M. Katsh

Studies of the Modern Corporation
Graduate School of Business
Columbia University

MACMILLAN PUBLISHING CO., INC.
NEW YORK

Collier Macmillan Publishers
LONDON

Macmillan Publishing Co., Inc.
866 Third Avenue, New York, N.Y. 10022

Collier Macmillan Canada, Ltd.

Library of Congress Catalog Card Number: 80–69280

Printed in the United States of America

printing number

    3   4   5   6   7   8   9   10

Library of Congress Cataloging in Publication Data

Millstein, Ira M
  The limits of corporate power.

  (Studies of the modern corporation)
  Includes index.
  1. Corporations—United States. 2. Industry and state—United States. 3. Decision-making. I. Katsh, Salem M., joint author. II. Title. III. Series.
HD2795.M54   1980   658.4'03   80-69280
ISBN 0-02-921490-4

THE PROGRAM FOR STUDIES
OF
THE MODERN CORPORATION

Graduate School of Business, Columbia University

The Program for Studies of the Modern Corporation is devoted to the advancement and dissemination of knowledge about the corporation. Its publications are designed to stimulate inquiry, research, criticism, and reflection. They fall into three categories: works by outstanding businessmen, scholars, and professional men from a variety of backgrounds and academic disciplines; annotated and edited selections of business literature; and business classics that merit republication. The studies are supported by outside grants from private business, professional, and philanthropic institutions interested in the program's objectives.

RICHARD EELLS
Director

Contents

Foreword

In writing this Foreword I have the privilege of introducing the reader to a book important in at least two key dimensions. Not only is the subject of deep interest and concern to our times, but it is treated from a perspective likely to increase its usefulness in the years to come. The book provides an analytical framework for understanding the basic issues in a complex, emotional and occasionally strident debate cutting across our economic, social and political lives.

The central issue is corporate control: those forces which operate to constrain the discretionary acts of business corporations—especially, but not exclusively, large corporations. Clamorous positions are often taken at the extremes. There are those for whom no amount of corporate control is enough; and there are those for whom any control is too much. It is between these two extremes that most of us—as voters, customers, taxpayers, investors and enlightened citizens—are called upon daily to take positions and endorse or deny exploratory efforts in a complex web of activities. Most of the decisions we make are communicated by our behavior or response, rather than by formal vote. Most of our decisions involve relatively small, "nitty gritty" problems dealing with seemingly minor elements of our daily lives.

It is difficult to perceive the multiplicity of these small, scattered decisions as crucial forces in molding and shaping a vast, incredibly complex, and constantly evolving structure designed to channel the great talents and resources of the business corporation in the direction of the common good. It is even more difficult to impose a rational or historical perspective on our choices. We are almost always asked to make our decisions on an *ad hoc* basis; that is, to reach decisions about quite specific means of achieving some particular goal at a given point in time. We seldom realize that today's decisions may overturn yesterday's, or inhibit tomorrow's.

In achieving a sense of perspective, this book can be of great help. It classifies in the fashion of an encyclopedia the constraints we have so far erected for business activities. It provides the background panorama against which we can better judge both specific proposals and general philosophies about the conduct of our economic affairs. By "restoring the context" it gives much needed protection against demagogues and special pleaders of whatever persuasion.

Five basic approaches for exercising control over the behavior of corporations are discussed in the book's five chapters. The theories behind each approach are set forth; and its mechanics are described in detail. First come the corporate chartering laws of the states, limiting *de jure* what the corporation does and how it does it. Chapter 2 begins with the *de facto* limitations the corporation faces in the laws of supply and demand operating through the market mechanism and the profit incentive. Appropriately, the chapter goes on to discuss antitrust and securities regulation, intended to protect the workings of competitive markets for goods, services and capital.

In Chapter 3 we meet the incentives and deterrents for corporations stemming from the tax system. Especially useful is the systematic cataloging of collateral effects of tax rewards and penalties. In such major corporate decisions as debt versus equity financing, and commitments of resources for the future, these collateral effects can impart a substantial and often disquieting skew to what would otherwise be logical responses to free market forces. Tax legislation clearly demonstrates the dangers of tinkering with powerful economic forces without considering the entire matrix of incentives and constraints which determine economic behavior. Chapter 4 introduces the direct, command-type controls imposed on corporations by federal and state regulatory statutes and administrative codes. The chapter first outlines the theories underlying most regulation (such as natural monopoly, so-called "externalities," overriding social objectives, etc.). It then classifies major regulatory programs in terms of these theories, and finally illustrates their significance by considering their impact on such arenas as labor relations; equal employment opportunity; occupational safety and health; environment; consumer protection; political activity; and energy consumption. Here, too, it becomes clear that government controls often influence the economy in many unintended ways.

Finally, the book concludes with an illuminating chapter on the formative impact of social forces on corporate conduct—with particular attention to public opinion in general and to activist special-interest groups in particular.

Of great value is the book's clear presentation of major anomalies, inconsistencies and incompatibilities which have crept into the system over time, as well as the growing divergence between the intentions of Congress and the empirical results of its actions.

As we move through the 1980's, the public policy decisions we make—about corporate size and governance, industry structuring, regulation and reform, tax incentives, protectionism, government bailouts and the like— will have increasing leverage for good or ill on free enterprise as we have known it in this country. Before we conclude that what exists is inadequate, or move in panic to plug loopholes, thorough understanding of controls we already have put in place is essential.

For this reason especially I would hope this volume finds its basic and broadest use in the classroom. The curricula of today's business and law schools would be greatly enriched by this kind of vivid picture of the environment in which the business corporation is created, grows and evolves over time. We have here a basic text for all serious students of the corporation and for all with sincere concern for its future.

BORIS YAVITZ
Dean, Graduate School
of Business
Columbia University

Acknowledgments

This book embodies the efforts of many of our colleagues at Weil, Gotshal & Manges, with whom we approached its preparation as a project calling upon many of the areas of expertise the law firm comprises. Philip J. Harter deserves singular mention for the concept and substantial drafting of Chapter 4, as does Jeffrey L. Kessler for both his drafting and editorial contributions. Substantial contributions were made by Nancy L. Buc, Howard Chatzinoff, Michael R. Cooper, Mark H. Gallant, Joseph W. Gelb, Martin D. Ginsburg, Simeon Gold, Bennett S. Gross, Mark A. Jacoby, M. Stuart Madden, Robert L. Messineo, Kenneth Rubin, Bruce H. Turnbull, Mark A. Vogel, and Alan J. Weinschel, all of whom either drafted or reviewed important segments of the manuscript. The assistance of our paralegal supervisor, Deborah J. Lee, in proofreading and processing drafts of the manuscript is also gratefully acknowledged.

Additionally, we wish to thank: L. Earle Birdzell, Jr., for his valuable editorial comments on the entire book and his preparation of an initial draft of the section on market constraints in Chapter 2; David C-H Johnston, who prepared an initial draft of Chapter 5; and The Business Roundtable, for its financial contribution in covering a portion of the expenses incurred in the preparation of this book. We wish to emphasize, however, that all views and statements set forth in this book are our sole and exclusive responsibility, and do not necessarily reflect the views of Weil, Gotshal & Manges, any other organization, Messrs. Birdzell and Johnston, or any other individuals.

IRA M. MILLSTEIN
SALEM M. KATSH

Introduction

The large corporation promises to remain at least as much center stage in the next decade as it has in the recent past. It will be dissected, debated, reviled and revered; it will receive advice and admonition. It will certainly be the subject of further regulation and quite possibly of further legislation on its size, governance, accountability, and responsibilities, as well as its legal, political, economic and social performance.

The public has generally appreciated that the corporation's *raison d'être* is the efficient provision of useful, needed goods and services—spurred by the profits essential to produce and provide them. Now, however, there is a growing insistence on the rationalization of that corporate purpose with expanding social demands concerning the environment, employees, the consumer, the community, and the political process. But just how this is to be brought about remains vague—even in the minds of the most vocal critics of the *status quo*.

The historic discomfort with large corporate size and the assertion of a need for new means of corporate governance appear to us to be opposite sides of the same coin; they are part of an historical and philosophical love/ hate relationship toward private ownership which is unique to this country. On the one hand, the nation traditionally leans toward pluralism, of which private ownership and enterprise is a key part; and, accordingly, it has knowingly afforded private enterprises vast opportunities throughout the economy, even in such key areas of national concern as energy distribution, communications and transportation. (We are one of only a few countries which have done so.) On the other hand, our society is increasingly suspicious of the uses to which the very opportunities it has granted private enterprises are being put. The nation is repelled by the nationalization of business or by its over-regulation, but is equally repelled by corporate libertinism. This has been and is the historic/ philosophic climate in which the debate has evolved; the larger corporations grow, especially as their economic performance becomes totally intertwined with the national interest, the more severe the philosophical schizophrenia.

We believe a continuing examination of corporate size and governance is healthy; every major institution in our pluralistic society must be able to justify its existence, in present or modified form, as the society continues to develop. One thing the sixties and seventies have taught us all is that no institution is sacrosanct. But it is equally apparent that the issues raised must be examined through analysis and reasoned debate. The issues are too complex, and the ultimate actions too important, to relegate them to sloganeering, rhetoric and demagoguery.

Today, however, with increasing momentum, we are urged to reject the kind of reasoned analysis needed to chart a course in these murky waters in favor of a visceral "corporate power" argument. Large corporate size, it is now asserted, brings with it discretionary powers which can be—and are being—undemocratically used in disregard of societal objectives and the public interest.

Ralph Nader, the consumer advocate, and Mark Green, director of Public Citizen's Congress Watch, articulated the extreme view of this "power" contention on the Op-Ed page of *The New York Times* (December 28, 1979):

> We must redesign the law to keep up with the economic and political evolution of giant corporations, which are tantamount to private governments. One definition of "government" would be "an entity that can tax, coerce or even take life. . . .
>
> They [giant corporations] can spend decisive amounts in elections determine which towns thrive and which gather cobwebs, corrupt or help overthrow foreign governments, develop technology that takes lives or saves lives. . . .
>
> . . . The economic government [giant corporations] is largely unaccountable to its constituencies—shareholders, workers, consumers, local communities, taxpayers, small businesses, future generations.

This strident and partisan concept of substantially unrestrained corporate power and discretion is, in a more moderate form, among the most important fundamental public concerns with large corporations. However expressed, there appears to be widespread fear that corporate managers have significant *unrestrained* discretion to make critical choices regarding a myriad of economic, social and political issues touching the lives of every citizen—including, to name but a few: what products and services to offer; what prices to charge; whether to invest in existing lines of business, to build new lines or buy out existing companies; where to locate corporate headquarters and new facilities; what plants to open and close; whether to adopt measures to protect the environment and conserve energy; whether to adopt worker benefit, safety and health programs; which philanthropic endeavors to favor; and so on.

At issue ultimately is whether the nation, in responding to these concerns, will essentially continue its traditional preference for pluralism. Will it accept larger private corporate size as it does larger governments and seek only to adjust the corporation's relationship to society where absolutely necessary? Or will it, instead, accelerate the decline of pluralism either by relegating ever greater responsibility in all areas to government, or by requiring fundamental changes in the internal government structure of our major corporations? Or will the nation adopt some combination of the above courses of action?

How then to select directions? We believe the essential first task is to examine closely the environment which presently circumscribes the ambit of corporate choices, and to determine whether there are identifiable and specific problems beyond the claims of "power" and "discretion." Certainly, in developing a reasoned analysis of the power and discretion concerns, it will not suffice to contend that corporations do not possess discretionary power. The function of a corporation being the assembly of capital and labor to produce goods and services, it necessarily must possess the "power" to make and implement a host of decisions, ranging from the most insignificant (the color of the carbon copy) to the potentially global (the opening or closing of a mine or plant in Montana or Gabon), with a full range in betweeen (the TV or radio program to sponsor; the research and development funds to expend; the safety of products; employee benefits; participation in local community affairs, charitable institutions, political activity). But acknowledging the existence of corporate discretionary powers does not logically compel or even support the contention that the discretion is of an *unlimited* and *unrestrained* character.

The existence of discretionary powers and the existence or absence of limitations on how they are exercised are two very different matters.

It becomes, therefore, of enormous importance in the

first instance—and it is the purpose of this book—to classify and describe the types of existing limitations on corporate discretionary powers. Finding "uncontrolled discretion" and "private governments" would be one thing, and might suggest one realm of solutions, such as size limitations, broad-scale divestiture, centralized government planning, etc., some or all of which might alter irrevocably the balance in our pluralism. Finding limits on discretion would be quite another matter, and might suggest a different realm of solutions more readily accommodated within the nation's traditional framework. The severity of the "solutions" must be related to the urgency of the identified problems.

Examining existing constraints and limitations on discretionary corporate power has an added benefit for the current debate on corporate size and governance questions, and hence on the future of the large corporation. We believe the public finds the large corporation an enigma; there is a difficulty in perceiving its decision-making process. In contrast to a debate in Congress on a new law or to a hearing in court on a contested issue, or to the visible checks and balances in our constitutionally created government, opportunity for public examination of the forces that mold corporate conduct is rare. Thus, the more closed process of corporate decision making fuels suspicion and fears of autocracy—fears that corporate discretion is subject to no meaningful checks and balances. An inquiry into the constraints that do exist on the exercise of corporate powers will help to illuminate the corporate decision-making process, and, we hope, remove simple suspicion as a basis for such corrective action as may be needed.

At the same time, it is important to emphasize that the essentially empirical analysis set forth in this book cannot and does not adopt normative positions on the further questions whether the large corporation is "sufficiently" limited in the exercise of its powers in any or all areas, or whether particular constraints are "good" or "bad" either in some absolute sense or as measured against alternatives. Undoubtedly, some readers will conclude that a sufficient number of effective constraints exist in all (if not too many) areas, while others will assert the inadequacy of the present matrix on both quantitative and qualitative grounds. And there will obviously be a wide spectrum of opinion in between. What we stress here is only that a complex matrix of constraining forces does exist, and that if the country is seriously concerned about the issues of corporate size and governance, it behooves us all to enter the discussion with a solid basis of facts about the accountability of corporations today.

1

Organic State and Federal Constraints Relating to the Creation, Structure, and Management of the Business Corporation

A description and analysis of the environment within which the modern corporation functions, and the manner by which that environment controls corporate activities, must begin with those state and federal laws which govern the creation of the corporate entity and define its organic powers and responsibilities.

This chapter outlines the basic, representative provisions of those state and federal laws. Particular emphasis will be given to trends in the responsibilities and accountability of directors, arising from judicial interpretation of state corporation laws and from the activities of the Securities and Exchange Commission. From this analysis,

1

it will be seen that organic laws set limits on the corporation's discretion by directing that it be created and governed as specified by law, and no other way.

The business corporation is fundamentally a creature of the law,[1] which evolved as a mechanism to enable many investors to share the large-scale risks in such business ventures as railroad and canal companies, banks and post-Industrial-Revolution manufacturing. The corporate form offered the further advantage of limited "owners' " (i.e., shareholders') liability for the corporation's debts and obligations—in contrast to the unlimited exposure of sole proprietors and partners.

Initially, charters were granted only by act of state legislatures; general incorporation laws, permitting chartering by a simple registration procedure, came about late in the nineteenth century. Nearly all domestic business corporations have been created under state law.

State corporation laws set forth the procedures and formalities for corporate action. They allocate certain decisions to the board of directors and others to the shareholders. They describe the duties and liabilities of corporate directors to shareholders and the public. They specify procedures for resolving shareholder challenges to director decision making. They reflect the basic bargain essential to the corporation's mobilization of the funds of its investors: the managers of the corporation will conduct the business in the interests of their many principals.

Overlaid on state corporation law are a variety of federal standards which further influence the processes of corporate management and decision making, e.g., the federal securities laws and regulations of the Securities and Exchange Commission ("SEC").[2]

Recently, the SEC has required increased disclosures on such matters as "management integrity," to enable

2

shareholders better to control management's exercise of its discretionary powers. The same policy has given rise to the emergence of the "independent audit" committee of the board of directors to oversee management decision making, and to increased supervisory responsibilities for specialists—particularly lawyers and accountants—who deal on a regular basis with corporate managers.[3]

State Law

The most comprehensive organic constraints on the business corporation are found in state corporation statutes.

1. Regulatory Approaches

Viewed practically, an analysis of these organic constraints must have as its focal point the General Corporation Law of the State of Delaware.[4] Aside from being most often selected by large public companies as the State of incorporation, Delaware has had a substantial effect upon the enactment, implementation and revision of the corporation laws in other states. All state corporation statutes follow similar lines insofar as they establish that corporations are chartered by the state and are free to act only in accordance with their organic charter and the state's statutory requirements. While the statutes generally authorize broad discretion to corporate management (i.e., directors and officers) in the normal running of business operations, they differ in the degree of protection accorded minority stockholders and in the types of corporate action for which specific stockholder approval is required.

Historically, the Delaware statute minimized restrictions on corporate management; this led to Delaware's becoming the most popular state of incorporation. Recently, however, judicial determinations have cut back on the Delaware statute's liberality.[5]

New York, the second most popular state of incorporation for large corporations, is considered to have a rather "restrictive" statute; management's discretion is more limited and the interests of shareholders and creditors are given more weight. California's corporation law is even more restrictive, maintaining a policy in favor of shareholders and creditors at the expense of management discretion.[6]

The Model Business Corporation Act (the "MBCA"), which has been adopted in substance by 35 states, has become a major point of reference in the continuing revision of state corporation statutes. The MBCA reflects the liberal attitude toward management discretion evidenced by the Delaware statute, but is somewhat more responsive to the interests of shareholders.[7]

2. Corporate Formalities

State corporation laws are almost exclusively concerned with the creation and internal governance of the corporation; in particular, with the relationship of shareholders to management. The older practice of restricting a corporation's powers to specifically defined lines of business often raised questions as to whether its managers were acting *ultra vires*. Today, this restriction is usually limited to special fields of corporate activity, such as banking or public utilities.

Certain corporate powers have always been reserved to

4

the shareholders exclusively; shareholders have clearly defined legal rights to review, and in some cases to initiate, proposed corporate actions. Typical kinds of corporate actions which management normally may not implement absent prior shareholder approval (unless otherwise provided in the corporate charter and/or bylaws) include: election and removal of directors, adoption and amendment of bylaws, and approval of so-called "organic" changes. These formalities are intended to limit management's ability to alter unilaterally the corporation's basic structure and scheme of governance.

Election of Directors

Most states require that directors be elected by the shareholders at annual meetings.[8] A majority of state corporation laws provide that vacancies occurring during a director's term of office may be filled by the remaining members of the board of directors; the remaining states require that vacancies and newly created directorships be filled exclusively by the shareholders.[9] In general, a director may be removed by the shareholders for cause; some certificates of incorporation permit a director to be removed without cause by a majority vote of the shareholders.[10] State corporate laws also set standards for membership on the Board of Directors and for membership on committees created by the Board.

Adoption of Bylaws

Many modern statutes provide that in certain circumstances bylaws may be adopted by the directors.[11] Historically, however, the power to make or amend bylaws has belonged to the shareholders.[12]

Merger, Consolidation, or other "Organic" Changes

In all states, shareholder approval is required to merge the corporation into or consolidate it with another corporation, to sell all or substantially all of its assets, to dissolve the corporation, to reduce its capital, or to amend its certificate of incorporation.[13] Moreover, in many states, the shareholders may themselves initiate an action to dissolve the corporation.[14] A similar limitation on the powers of the board is that the shareholders generally must approve all increases in the authorized number of shares of the corporation's stock. Finally, most states provide shareholders with an opportunity to dissent from proposed corporate actions which would affect their rights and preferences, and to obtain the appraised value of their shares in cash.

Nondelegable Board Responsibilities

Certain corporate actions are reserved for the sole consideration of the entire board of directors and may not be delegated to any board committee.[15] These include, for example, such matters as initiating amendments to the certificate of incorporation or adopting an agreement of merger or consolidation. Moreover, while the conduct of the corporation's day-to-day operations is generally delegated by the board to the corporation's officers, transactions "outside the ordinary course of business" are usually treated as nondelegable. Major capital investments and entry into new lines of business are common examples of such transactions.

Disclosure Requirements

State disclosure requirements have a significant constraining impact on actions by corporate management. For example, with regard to "interested director transactions,"[16] state laws generally provide that contracts or transactions between a corporation and one or more of its directors or officers may be void or voidable unless proper advance disclosure is made to the corporation.

Shareholders may also have the right to require disclosure of the corporation's stock ledger and certain other of its books and records, and to make copies or extracts. This right has frequently been invoked in shareholder derivative suits.[17] Many states allow shareholders to invoke court action to compel such inspection, should the corporation's management refuse.[18] The scope of "proper" interests for which such inspection may be ordered (e.g., to ascertain whether the corporation is being mismanaged, or to obtain information for use in litigation against or in the name of the corporation) is expanding. So are the types and numbers of records subject to inspection on request. Both phenomena are evidence of the recent trend toward greater public scrutiny of the inner workings of corporations.

State corporation statutes also require corporations to give notice of all meetings of shareholders;[19] and in the case of special meetings, most statutes require that the purposes for which the meeting is called be stated in the written notice. Formalities such as the maximum and minimum time for giving notice exist in order to prevent management from attempting to evade notice requirements either by giving notice too late for shareholders to formulate a response, or so early that the circumstances may change or the issue may not be fresh in the shareholder's mind.

Whenever action is to be taken at a meeting of shareholders with respect to an amendment of the certificate of incorporation, the notice of such meeting, whether it be a special or an annual meeting, must set forth the amendment in full or a summary of the changes to be effected thereby.[20] Corporations are prevented from putting into effect such amendments unless they are first filed with the appropriate authority in the State of incorporation.[21] Similarly, in the case of mergers, certain documents must be filed, and official tax clearance must frequently be granted, before the merger can be consummated.[22]

Finally, many states require that an annual franchise tax report be filed.[23] Such reports generally require the disclosure of the registered office of the corporation; the name of the corporation's registered agent for the receipt of service of process; the location of its principal place of business; the names and addresses of all of its officers and directors and the dates their terms expire; the date selected for the next annual meeting of shareholders for the election of directors; and the capitalization of the corporation. These requirements, along with the other filing and notice obligations delineated above, are intended to insure that the shareholders, and in certain instances the State of incorporation, are aware of actions taken or proposed to be taken by the corporation.

3. Recent Procedural Trends

An area of potentially influential state regulatory power over corporate management has recently developed in relation to the principle of "choice of law." Historically, the internal affairs of a corporation have been constrained solely by the law of the State of incorporation, without regard to where the corporation actually conducted most of its business. Recently, however, a flexible "choice-of-law" principle has begun to develop which would permit "host" states—where the corporation is doing a substantial amount of business—to apply their own laws to internal corporate disputes when such states have a significant interest therein—for example, when a significant number of the corporation's shareholders are citizens of the host state.[24] Another approach would require a foreign corporation, as a condition of doing business within a state, to consent to be governed by the local law.[25]

The significance of these trends is that corporate management may no longer be able to rely upon the corporate law of its State of incorporation for principal guidance; the company's activities may be circumscribed as well by the laws of states where it does business, or where a certain percentage of its shareholders reside. This choice-of-law movement may add significant limitations on the exercise of management discretion; it may also create serious problems of equality in the rights of shareholders residing in different states.

4. Duties of Loyalty, Care and Fairness

The discretionary powers of management are subject to a number of specific duties.[26] The New York statute

9

sets forth a typical standard defining a director's duties of loyalty and care:

> Directors and officers shall discharge the duties of their respective positions in good faith and with that degree of diligence, care and skill which ordinarily prudent men would exercise under similar circumstances in like positions.[27]

Delaware does not have a specific statutory test, but indirectly provides one by allowing indemnification of a director only "if he acted in good faith and in a manner he reasonably believed to be in or not opposed to the best interests of the corporation."[28] California combines the Delaware "good faith" and "best interests" tests with New York's "prudent man" standard. However, California imposes an additional burden of "reasonable inquiry" on the director, a provision which is implicit in the MBCA as well.[29]

In addition to statutory requirements, directors are subject to common-law duties of loyalty and due care. The concept of loyalty is reflected in the prohibition against personal gain by the director, either by taking personal advantage of a business opportunity arising through his relationship with the corporation or by taking part in a business transaction with the corporation. The director's duty of care includes the obligations of attending meetings and ensuring that there are good faith bases for relying on counsel or upon the books or records of the corporation.

The director's duty of loyalty to his corporation has many ramifications and is a basic factor influencing and constraining his conduct. Violation of this duty constitutes grounds for invalidating contracts between a corporation and a director (including contracts relating to the director's compensation), and for the recovery by the corporation of the profits made by a director (and any resulting damages to the corporation) arising from transactions with the corporation or with others where the director's fiduciary duty to the corporation makes it improper for him to engage therein.

The "corporate opportunity" doctrine is one facet of this broad concept of fiduciary duty which deserves special mention. This conflict-of-interest rule provides that an officer or director of a corporation may not acquire for personal profit a business opportunity which rightfully belongs to the corporation. Any profits derived by corporate officials in breach of this duty are held in constructive trust for the benefit of the corporation, and, in certain cases, damages also may be recovered from such corporate officials. In ascertaining whether the appropriation of the opportunity violated the official's fiduciary duty to the corporation, some states scrutinize the good faith and loyalty of the officer or director in light of the surrounding facts and circumstances.[30] Other states, however, apply a "strict-trust" approach which imposes a more rigorous standard of fiduciary responsibility. Once a corporate opportunity is identified, this strict-trust approach penalizes personal appropriation of the opportunity regardless of the fairness of the official's conduct.[31]

A related subject concerns the duties of majority shareholders in so-called "corporate freezeouts," in which a majority of shareholders vote for a merger in order to eliminate minority shareholders. Two recent decisions of the Delaware Supreme Court have given assistance to minority shareholders by holding that the majority had the burden of establishing the "entire fairness" to the minority of the freezeout merger.[32] Subsequent lower court decisions have interpreted these cases to permit judges to pass upon the economic necessity, desirability and feasibility of the contested action.[33]

11

5. Recent Limitations on the Scope of the Business Judgment Rule

The so-called "business judgment rule" was developed to distinguish between those actions by directors which should be subject to judicial challenge and those which should not. The rule is based on the principle that, unless the board of directors acted in bad faith, their business judgments should not be displaced by those of an individual shareholder, or by the courts.[34]

Recent developments with respect to the business judgment rule are integrally related to the recent increase in the number of shareholder derivative suits. Traditionally, derivative actions could be maintained only if the shareholder demonstrated that the directors were personally involved or interested in the alleged wrongdoing in a way which impaired their exercise of an independent judgment in deciding not to commence a suit on behalf of the corporation, or that the directors' refusal to sue reflected a breach of trust or similar act of bad faith. Derivative actions were therefore defeated when the board's refusal to sue represented an honestly exercised business judgment, even if it proved to be an unsound one.[35]

A number of recent cases, however, indicate that, in certain circumstances, the business judgment rule may not necessarily be applied to shield unreasonable decisions, even assuming good faith on the part of the board.[36] It has been suggested that the presence of "interested directors" on the board may taint the independence and integrity of the outside directors whom they appoint, so as to preclude application of the business judgment rule. To be sure, a 1979 Supreme Court decision[37] recognized the continued general application of the business judgment rule; but even there, the court left open the possibility that some overriding federal policies, including, perhaps, certain provisions of the federal securities laws, may prohibit application of the business judgment doctrine in certain circumstances.[38]

In connection with the foregoing, it is relevant to note that the number of derivative lawsuits by disgruntled shareholders alleging director mismanagement has escalated tremendously in recent times. One source reports that within the thirty-month period preceding August 1973 "some 4,500 securities law suits, charging everything from false earning statements to unfair merger terms, have been filed in the federal courts."[39] On the rise were not only suits predicated on well-established and long-identified director liabilities, but also those seeking the creation of new liabilities by judicial construction. Indeed, the threat of litigation has caused many potential directors to decline, and many elected directors to resign, board membership rather than face the possible hazard of loss of business reputation and personal fortune.[40]

The derivative cases have also had the effect of imposing judicially-enforced requirements on boards of directors to investigate alleged management wrongdoing. For example, based upon certain recent decisions, a board faced with knowledge of potential wrongdoing on the part of corporate officers or directors may be obliged to impanel a special audit committee of independent directors to conduct a full-scale investigation.[41]

Federal Law

1. Regulatory Approach

In recent years, the federal securities laws have played an expanding role in the extension of management's fiduciary duties and in investor protection. The cornerstone of these laws is the broad disclosure requirements imposed by both the Securities Act of 1933 (the "1933 Act") and the Securities Exchange Act of 1934 (the "1934 Act").

The purpose of the federal disclosure requirements is to protect the investor by enabling him to make an informed decision before engaging in any securities transaction. But in addition, the federal disclosure requirements have had the concomitant effect of constraining public corporations from engaging in wrongful practices they would be required to disclose. They encourage more informed and reasonable corporate decision making—and at higher organizational levels—than might otherwise be the case.

2. Proxy Regulation

The proxy rules adopted by the SEC under the 1934 Act impose full disclosure requirements upon management in soliciting shareholder proxies in respect of listed and registered securities. Rule 14a-3 states that no solicitation can be made unless each person solicited has been furnished with a written proxy statement containing information with respect to, among other things, (i) any interest by certain persons (directors, nominees, etc.) in matters to be acted upon, (ii) principal shareholders, (iii)

the identities of directors and executive officers, (iv) remuneration of directors and officers, (v) relationships
with independent public accountants, and (vi) certain financial matters.[42] In addition, if the solicitation is made
on behalf of management and relates to an annual meeting of security holders at which directors are to be
elected, an annual report, including financial statements
audited by independent certified accountants, must be
furnished to shareholders. Further, Rule 14a-7 provides
that the corporate issuer must provide to a shareholder
who desires to communicate with other shareholders a
list of all persons solicited.[43]

Rule 14a-8 relates to shareholders' rights to raise social
issues and other proposals through the medium of the
corporation's proxy materials.[44] The rule provides that a
proposal is not a proper subject for action by security
holders "[i]f it clearly appears that the proposal is submitted by the security holder . . . primarily for the purpose of
promoting general economic, political, racial, religious,
social or similar causes," as distinguished from promoting the corporation's welfare. Not surprisingly, the question of what constitutes a "proper subject" has been the
source of a great deal of controversy; but, with certain
exceptions, the general trend has been to liberalize the
scope of matters which the shareholder may propose.[45]

3. "Negative Disclosure" Requirements

Corporations have become subject to increased reporting requirements under the 1934 Act with regard to so-
called "negative disclosures." These requirements have
the effect of deterring various corporate actions believed
to be undesirable. For example, the summary of operations required in a public corporation's Form 10-K annual

report filed with the SEC must be accompanied by a management discussion and analysis of all material negative factors explaining why historical operations may not be indicative of future operations or earnings.[46] Similarly, Form 10-Q, the quarterly SEC form for reporting interim and unaudited financial information, explains the significance of the operating results reported, including footnote or other disclosure of negative sales and earning developments.[47] The format of this disclosure is similar to the management discussion and analysis required by Form 10-K. And, in the monthly "special-events" reporting form—Form 8K—material defaults upon senior securities must be reported.[48]

The Arab Boycott of the mid-1970's is a contemporary case in point illustrating how such "negative disclosure" requirements tend to limit corporate discretion. SEC Form S-1, which must be filed in connection with the registration of securities, requires the disclosure of information with respect to significant corporate operations and interests in foreign countries. For companies with material interests in Arab countries, compliance with the boycott would appear to be an item of required disclosure under Form S-1. Further, since the description of the registrant's business in the Form 10-K annual report must specify the emphasis, if any, on foreign operations, information as to boycott participation may be necessary to release a report that is not misleading. In addition, to the extent that the definition of "materiality" with respect to disclosure is expanded to include matters beyond financial relationships and data, such as the quality and integrity of management, participation in the Arab Boycott may be considered a reflection on management integrity and disclosable as such.[49] In each case, the existence of such disclosure requirements will tend to deter management from participating in a boycott or similar type of activity which it believes investors, the SEC, the media or other corporate constituencies might consider improper. In this connection, the SEC's role in administering the Foreign Corrupt Practices Act has had the practical effect of expanding the role of the SEC in constraining management activity through the use of disclosure tools.

4. Corporate Governance

Various proposals have been advanced to enhance the part played by stockholders and directors in the management of the corporation and to narrow correspondingly the role of corporate officers. Certain disclosure requirements have added the real but imponderable force of public opinion to the influences guiding the corporate decision-making process. These developments constitute trends affecting the structure of the corporation, its sensitivity to legal constraints imposed by other laws, and its responsiveness to public opinion (see Chapter 5).

SEC consent decrees mandating organic changes in corporate management are part of this picture. So too are the SEC's voluntary disclosure program on questionable payments,[50] its disclosure procedures with respect to defensive tactics in connection with potential takeover bids,[51] "going private" transactions,[52] and its regulations requiring shareholder consent to remuneration plans. Also prominent on the scene are federal judicial decisions promoting the maintenance of objective procedures for decision making and disclosure of management and controlling shareholder practices.

The SEC has also used its proxy rules to further corporate governance objectives. In December 1978, it issued proxy rule, form, and schedule amendments to provide shareholders with information about the structure, composition, and functioning of the corporation's board of directors. These rules require a proxy issuer to list specified relationships it may have with all nominees for its board of directors. In addition, issuers now are required to furnish information in the proxy statement about director resignations, committee functions, directors' attendance at board and committee meetings, the terms of settlement of proxy contests, and the functions and independence of the corporation's auditors.

In late 1979 the SEC amended the proxy rules to provide shareholders a still greater voice in corporate governance. Management is allowed to vote the proxies of shareholders only after the shareholders have been given the opportunity to expressly abstain from voting on each proxy matter, as well as to approve or disapprove each matter other than the election of directors. The new amendments also require that the shareholders be provided with a proxy card which indicates whether it is solicited on behalf of management and which permits shareholders to vote for or against individual board candidates.[53]

While these new disclosures are clearly intended to constrain the conduct of corporate management, it is noteworthy that they appear to depart from the mainstream of historical SEC regulations, which focused on the disclosure of information material to stockholder investment decisions. The new disclosure requirement with respect to director attendance at meetings, for example, seems primarily designed to encourage better attendance. The SEC's rules requiring the disclosure of remuneration paid to top corporate officials seem intended to inhibit corporations from adopting what shareholders might consider "excessive" compensation programs. Finally, the limitations on discretionary voting by management seem to require certain democracy standards not ordinarily associated with the operations of a public company.

Notes

1. For another view, *see* Henssen, *In Defense of the Corporation* (1970).

2. Other provisions of the securities laws, such as the disclosure requirements applicable in connection with the issuance of stock, and proscriptions on capital market manipulations, are dealt with in Chapter 2, relating to the free market system and the antitrust and securities laws.

3. *See* p. 13 *infra*.

4. *Del. Code*, tit. 8, §§101 to 398 (1979).

5. *See, e.g., Singer* v. *Magnavox Co.*, 380 A.2d 969 (Del. Sup. Ct. 1977).

6. *See N.Y. Bus. Corp. Law* §§101 to 2001 (McKinney 1963 Supp. 1979–80); *Cal. Corp. Code* §§1 to 2300 (West 1977 and Supp. 1979).

7. ALI-ABA Model Business Corporation Act §1–152 (1979 rev.).

8. *Cal. Corp. Code* §600(b) (West 1977); *Del. Code*, tit. 8, §211(b) (1979); N.Y. Bus. Corp. Law (McKinney 1963); MBCA §36 (1979).

9. *Cal. Corp. Code* §305 (a) (West Supp. 1979); *Ill. Ann. Stat.* ch. 32, §36 (Smith-Hurd Supp. 1979); *N.Y. Bus. Corp. Law* §705 (McKinney Supp. 1978-79) (vacancies created by the removal of directors); MBCA §38 (1979) (vacancies may be filled by directors).

10. *Cal. Corp. Code* §303 (West 1977); *Del. Code*, tit. 8, 141(k) (1979); *N.Y. Bus. Corp. Law* §706(b) (McKinney 1963); MBCA §39 (1979).

11. *E.g., Del. Code*, tit. 8, §109(a) (1979); MBCA §27 (1979).

12. *N.Y. Bus. Corp. Law*, §601(a) (McKinney Supp. 1978–1979); MBCA §27 (1979) (power to alter, amend or repeal by-laws shall be vested in the directors unless reserved to the shareholders in the certificate of incorporation).

13. *E.g., Cal. Corp. Code* §§903, 1201 (West 1977 and Supp. 1979); *Del. Code*, tit. 8, §§241, 251, 271 (1979); *N.Y.*

Bus. Corp. Law §§804, 903, 909 (McKinney 1963 and Supp. 1979-1980); MBCA §§59, 65, 79, 83 (1979).

14.   *E.g., Cal. Corp. Code* §1903 (West 1979); *N.Y. Bus. Corp. Law* §1103 (McKinney 1963); MBCA §83 (1979).

15.   *Cal. Corp. Code* §311 (West Supp. 1979); *Del. Code*, tit. 8, §141 (c) (1979); *N.Y. Bus. Corp. Law* §712 (McKinney 1963 and Supp. 1978-79); MBCA §81 (1979).

16.   *See, e.g., Cal. Corp. Code* §310 (West 1977); *Del. Code*, tit. 8, §144 (1979); *N.Y. Bus. Corp. Law* §713 (McKinney Supp. 1978-79); MBCA §41 (1979).

17.   Such a suit is in the name and on behalf of the corporation alleging wrongdoing on the part of directors and/or majority shareholders and seeking an accounting to the corporation from third persons. *See* Goldman, *Delaware Corporation Law —Shareholders' Right to Make an Informed Judgment*, 32 Bus. Law. 1805 (1977).

18.   *Del. Code*, tit. 8, §220 (1979); *N.Y. Bus. Corp. Law* §624(d) (McKinney 1963); MBCA §52 (1979) (refusal of right of inspection also creates liability to corporation for 10% of value of shareholder's shares).

19.   *Cal. Corp. Code* §601 (West Supp. 1978); *Del. Code*, tit. 8, §222 (1979); *N.Y. Bus. Corp. Law* §605(a) (McKinney Supp. 1978-79); MBCA §29 (1979).

20.   *Del. Code*, tit. 8 §242(c) (1979); MBCA §59(b) (1979).

21.   *Cal. Corp. Code* §906 (West Supp. 1979); *Del. Code*, tit. 8, §241 (1979); *N.Y. Bus. Corp. Law* §805(c) (McKinney Supp. 1979-80); MBCA §62 (1979).

22.   *E.g., Cal. Corp. Code* §1103 (West Supp. 1979); MBCA §§74(b), 128(d) (1979).

23.   *E.g., Cal. Rev. Tax Code* §23501 (West Supp. 1979); *Del. Code*, tit. 8, §502 (1974); *N.Y. Tax Law* §211(1) (McKinney Supp. 1979-80); MBCA §132 (1979).

24.   *See, e.g.,* Note, *Corporate Regulation*, 46 Cincinnati L. Rev. 846, 851 (1977).

25.   *Cal. Corp. Code* §2115 (West Supp. 1979); *N.Y. Bus. Corp. Law* §§1301-1320 (McKinney 1963 and Supp. 1979-80); MBCA §107 (1979).

26.   Without specifying minimum standards itself, the Federal securities laws have, in effect, adopted the state standards by the application of Rule 10b-5 under the Securities Exchange Act of 1934, which prohibits fraudulent practices. *See* Chapter 2 *infra*.

27.   *N.Y. Bus. Corp. Law* §717 (McKinney 1963).

28.   *Del. Code*, tit. 8, §145(a) (1979).

29. *See Cal. Corp. Code* §317(c) (West Supp. 1979); MBCA §5(c) (1979) (indemnification shall be made by the corporation only upon a determination that indemnification is proper because the director, officer, employee or agent has complied with the standard of conduct set forth in the statute). Some of the corporation laws, such as New York's expressly, establish similar standards of conduct for corporate officers.

30. *Schreiber v. Bryan,* 396 A.2d 512 (Del. Ch. 1978).

31. *Tennessee Dressed Beef Co. v. Hall,* 519 S.W. 2d 805 (Tenn. Ct. App. 1974).

32. *Singer v. Magnavox Co.,* 380 A.2d 969 (Del. Sup. Ct. 1977); *Tanzer v. International General Industries, Inc.,* 379 A.2d 1121 (Del. Sup. Ct. 1977). *See also* 44 Fed. Reg. 46736 (1979).

33. *See Bell v. Kirby Lumber Corp.,* 395 A.2d 730 (Del. Ch. 1978); *Najjar v. Roland International Corp.,* 387 A.2d 709 (Del. Ch. 1978), *aff'd,* 407 A.2d 1032 (1979).

34. *E.g., Karasik v. Pacific Eastern Corp.,* 21 Del. Ch. 81, 180 A. 604 (Del. Ch. 1935).

35. *See, e.g., Blish* v. *Thompson Automatic Arms Corp.,* 30 Del. Ch. 538, 64 A.2d 581 (Del. Supreme Court 1948); *Abbey* v. *Control Data Corp.* 460 F. Supp. 1242 (D. Minn. 1978); *McKee* v. *Rogers,* 18 Del. Ch. 81, 156 A. 191 (Del. Ch. 1931). *See also, The Demand and Standing Requirements in Stockholder Derivative Actions,* 44 U. of Chi. L. Rev. 168, 171–172 (1976).

36. *See, e.g., Gall* v. *Exxon Corp.,* 418 F. Supp. 508 (S.D.N.Y. 1976); *Bernstein* v. *Mediobanca Banca di Credito,* 69 F.R.D. 592 (S.D.N.Y. 1974).

37. *Burks* v. *Lasker,* 99 S. Ct. 1831 (1979).

38. *See Galef* v. *Alexander,* 615 F.2d 51 (2d Cir. 1980); *Lewis* v. *Anderson,* 615 F.2d 778 (9th Cir. 1979).

39. Marget, *Accounting—The Audit Committee—A Progressive Move toward More Meaningful Financial Reporting,* 3 J. Corp. L, 400, 408 (Winter 1978), quoting Hershmann, *Sue, Sue, Sue: The Angry Stockholders,* Dun's Rev., at 25 (Aug. 1973).

40. Sloate, *Outside Corporate Directors: Will Increasing Liability Send Them Running Out of Boardrooms?,* 48 N.Y.S. B.J. 618 (1976).

41. *See, e.g., Report of Investigation in the Matter of Stirling Homex Corporation Relating to Activities of the Board of Directors of Stirling Homex Corporation* [1975–1976 Transfer Binder] Fed. Sec. L. Rep. (CCH) ¶80,219.

42. 17 C.F.R. §240.14a-3 (1979).

43. 17 C.F.R. §240.14a-7 (1979).

44. 17 C.F.R. §240.14a-8 (1979).

45. See Exchange Act Release No. 12999 (Nov. 22, 1976); Roth, *The Arab Boycott and the Federal Securities Laws*, 5 Sec. Reg. L. J. 318 (1978).

46. Securities Release No. 5992 (Nov. 7, 1978), 43 Fed. Reg. 53250 (1978).

47. Exchange Act Release No. 10547 (Dec. 13, 1973), 39 Fed. Reg. 1261 (1973).

48. 4 Fed. Sec. L. Rep. (CCH) ¶31,001.

49. Roth, *The Arab Boycott and the Federal Securities Laws*, 5 Sec. Reg. L. J. 318 (1978).

50. For a description of the SEC's voluntary disclosure program on questionable payments, see BNA Sec. Reg. & L. Rep. No. 353 (1976).

51. Exchange Act Release No. 16385 (Nov. 29, 1979), 44 Fed. Reg. 70349 (1979); Exchange Act Release No. 15230 (Oct. 13, 1978).

52. 44 Fed. Reg. 46736 (1979).

53. Exchange Act Release No. 16356 (Nov. 23, 1979).

2

The Economic Constraints Imposed on Corporate Decision Making by the Free Market System and the Antitrust and Securities Laws

THE bodies of state and federal law which define the corporation's organic powers and responsibilities constitute a first tier of constraints on its discretionary powers. The corporation, being wholly a creature of the law, must exist and govern itself as provided by law, and in no other way. In turn, a second tier of constraints comes into play as the corporation commences its operations and begins to fulfill its entrepreneurial function.

The United States has traditionally been committed to a free enterprise economy. This chapter will first describe the free market system's complex array of checks, balances, rewards and punishments which pervasively influences business activity and constitutes the most fundamental limitation on the exercise of corporate discretionary powers. Thereafter, it will discuss the antitrust and securities laws, which were passed to protect the free market system. The antitrust laws were designed to prohibit corporate conduct which limits the operation of free market forces in the product and service sectors of the economy. Thus they proscribe price-fixing agreements, market divisions, collusive output restrictions and bidding arrangements, anticompetitive mergers and other kinds of commercial agreements which tend to displace consumer choices by producer choices.

The securities laws, similarly, were designed to ensure that the allocation of capital resources is directed by market forces, and to that end they compel the disclosure of a broad range of information required by investors and they outlaw various practices, such as insider trading, which tend to subvert the operation of market constraints.

The System of Market Constraints

1. The Market System—An Overview

The day-to-day operations of corporations organized for the purpose of conducting a business are guided by what business people call "business considerations" and what economists call "market constraints."[1] Market constraints are the dominant forces guiding business decision making in our economy. Examples of the market's effectiveness are commonplace. Almost every large company has an "Edsel" in its past, a reminder of the penalties the market will impose when consumer preferences

24

are miscalculated. The initial high prices and then the rapid decline in the prices of calculators and other consumer electrical products is a more recent example of the market in operation. It demonstrates how the market induces efficiency and technological progress by rewarding with high profits those who innovate successfully. It also shows how the market then reduces prices; new firms are lured into the market by the high profits being earned, with the resulting increased competition forcing prices down.

To be sure, if particular business problems (e.g., what mix of widgets and gidgets to produce) are looked at in isolation, it may not always be possible to perceive that the market provides a clear, unequivocal answer. This is as much true for a farmer as it is for the chief executive officer of a large corporation. What market constraints in fact constrain is not so much single decisions as the stream of decisions by which the business corporation is operated and controlled. One of the merits of a free market system is that it allows traders a wide latitude for mistakes; and, given that latitude, business executives make mistakes aplenty. What determines the ability of a corporation to survive and to prosper more (or less) than its rivals is its capacity to maintain a higher over-all percentage of positive decisions: more right ones and fewer (and less costly) wrong ones. The tests of "right" and "wrong" in this context are market tests.

The decision stream has to be channeled along two main lines. One is toward keeping the corporation's costs (production, marketing, etc.) as low as possible, and the other is toward keeping the corporation's productive resources centered on those products for which customer demand is high and customer willingness to pay money, in the face of competing product and service offerings, is also high. These objectives are socially desirable: the first reflects the desirability of not wasting economic resources, and the second reflects a preference for giving consumers that pattern of output most nearly in conformity with their wants.

The market system provides reward and penalty motivations which constrain corporations to stay in these channels. The reward is higher profits; the lower the corporation can get its production costs, the higher will be its returns at *any* given price. The penalty is provided by the fact that a corporation which fails to keep its costs under as close control as its competitors will find itself underpriced and in competitive difficulty. Thus, while the market obviously does not prevent businessmen from making bad moves, nor tell them what are the good moves—except in retrospect—it furnishes both profit incentives and loss penalties for keeping the decision process in channels defined by market constraints.

Of course, the free market system is not the only means used to achieve business sector conformity with societal objectives. Sometimes the solution which would be tendered by market forces is undesirable or inconsistent with overriding public policy objectives, as described in Chapter 4. But, as the following brief outline of the principal elements of the system shows, its constraining powers are the ones which society relies upon in most situations —and nearly always in the first instance—to steer corporate behavior.

2. The Principal Elements of the Market System

Voluntary Trading and Private Property

Most of conventional economics is based on the proposition that trade will not take place unless both parties believe they will be benefitted. A market system also pre-supposes that the seller and buyer each own what they are trading. Ownership implies that the goods or services in question will have a value to the buyer and the seller; this value in turn will directly influence the traders' perceptions of the benefits they can derive from trading.

Alternatives and the Right of Withdrawal

In a market system, trading is a right, not an obligation. If B does not wish to do business with A, there is assumed to be a C, D, or E, with whom he can do business instead; or, he can decline to do business at all and even withdraw from the market. The proposition is basic that in a competitive market a seller lacks the power to force upon a buyer a product the buyer does not wish to buy (or a price the buyer is unwilling to pay). This may be contrasted with the public sector, in which there is usually only a single source of government services, with no right of withdrawal (refusing the services and returning the tax bill unpaid). It is the availability to consumers of alternative traders and offerings—different producers offering alternative products and services which can be substituted for one another at different points along a continuum of interchangeability—that underlies the forcefulness and constraining power of the market system.

Conflict Resolution

The market system is filled with conflicts convention-ally subsumed under such headings as intra-industry competition, inter-industry competition, international competition, competition among buyers for limited supplies of goods, competition among workers for jobs and promotions, and competition among employers for limited supplies of human skill and competence—to name a few. There is, for example, a conflict among hundreds of shoe manufacturers, located both in the United States and abroad, for hundreds of millions of shoe orders annually in the U.S. When properly functioning, the market continuously resolves the conflict of how much will get produced, by whom, and at what prices; and it respectively rewards and penalizes those companies that do and do not respond effectively to changes in consumer demand.

The market likewise plays a substantial part in conflict resolution internal to business corporations and other organizations. For example, competent managers of a corporation will seek the services of the best employees at the lowest possible cost consistent with the company's employment policies and objectives.[2] But they operate under the market constraint that valuable employees can frequently obtain employment from other businesses. A corporation thus finds itself limited by a market which could deprive it of the labor force it desires if its terms of employment are not competitive. While nominally "free" (within certain legal parameters) to offer any wage, the corporation's discretion in this regard is constrained by the threat of substantial market penalties if it does not offer terms of employment, including job security, retirement benefits, and the like, that are competitive with those being offered by other businesses (as well as by opportunities for self-employment).

Conflict resolution in the capital market operates in much the same way. Good investment and managerial decisions, resulting in higher profits to the corporation, will tend to attract capital; poor managerial decisions leading to poorer financial results, will discourage capital investment. Again, the corporation's management has the nominal freedom to make poor choices; if it did not, it would lack the ability to make any decisions. But, in a market system, the penalties for poor decisions will be as real as the rewards for managing resources and innovating effectively and for correctly anticipating and responding to supply and demand factors. To remain viable, a corporation is forced, on average, to make economically sound choices.

The Complexity of Economic Organization

A modern economy offers consumers an enormous variety of goods and services. It is no longer a simple question of producing enough "food"; consumers as a class constantly express preferences for thousands of different kinds of food, ranging from beans (of numerous kinds) to Bordeaux of the 1970 vintage.

Moreover, the determination of what mix of products to produce is only the beginning of a series of enormously complex and interrelated equations facing the corporation. Every consumer is constantly trying to answer questions of the form, "How much more of X could I buy if I cut back a bit on Y or substituted some of Z?" To succeed, corporations must correctly anticipate when and where consumers want certain products to be produced and made available.

Further, the corporation must make intelligent choices among the various combinations of capital, equipment, labor and raw materials that can produce similar quantities of output. Broadly speaking, an economic input, such as labor, is said to be priced "efficiently" when there is no alternative use which will yield a greater return and when the substitution of greater quantities of other inputs (such as capital or raw materials) will also not yield a greater return. If the two conditions are not met—if corporation A, for example, fails to solve this problem effectively—the system presents obvious opportunities for corporations B, C, D, etc. to meet consumer demand in a way that uses up fewer total resources. Corporation A will thus be constrained to become as efficient as its competition; if it does not, it will face substantial economic penalties.

Decisions relating to the use of resources must be made by business organizations and other market participants for millions of differently related inputs—the infinite varieties of human skills, raw materials, components, and capital equipment that are available. Entrepreneurs are constrained continuously to rethink their investment strategies, production processes and product plans in an attempt to come up with the optimum choices that will satisfy consumers at the lowest cost today and tomorrow. (A product that is very desirable to consumers at one point in time, may be far less desirable only a few years later—e.g., hulahoops, convertible cars, miniskirts).

Innovation

The market likewise disciplines corporate management to be innovative by rewarding the trader who discovers successful products, new production methods and forms of business organization. The hundreds of millions of R&D dollars spent annually by business corporations in fact represent only a small portion of their total efforts to find the better mousetrap, or better ways of making it, or better ways of selling it or more attractive substitutes for it.

Constraints on Investment

Business corporations customarily test investment proposals by estimating future net cash flows resulting from each proposed investment project, and comparing the return on investment implied by these flows to the stockholders' opportunity cost of capital. The value of a stockholder's shares is increased if the (hoped for) rate of return on a project exceeds that which the stockholder could obtain elsewhere. If a project is adopted which fails to meet this test, the value of outstanding shares in the corporation is diminished.

These facts have far-reaching implications in that they limit the discretion of management in allocating corporate resources. The reduction of firm value resulting from bad investment decisions creates powerful incentives to "eliminate" the source of that loss, i.e., current management. This can be accomplished either by action of present stockholders via their board of directors, or by takeover bids from outsiders. These considerations also explain, in part, such phenomena as corporate diversification. The focus is on the magnitude of future net cash flows rather than on the nature of the project creating them. Thus, once it becomes evident that further investment in a corporation's traditional line of business will not generate earnings equal to those which may be achieved in another line using the same corporate resources, the corporation will be constrained to deploy its resources into such other fields.

Legal Regulations Designed to Preserve the System of Market Constraints

Because of the principal reliance placed on the free market system to allocate economic resources in the product, service and capital sectors of the economy, Congress and the states have enacted comprehensive schemes of antitrust and securities laws designed to protect against monopolies, unreasonable restraints of trade, fraud, stock manipulations, and other acts and practices which would prevent the system's effective operation. These laws form a matrix of norms which have become an integral part of our economic system; they are rules of the road and substantially influence innumerable corporate decisions which take place on a day-to-day basis—whether having to do with raising, cutting or maintaining the level of prices; opening or closing plants; acquiring or merging with another company; selling stock or assets; entering into licensing agreements involving know-how, technology, patents, trade marks or copyrights; organizing and participating in joint ventures; organizing distribution through wholly-owned or franchised dealers; doing business in South Africa; participating in trade association functions; or the like.

1. The Antitrust Laws

The antitrust laws protect the operation of market constraints in the product and service sectors of the economy. They have been described as "a comprehensive charter of economic liberty aimed at preserving free and unfettered competition as the rule of trade."[3] They apply, with only limited exceptions,[4] to virtually every aspect of business behavior in interstate commerce—from the operation of a professional sports league[5] to the manufacture and distribution of sanitary pottery.[6]

The primary objective of antitrust regulation, as noted above, is to prevent corporations from taking any action which might significantly weaken the constraining force of the market system. For example, the antitrust laws: compel corporations to price their products unilaterally rather than through agreements with other producers; prohibit them from merging with their principal competitors, or setting the resale prices of articles they distribute, or conditioning the purchase of one article on the sale of another; and generally restrict them from discriminating in price among customers, or limiting the territories of their distributors, or engaging in joint ventures, where the effect of such activities may be to restrain trade unreasonably. Backing up these prohibitions are numerous and substantial enforcement mechanisms, including criminal penalties, injunctions, and treble damages. Indeed, the potential repercussions are so substantial in their cumulative impact that some corporations may actually run the risk of bankruptcy if they participate in activities which are found to contravene the antitrust laws. Many corporations, therefore, have instituted special antitrust compliance programs which often go beyond the prohibitions directly spelled out by the antitrust statutes themselves.

The following discussion will first describe the principal substantive provisions of the federal antitrust laws and will then outline the public and private mechanisms established by Congress for their enforcement.

Substantive Standards

The basic framework of antitrust regulation is set forth in four statutes: the Sherman Act, the Clayton Act, the Robinson-Patman Act, and the Federal Trade Commission Act.[7] These federal statutes have counterparts in many state statutory schemes, which in general have been construed and applied by state courts in a manner consistent with federal court decisions.

1. Section 1 of the Sherman Act

The first and most fundamental axiom of U.S. antitrust law is that private businesses may not jointly agree unreasonably to restrain competition. Section 1 of the Sherman Act, the most basic of all of the antitrust provisions, prohibits "every contract, combination . . . or conspiracy" which unreasonably restrains trade.[8] This broad prohibition directly prevents businesses from entering into any transaction—be it an ordinary marketing agreement between franchisor and franchisee, a joint venture to develop a new product, or a patent licensing agreement—where the effect may be unduly to weaken the vitality of market forces.

A determination of the legality of a particular arrangement under Section 1 initially turns upon the category into which the arrangement is classified. In one category are a group of restraints which "so often lack any virtue" and are so "plainly anticompetitive" that they are conclusively presumed to be unreasonable.[9] These arrangements are treated as *per se* unlawful and are banned irrespective of any purported justification or defense. In the second category are other restrictive arrangements, which are tested under the so-called "rule of reason."

The list of *per se* unlawful practices encompasses

those which are most blatantly anticompetitive. These practices, which are totally "off-limits" to a business enterprise, include: agreements to fix prices;[10] agreements among competitors to divide territories or allocate customers;[11] group refusals to deal among competitors which deprive another competitor of access to the market or an essential resource;[12] and "tying" arrangements, in which the market power of a seller over one product is used to coerce customers into buying undesired products.[13] Once a court determines that a challenged arrangement can be characterized as one of the *per se* unlawful practices, no defense is possible based on the asserted reasonableness of the conduct.

The most stringent of all the *per se* rules is that which prohibits price-fixing. The rule has been held to apply to any arrangement which has the purpose or effect of raising, depressing, fixing, pegging or stabilizing prices.[14] Since price is the "central nervous system of the economy,"[15] the "protection of price competition from conspiratorial restraint is an object of special solicitude under the antitrust laws" and any restraint upon such competition is *per se* unlawful even "when the effect upon prices is indirect" or assertedly beneficial.[16] In this regard, it should be noted that the *per se* unlawful designation has been applied not merely to the classic cartel situation where producers meet clandestinely to raise prices, but also to such practices as the exchange of non-public price information in a concentrated industry involving fungible products,[17] a ban on competitive bidding among professional engineers,[18] and the agreed-upon restriction of supply of a product whose price was falling.[19] It is the policy of the Antitrust Division primarily to devote its criminal enforcement resources to cases involving *per se* unlawful restraints of trade.

Beyond the *per se* rules, Section 1 of the Sherman Act

has an even broader (if more subtle) impact on the exercise of corporate discretion. As noted, arrangements engaged in by two or more businesses which do not fall within the *per se* category are scrutinized under Section 1 according to the "rule of reason." Because it may not be clear, in a particular factual context, whether a practice will be found to violate the rule, and because of the massive liability which can result from antitrust violations (discussed below), Section 1 of the Sherman Act tends to constrain corporations to err on the side of choosing those business strategies which pose the least risk of antitrust exposure. For example, such basic business decisions as whether or not to ask the distributors of a product to assume primary responsibility for a particular geographic area, or to insist that they limit their sales to particular territories or customers, can be significantly influenced by considerations of potential liability under Section 1, depending on the circumstances involved.

Under the rule of reason, artfully described in a landmark Supreme Court opinion of Justice Brandeis in 1918, a detailed examination of the history, purpose, and effects of a restraint must be conducted in order to determine whether it is one that "promotes competition or whether it is such as may supress or even destroy competition."[20] Broadly speaking, restrictive arrangements will be permitted under this standard only if they further legitimate procompetitive objectives whose benefits outweigh their anticompetitive effects.[21] Many business decisions may be unable to pass this test, as is illustrated by the application of Section 1 to strike down such practices as: an agreement among professional sports teams to provide compensation for signing a player whose rights have been assigned to another team;[22] a warranty program by a manufacturer of electronic dictating equipment under which dealers who found equipment within their territories that they had not sold were entitled to warranty payments extracted from the dealers who sold the products outside of their territories;[23] and the use of restrictive licenses by copyright or patent holders to restrain competition beyond the legitimate confines of their statutory monopolies.[24] In each of these illustrative cases, the courts found that the practice, on balance, was unduly restrictive of competition.

2. Section 2 of the Sherman Act

Section 2 of the Sherman Act prohibits "monopolization," attempts to monopolize, and conspiracies to monopolize.[25] This section has particularly constrained the market behavior of large corporations, which often may have significant shares of one or more product or service markets.

The Supreme Court has held that the offense of monopolization consists of the "willful" acquisition or maintenance of monopoly power in a relevant market.[26] Monopoly power has been defined as the power to control prices or exclude competition.[27] And the term "relevant market" has been construed as encompassing both broad product areas (e.g., packaging materials) and smaller submarkets (e.g., retail shoe outlets in a particular city); this means that Section 2 will also constrain the conduct of relatively small firms, which frequently can be significant factors in individual regional or product submarkets.

The vagueness of the criteria governing the offense of monopolization has plagued both the courts, which are required to administer them, and the corporations, which are required to obey them. Beyond the critical issue of relevant market definition (a corporation may be a monopolist under one market definition and one of thousands of competitors under another), there is a very fine and unsettled line between conduct which may lawfully be used to achieve and maintain monopoly power and that which may not.[28] For example, while it is clear that it is unlawful to acquire or maintain such power by practices that would violate any of the other antitrust statutes,[29] it is often difficult, with respect to other conduct, to distinguish between that which is legitimate and that which is inappropriate behavior for a firm which is dominant in a particular market.[30] In this connection, Section 2 has often been applied quite stringently, condemning such otherwise lawful behavior as the expansion of operating capacity to meet the projected total demand of the marketplace,[31] and the use of a long-term, "lease-only" policy,[32] when this conduct has had the effect of entrenching a firm's monopoly power. Further, the courts have held that it constitutes a violation of Section 2 to use monopoly power lawfully acquired in one market to foreclose competition or to gain a competitive advantage in another market.[33] On the other hand, recent cases involving IBM and Kodak, for example, have indicated a more hospitable attitude toward large firms who compete aggressively on the merits with smaller rivals.[34]

In all events, because of the still undefined and broad reach of Section 2, and the risk of Draconian remedies such as divestiture and treble damages if a violation is found, the constraining effects of the statute may well extend beyond practices which are clearly objectionable for a dominant firm (e.g., predatory price cuts below cost; special exclusionary deals with suppliers) to practices which in other contexts, for smaller firms, would represent no more than aggressive competition. To put it another way, the mere risk of a Section 2 action represents an additional cost which must be borne by the large firm; and in a situation presenting a close question whether the corporation should go forward with a particular practice, Section 2 concerns could well tip the scales against proceeding. For these same reasons, the statute may also be a contributing factor in a large firm's decision whether to diversify into new areas of endeavor, in which it is not dominant, rather than to expand its efforts in markets in which it is a substantial factor and thus increase its risks under Section 2.

Section 2, moreover, not only prohibits the act of monopolization itself, but also bars attempts and conspiracies to achieve that end. This has had the effect of extending the prohibitions of Section 2 to firms that are less than dominant in their markets. Most courts hold "exclusionary" or "predatory" conduct to be an unlawful "attempt" to monopolize when the defendant has a "specific intent" to monopolize a relevant market and there is a "dangerous probability" that it might succeed in achieving this unlawful objective.[35] It is uncertain whether proof of such a probability of success is similarly required in an action charging a conspiracy to monopolize or whether the mere proof of an actionable conspiracy and specific intent to monopolize is enough to violate this particular ban.[36] Regardless, the standards are sufficiently broad and uncertain under both of these prohibitions so as to add additional constraining pressures on the competitive strategies of dominant and nondominant firms alike.

Finally, it may be noted that the Antitrust Division of the Department of Justice and the Federal Trade Commission have announced their intention to try to use the Sherman Act and Federal Trade Commission Act to regulate so-called "shared monopolies."[37] These are industries in which a small group of firms account for a large percentage of sales and are alleged to behave as if they were a single firm monopoly. The economic merits of this untested theory are currently subject to much debate.[38]

The FTC, however, has already brought one such action against the makers of antiknock compounds, charging that they have unlawfully coordinated their pricing activities by means of public statements to the press and certain clauses in their contracts with customers.[39] Should the FTC prevail in this case, corporate discretion in the area of pricing would be further affected to the extent that in many industries it would not be prudent or lawful for a company publicly to announce its prices. In this connection, the E.I. du Pont company, one of the respondents in the FTC's case, sought an immediate court ruling on the constitutionality under the First Amendment of the FTC's "price signalling" theory. The du Pont complaint charged that the FTC's action had *already* occasioned a "chilling effect" on the publication of price information; the court, however, dismissed du Pont's complaint, refusing to interfere in the FTC's pending action.[40]

3. The Clayton Act

To supplement and strengthen the basic prohibitions of the Sherman Act, the Clayton Act sets forth a number of specific limitations upon corporate conduct. Together with the Robinson-Patman Act discussed below, these prohibitions substantially regulate corporations in terms of what distribution and sales arrangements may lawfully be employed. They have had a special impact on the freedom of corporations to engage in mergers and acquisitions.

Section 3 of the Clayton Act prohibits exclusive distribution and sales agreements, requirements contracts, and agreements using market power over one commodity to coerce customers into purchasing an undesired commodity ("tying arrangements"), where the effect of such agreements "may" be to lessen competition substantially in a relevant market.[41] In combination with Section 1 of the Sherman Act, whose more general ban on all unreasonable restraints of trade also can be applied to these practices, Section 3 has had the effect of placing beyond the pale of corporate discretion a wide variety of distribution and sales practices.

For example, Section 3 has been applied to ban such diverse business arrangements as: a set of contracts between an oil company and certain retail gasoline stations providing that the stations would buy all their gasoline from the company;[42] an agreement by a pattern manufacturer with various retail outlets requiring the retailers to sell only the manufacturer's patterns;[43] and many other similar type arrangements with exclusivity effects. The tying prohibition, imposed by both Section 3 of the Clayton Act and Section 1 of the Sherman Act, has been even more stringently applied—restraining, as *per se* unlawful, such practices as the licensing of fast-food fried chicken franchisees on the condition that they purchase cooking machinery, packaging and certain ingredients from the franchisor;[44] the leasing of certain machinery on the condition that materials used in that machinery be bought from the lessor;[45] and the "block booking" of motion pictures in package licenses to television networks.[46]

The Clayton Act has also pervasively affected corporate conduct in the merger area, substantially curtailing the kinds of acquisitions corporations may undertake. Section 7 of the Clayton Act, as amended in 1950 by the Celler-Kefauver Act, prohibits all stock or asset acquisitions by corporations which may substantially lessen competition or tend to create a monopoly.[47] This prohibition has been applied with particular stringency to "horizontal" mergers (those between competitors), so that almost any such combination of significance may be barred.[48] For example, Section 7 has been held applicable to disallow a merger between two local grocery retailers with only 4.2 percent and 4.7 percent, respectively, of a relevant market which included over 4,000 other competitors, where there was a trend toward concentration and a history of acquisitions.[49]

Similarly, Section 7 has been applied to prohibit many mergers between suppliers and purchasers.[50] Indeed, in one case, it was applied by the Supreme Court retroactively to invalidate the purchase by du Pont (a major supplier of automotive paints and finishes) of a minority interest in General Motors some 25 years earlier.[51] The Court held that Section 7 can be applied *whenever* an acquisition threatens to restrain competition, even if the transaction had long ago been consummated and posed no significant competitive threat at that time.

In light of its broad reach and the government's historic success in enforcing the statute in a wide variety of merger contexts, it is generally agreed that Section 7 has had a substantial impact on the allocation of capital resources by corporate managements. Since Section 7 effectively precludes most horizontal and many vertical mergers of significance, it has given substantial impetus to foreign acquisitions and to the so-called "conglomerate merger waves" of the late 1960's and early and late 1970's. While conglomerate mergers are themselves subject to Section 7 scrutiny,[52] they raise fewer antitrust problems since they involve (by definition) firms in unrelated fields. However, even in this area or in other situations where the merger or acquisition does not appear clearly to contravene Section 7, the parties may nevertheless decline to consummate the transaction because of the risk of antitrust challenge.

Finally, Section 8 of the Clayton Act prohibits interlocking directorates between competing industrial corporations.[53] Specifically, it bars any person from serving as director of more than one competing corporation when one of the corporations is engaged "in commerce," has capital, surplus and undivided profits totalling over $1 million and "the elimination of competition by agreement between them" would violate any of the antitrust laws.[54] As applied by the courts, Section 8 imposes a virtual *per se* prohibition on any interlocking directorates between competing industrial corporations. Because of this, the statute has had a fundamental constraining effect on the process of selecting nominees for election to boards of directors, limiting the available universe of candidates to those in noncompetitive fields of activity.

4. The Robinson-Patman Act

The Robinson-Patman Act is a complex amendment to Section 2 of the Clayton Act. It outlaws various forms of price discrimination.[55] The statute was primarily designed to protect small businesses from competitive advantages believed to be possessed by larger rivals. As even a cursory description of the statute will show, this Act significantly limits corporate discretion in the area of product distribution and in particular limits the discretion of sellers in discounting from general price levels.

The basic prohibition set forth in the statute makes it unlawful for any person engaged in interstate commerce to discriminate in price between different purchasers of commodities of "like grade and quality" when the effect of that discrimination "may be substantially to lessen competition or tend to create a monopoly . . . or to injure, destroy, or prevent competition with any person who either grants or knowingly receives the benefit of such discrimination, or with customers of either of them."[56]

No illegality results, however, if the price discrimination can be justified by cost differentials, changing market conditions, or a good faith effort to meet the lower price of a competitor.[57] Because the courts have required substantiation that a price reduction was offered in good faith to meet competition, many corporations have initiated formal procedures to document both how they learned that a competitor was undercutting them and their efforts to verify this information. Ironically, procedures for contacting competitors for such price verification purposes have been challenged as evidence of price-fixing in violation of the Sherman Act.[58] As a result, corporations must delicately balance the dictates of these two statutes, whose inherent potential for conflict has been noted by the Supreme Court.[59]

The Robinson-Patman Act exposes the seller to possible liability at three distinct levels of distribution. First, a discrimination will be held unlawful if it substantially restrains competition between the seller and his competitors ("primary" level injury). This may be the case, for example, where discriminatorily below cost prices are being subsidized in one geographic region by higher prices in another region in order to drive the seller's local competitors out of business.[60]

Second, price discriminations will be held unlawful when they may have the effect of causing competitive injury between customers of the seller—at the so-called "secondary" level. This is the most common type of Robinson-Patman Act complaint; indeed, one line of cases holds that the required injury can be inferred from little more than the fact of discrimination in a price sensitive market[61] and damages have been awarded under this theory for treble the amount of the discrimination.[62] While a contrary line of authority requires a detailed inquiry to determine competitive impact,[63] under either standard a stringent constraint is erected against price discriminations which impair competition at the customer level.

Third, it has been held that price discriminations are unlawful under the Act when they may have the effect of lessening competition between customers of the customers of the seller (i.e., at the tertiary level of distribution) or possibly even between their customers.[64] Under this approach, the Act may be violated whenever competitive injury can be accurately traced to a price discrimination —virtually irrespective of what level of distribution may be involved. Sellers are thus deterred from offering price discounts anywhere in the chain of distribution if such discounts have the potential for causing an anticompetitive impact at any level.

In addition, the Act prohibits a number of nonprice discriminations. Section 2(c) of the Act, for example, prevents the parties to a sale from granting or receiving a brokerage commission, or any allowance in lieu thereof, except for services rendered in connection with the sale.[65] The principal purpose of this provision is to outlaw the practice of "fictitious" brokerages extracted by some large purchasers to get a price advantage over their competitors.[66] Sections 2(d) and 2(e) of the Act prohibit a seller from granting advertising or promotional allowances or services to a customer unless they are made available to all of the customer's competitors on proportionately equal terms.[67] This prohibition is absolute, except for the "meeting competition" defense, and requires no independent proof of competitive impact.

In sum, although the Robinson-Patman Act is disfavored by antitrust enforcement officials because of its tendency to deter price cutting/competition, its impact on the business community should not be underestimated. The numerous possibilities for liability, coupled with the ambiguous availability of defenses and uncertain damage calculations, have substantially influenced and constrained corporate distribution and pricing practices.

5. The Federal Trade Commission Act

The final element of antitrust policy derives from the sweeping language of Section 5 of the FTC Act, which broadly prohibits all "unfair methods of competition in or affecting commerce."[68] Although not technically an antitrust statute, it is clear that Section 5 covers all conduct in violation of the antitrust laws and "more"—the outer limits of which have not yet been defined.[69] Hence, even if a corporation has taken all necessary steps to ensure compliance with the antitrust laws themselves, its conduct might still be challenged as in violation of Section 5 of the FTC Act. For example, the statute has been held to bar:

(i) "leveraged" distribution arrangements that fall short of being an unlawful tying or exclusive dealing arrangement under the Sherman and Clayton Acts;[70]

(ii) actions by a purchaser to induce its seller to violate Section 2(d) of the Robinson-Patman Act (even though the statute itself only prohibits buyers from inducing a violation of Section 2(a));[71] and

(iii) noncorporate acquisitions which have anticompetitive effects (even though such mergers are beyond the purview of Section 7 of the Clayton Act).[72]

The FTC's shared monopoly case against the practice of so-called "price signalling," previously discussed (pp. 39–40), and its unsuccessful attack on the interdependent adoption of a delivered pricing formula by competing distributors of plywood, further illustrate the efforts of the FTC to expand the scope of Section 5; and the Commission has announced that it intends to continue to explore the limits of its authority under this statute, which it believes provides a "failsafe" for any gaps that may exist in antitrust coverage.[74]

Enforcement and Penalties

In order to maximize the effectiveness of antitrust legislation as a control on corporate conduct, Congress has backed up these laws with an impressive array of overlapping enforcement programs and sanctions.

Looking first at the federal government, two agencies —the Antitrust Division of the Department of Justice and the Federal Trade Commission—are charged with conducting extensive antitrust enforcement programs. The Antitrust Division is empowered to enforce the Sherman, Clayton and Robinson-Patman Acts. Violations of the Sherman Act can be prosecuted in both civil and criminal proceedings. Criminal violations now constitute a felony and may be punished by a fine of up to $1 million if the violator is a corporation or (if the violator is an individual) a fine of up to $100,000, or a jail term of up to three years, or both.[75] Civil proceedings brought by the Antitrust Division for violations of the Sherman and Clayton Acts seek injunctive or other equitable relief.[76] Such relief can be extremely varied in scope—ranging from a broad order compelling a company to divest itself of one or more of its divisions to various injunctive provisions (which may include prohibitions on otherwise lawful as well as illegal conduct) ensuring that the violation is stopped and will not be repeated. In addition, the Antitrust Division is empowered to sue for the recovery of actual damages sustained by the United States government as a result of antitrust violations.[77]

To carry out its enforcement authority, the Antitrust

Division has been given extensive investigatory powers. In a criminal proceeding, it can convene a grand jury with broad subpoena authority. In civil investigations, it has the authority to issue a "civil investigative demand" to any person who may be in possession of documentary material or information relevant to a civil antitrust investigation.[78]

The wide-ranging enforcement activities of the Antitrust Division[79] are in turn supplemented by those of the Federal Trade Commission, which separately conducts its own extensive antitrust enforcement program. The FTC has coextensive authority with the Department of Justice to enforce provisions of the Clayton and Robinson-Patman Acts, and exclusive jurisdiction to enforce the broad "unfair methods of competition" mandate of Section 5 of the Federal Trade Commission Act.[80] If the Commission has reason to believe that any of these statutes is being violated, it may issue an administrative complaint against the suspected violator and hold an adjudicative hearing. A finding of liability will result in a Commission cease and desist order prohibiting the violator from continuing its unlawful activity. Violation of such an order is punishable by a fine of up to $10,000 per day.[81] To meet its statutory responsibilities, the FTC has been granted broad powers to compel the production of documents and the appearance of witnesses, as well as the power to require businesses to file various informational reports and to answer questionnaires.[82]

In addition to the extensive programs of the Antitrust Division and the FTC, enforcement of the antitrust laws is aggressively furthered by private litigants. Section 4 of the Clayton Act[83] provides that "any person who shall be injured in his business or property by reason of anything prohibited in the antitrust laws" may recover three-fold the damages sustained by such violation as well as reasonable attorneys' fees. This combined incentive of treble damages and attorney's fees, along with the willingness of many attorneys to work for plaintiffs on a contingency fee basis, has resulted in the commencement of thousands of private antitrust cases.[84] The threat of such private treble damage actions is a major constraint on the large corporation, and substantially adds to the deterrent effect of the antitrust laws.

The constraining influence of private antitrust suits is heightened further by the fact that one or more representative antitrust plaintiffs can bring a class action on behalf of all persons similarly situated—seeking enormous treble damage sums for the entire class.[85] Moreover, a 1977 amendment to the Clayton Act authorizes each state Attorney General, as *parens patriae* on behalf of the natural persons residing within that state, to bring civil antitrust actions in which three-fold the total damages sustained by those natural persons, as well as the costs of suit, including attorney's fees, may be recovered.[86]

Further, although the discussion in this section is generally limited to the federal antitrust laws, it should be noted that those laws are complemented by numerous other federal laws protecting competition in various specified industries, as well as by state antitrust and so-called "little FTC" acts which provide for additional sanctions and enforcement mechanisms to preserve and protect the constraining force of the market system.[87] Many of these state laws contain their own private rights of action, further adding to the legion of potential antitrust litigants. Finally, business behavior affecting competition is also regulated by common law prohibitions of unreasonable restraints of trade[88] and by state laws that prohibit various forms of unfair competition (e.g., disparaging a competitor's products, stealing trade secrets).[89]

In summary, there is little a corporation can do competitively that is not subject to antitrust scrutiny. Moreover, the larger the corporation is, and particularly if it is a significant factor in a market, the greater will be its exposure to government investigation and private suits, and the greater will be its incentive to monitor its commercial activities carefully from an antitrust viewpoint. Because of the enormous potential damages attendant on an antitrust violation, counsel are frequently consulted by corporate managers in advance of any major commercial decisions; and it is clear that counsel play a major role in arresting many incipient antitrust problems. Even where activities present borderline questions under the "rule of reason," as discussed above, corporations in many cases will tend to choose those commercial strategies presenting the fewest antitrust risks consistent with the commercial objectives involved. Again, these considerations apply with special force to the large corporation.

2. The Securities Laws

The securities laws are designed to protect the operation of market constraints in the allocation of capital resources. They were enacted by Congress in the 1930's and 1940's—seven statutes in as many years—in response to the financial traumas of the 1929 stock market crash.[90] The most important are the Securities Act of 1933 ("1933 Act") and the Securities Exchange Act of 1934 ("1934 Act").[91] These laws prohibit public trading in securities unless specified rules are complied with:

principally rules concerning information disclosure by the corporation involved and rules prohibiting insider trading and market manipulation. As in the antitrust area, the potential penalties for failure to comply with the requirements of the securities laws are enormous.

Beyond specific prohibitions on insider trading and market manipulation, the federal securities laws seek to achieve their goal of maintaining an efficient, reliable capital market primarily through requiring disclosure of a broad range of information by corporations and other market participants. Reflecting Brandeis' aphorism that "sunlight is said to be the best of disinfectants; electric light the most efficient policeman,"[92] the disclosure policy underlying the federal securities laws seeks both to deter shady dealing and promote informed decisions by investors. Moreover, in an important sense, the securities laws act as a policeman of all of the significant legal requirements applicable to the public corporation, including those which do not directly bear upon the capital market system. For example, beyond the liabilities under the Clayton Act which confront a corporation that is party to an agreement which violates Section 1 of the Sherman Act, the securities laws present an additional deterrent by requiring that all material commercial agreements entered into by public corporations be disclosed in filings with the Securities and Exchange Commission ("SEC"). This same requirement also covers any other activity of material importance to investors—such as a strike, new discovery, plant breakdown, etc. Hence, a corporation which ignores antitrust requirements or similarly significant legal constraints will inevitably find itself trapped in a dilemma, since compliance with the disclosure requirements of the securities laws may create risks of liability under other statutes. That kind of "catch-22" dilemma operates in a very substantial way to restrict the activities of the large corporation, since it must make frequent disclosures of material activities to the SEC pursuant to the securities laws.

As discussed herein, securities regulation encompasses not only stock ordinarily issued by business corporations, but also the many other kinds of equity and debt securities, including long-term debt instruments (such as corporate debentures), stock warrants and options, interests in certain kinds of financial intermediaries (such as mutual funds), and, in general, all kinds of investment contracts, whether issued by corporations or any other nongovernmental entity.[93] Moreover, we will deal with both federal regulation and state "blue sky" regulation, which today exist side by side, and may be considered as one system of securities regulation.

As discussed in the subsections which follow, this regulatory system controls or limits corporate conduct in connection with three principal aspects of the processes of capital accumulation and investment: *first*, issuance of securities; *second*, trading in securities; *third*, though to a lesser extent, the withdrawal by business corporations of their securities from the publicly traded market.

Entry into the Public Capital Market by Corporations: Issuing Securities

The disclosure policy of the securities laws, embodied in the 1933 Act and roughly paralleled by state "blue sky" laws, is clearly reflected in the requirements applicable to corporations seeking to raise capital by issuing securities to the public.

1. Registration of Securities and Use of Prospectuses Under the 1933 Act

The core of the federal system of securities regulation lies in the disclosure requirements specified in the 1933 Act,[94] which, together with the 1934 Act (discussed *infra*), comprehensively control the trading process in corporate securities. Section 5 of the 1933 Act requires that new issues of securities be registered with the SEC. In addition, Section 10 of that Act requires that a prospectus, filed as part of the registration statement and containing much of the same information, be furnished to potential purchasers before the securities are sold or, in some cases, at the time of sale.[95]

Securities are registered under Section 5 of the 1933 Act by filing with the SEC a registration statement, which must disclose detailed information concerning:

(i) the principals of the corporation (including directors, officers, promoters and underwriters) and their interests in the corporation, such as their ownership of, or intention to subscribe for, securities of the corporation and their remuneration from the corporation in the past year;

(ii) the corporation and its business, including the corporation's capitalization, the rights of the holders of all of its securities, the dates of, parties to, and general effect of, every contract material to the corporation's business which was executed in the two years prior to registration or which is to be executed in whole or in part after registration, and the net proceeds derived by the corporation from the sale of any securities in the past two years; and

(iii) the particular issue of securities involved, including the "specific purposes in detail"[96] for which securities are to be issued, the estimated net proceeds of the issuance, the offering price, and all of the actual or estimated costs incurred in connection with the issuance and sale of the security.

All of these disclosures become public information when submitted to the SEC. With very limited exceptions, no corporation may issue securities to the public unless these disclosure requirements are met.

Beyond these basic disclosures, the registrant corporation must provide to the SEC a copy of the corporation's current certificate of incorporation and bylaws, all agreements affecting any of its securities, and a copy of the underwriting agreement or agreements for the offering.[97] Copies of the opinion of counsel with respect to the legality of the offering must also be submitted.[98] So must a current balance sheet and profit-and-loss statements for the preceding three fiscal years;[99] these financial statements must be prepared in conformity with SEC-approved financial accounting requirements (discussed below), and must be certified by independent public accountants.[100]

The 1933 Act also prescribes that a registration statement contain "such other information, and be accompanied by such other documents, as the [SEC] may by rules or regulations require as being necessary or appropriate in the public interest or for the protection of investors."[101] Pursuant to this provision, the SEC has issued many different registration forms for use in a variety of circumstances, and has ordered the disclosure of a great deal of information in line with the extremely broad requirements of the 1933 Act. As a result of all of these requirements, the preparation of the materials required to be filed with the SEC has aptly, if not conservatively, been described as "a demanding and intricate undertaking,"[102] and the cost of obtaining registration for a large company at times runs over $1 million.[103]

In this connection, it is relevant to point out that while registration statements become effective automatically twenty days after filing with the SEC (unless the SEC rejects the filing or issues a "stop order"),[104] every amendment to a registration statement starts the twenty-day waiting period anew. Since virtually every registration statement inevitably requires some amendment, the registration process in practice takes much longer. In a typical situation, after reviewing a registration statement, the SEC staff will send a "Letter of Comment" to the issuer requesting additional information and suggesting changes in the statement. The corporation then will respond to the SEC's comments and, if necessary, will amend the registration statement. The SEC staff will then review the statement as amended, and may make further comments. This process continues until both the issuer and the SEC are in agreement—a process which, in practice, usually takes several months.[105]

It is also relevant to point out here that, for purposes of their employee benefit plans, most large corporations keep a registration statement (albeit a much abbreviated version) continuously in effect.

The registrant corporation is subject to stringent liability if a registration statement or prospectus contains any "untrue statement of a material fact or [omits] to state a material fact required to be stated therein or necessary to make the statements therein not misleading. . . ."[106] In addition to specific criminal sanctions, substantial civil liability exists in the event a registration statement or prospectus is found to violate these criteria. Among other things, in such circumstances (subject to certain limited defenses which are not available to the issuing company), all of the following persons may be jointly and separately liable to any person acquiring such securities in reliance on the registration statement for an amount up to the offering price of the securities:

(i) every person who signed the registration statement,
(ii) every director of the corporation,
(iii) every accountant or other professional who prepared any part of the registration statement or any report used

in connection with the registration statement, with respect to such statement or report,
(iv) every underwriter of the securities, and
(v) any person controlling any of the foregoing.[107]

That the sanctions applicable for violations of the 1933
Act's disclosure requirements are so substantial is under-
standable in light of the purposes of the securities laws
—which reach far beyond the formal requirements for
filing a registration statement and mailing out a prospectus. Fundamentally, as noted earlier, a corporation must
continuously be concerned about engaging in activities
which it would not want disclosed publicly or to the SEC,
including both activities which directly affect the securities market (e.g., misstatement of financial results) and
activities relating to other areas material to the corporation's business in general. It is noteworthy in this connection that the "foreign payments" scandals have come to
light largely as a result of SEC disclosure requirements.
So, too, with corporate participation in boycott activities,
trading with South Africa or Rhodesia, etc. Thus, particularly for large corporations, the SEC's disclosure laws
constitute a very basic limitation on management's freedom of action.

2. Requirements Under the Blue Sky Laws

State regulation of the issuance of securities by ordinary business corporations is similar to federal regulation. Virtually every state has some sort of registration
requirement, calling for disclosure of basically the same
kinds of information that are required for federal registration. (In fact, many states provide for "registration by
coordination," whereby material filed with the SEC may
be filed with them.) Also, many of the states which require detailed registration statements provide a simpli-

fied form of registration for securities issued by corporations which have been in continuous operation for a certain number of years during which they have had favorable earnings records.

Under most state blue sky laws, securities may not be issued until the registration statements have been qualified by the administrator of their securities laws—the applicable standard in such states being whether the issuance of the securities would be contrary to the public interest.[108] A few states give their administrators wider powers by requiring that the terms of the securities issue be "fair, just and equitable" and that the issuer's business be conducted "fairly and honestly."[109] In all states the administrator of the securities laws may investigate the issuance of securities.[110]

State blue sky laws contain their own sets of substantial penalties—generally applicable to both the corporation and relevant individuals—for violations of their requirements. They thus complement the federal system of securities regulation in constraining what the corporation may do and say when it goes to the public markets for money.

Trading of Securities in the Public Capital Market

The process of initial capital accumulation is only the starting point of securities regulation. The federal securities laws even more pervasively influence trading in securities already issued. Here again, both federal and state requirements come into play. And, here too, the specific goal of regulation is to preserve and promote a free market in capital by constraining what may be done or said by those who deal in securities and by the corporations whose securities are traded. To this end, as discussed below, the securities laws specifically and directly: regulate the constituent elements of the securities markets—brokers, underwriters, exchanges, etc; control and oversee the accounting practices of corporations; directly prohibit insider trading, fraud, and other forms of market manipulation; and subject corporate acquisitions to special scrutiny.

1. Regulation of the Constituent Elements
of the Securities Markets

Under the 1934 Act, the elements that constitute the securities market—exchanges, brokers, dealers, specialists, securities information processors and clearing agencies—must be registered with the SEC, and the SEC is given substantial authority to determine the requirements for registration.[111]

Though not directly applicable to corporations, regulation of these market elements acts to constrain the activities of the corporations whose securities are being traded. For example, underwriters of an offering of securities are liable to the purchasers of those securities for false or misleading information contained in a registration statement or prospectus and for the omission of any material information, unless they can show that they used due diligence in investigating the corporation to see that the information contained in the registration statement was not misleading and that all material information was revealed—in other words, that the corporation met its disclosure requirements.[112] Accountants and lawyers, who are in large part relied on in making such investigations, are similarly liable.[113] Likewise, underwriters and brokers can be liable under the 1934 Act if they effect transactions in securities when the corporations involved have not made adequate disclosure of public information.[114]

The substantial liabilities to which these constituents of the securities market are subject provide a strong motivation for them to require the corporations with which they deal to adhere strictly to the letter and spirit of SEC disclosure regulations. This illustrates a principal strategy of the securities laws—to "piggyback" one layer of regulation on another. Brokers, underwriters and others trading a particular corporation's stock thus act, in effect, as a private police force requiring compliance by corporations with SEC disclosure rules.

Beyond disclosure, the various entities which make up the securities market, especially brokers and dealers, are subject to a comprehensive pattern of direct regulation designed to prevent market manipulation and use of their position for private advantage.[115] Brokers and dealers also have fiduciary obligations to their customers, which further tend indirectly to regulate the actions of corporations by requiring such brokers and dealers to buy only those securities which are suitable for their clients and to supervise the execution of transactions by and for their clients to prevent frauds.[116] Obviously, these obligations tend further, if indirectly, to regulate the actions of corporations, which wish to see their shares traded as broadly as possible.

Investment advisers and investment companies—in living up to their own obligations under the securities laws—constrain corporate behavior. The activities of investment advisers, often closely associated with the operation of investment companies and other institutional investors, are crucial to the functioning of the market. They are required to register with the SEC under the Investment Advisers Act of 1940, and the SEC may deny or revoke such registration.[117] They must keep certain records and make certain periodic reports to the SEC.[118] Further, the SEC regulates the terms of contracts for investment advisory services,[119] and there are separate provisions in the Investment Advisers Act barring manipulative activities by investment advisers.[120] The Investment Company Act of 1940 also directly limits the role of investment advisers in the management of investment companies; it prohibits certain classes of transactions between them which create potential conflicts of interest; it regulates investment advisory contracts; and it establishes a code of ethics for those investment advisers who advise investment companies.[121]

Furthermore, corporations seeking access to important classes of investors, such as investment companies, pension funds, educational institutions, and the like, are subject as a practical matter to criteria far beyond simple corporate compliance with SEC disclosure rules. Because such investor entities have fiduciary duties of their own, plus potential liability for imprudent investments, their investment criteria by and large reflect a preference for conservative corporate management philosophies and operational strategies. This in turn tends to influence corporation management in the same directions.

2. Regulation of Financial Accounting Practice

Since much information about corporations is of a financial nature, the system of securities regulation has from the outset involved governmental supervision of financial accounting practices. In short, once a corporation goes to the public for funds, it loses its discretion to define the accounting practices it uses in preparing financial reports.

Both the 1933 and 1934 Acts authorize the SEC to de-

fine accounting terms, and to prescribe their use in reports filed with it,[122] viz:

> the items or details to be shown in the balance sheet and
> earning statement, and the methods to be followed in the
> preparation of accounts, in the appraisal or valuation of as-
> sets and liabilities, in the determination of depreciation and
> depletion, in the differentiation of recurring and nonrecur-
> ring income, and in the preparation, where the Commission
> deems it necessary or desirable, of consolidated balance
> sheets or income accounts.

The SEC has generally limited its formal rulemaking in
this area to prescribing the form and content of financial
statements—e.g., what kinds of financial information
should be included, how data should be displayed—and
to requiring that such information be prepared in accordance with generally accepted accounting and auditing
standards.[123]

The SEC has in effect required corporations to use the
accounting principles developed or endorsed by the
Financial Accounting Standards Board ("FASB"), a
non-profit quasi-public body. It has done so through a
formally promulgated statement that financial disclosures which are contrary to FASB standards will be presumed by the SEC to be misleading, and *vice versa*.[124]
Furthermore, by its positions taken in specific cases or on
specific issues, the SEC has influenced many specific accounting procedures. Occasionally, it has overruled the
FASB (or its predecessor, the Accounting Principles
Board). For example, in 1978 the SEC overruled the
FASB with regard to the accounting principles to be used
by oil and gas producing companies, and went ahead to
propose its own standard.

Traditionally, accounting data as publicly reported in
annual reports, filings with the SEC, prospectuses, and

the like—especially data on periodic and annual earnings—have been regarded as of critical importance to investors. Hence, one of the SEC's principal goals in recent years has been to take away from corporations the discretion to "manage earnings"; that is, to make them appear higher or lower by taking advantage of accounting quirks. For example, in the dispute cited above over accounting procedures for the oil and gas industry, substantial testimony was presented to the SEC that one of the two prevalent methods of accounting was used to boost earnings by limiting the numbers of oil wells drilled or by artificially timing drilling activities. The other method in general use was criticized as encouraging unjustified well-digging because of the resulting "smoothing out" of earnings fluctuations. In rejecting both approaches, the SEC proposed a novel method that would attempt to portray the earnings of oil and gas companies in terms of the value of their proven reserves, rather than their receipts in a given period.[125] This approach—which aroused a great deal of controversy—illustrates the SEC's overall efforts to encourage the adoption of uniform accounting principles and to curtail corporate options in the preparation and presentation of financial reports.[126]

In addition to its direct involvement in the substance of accounting rules, the SEC also has strictly required that the accuracy of financial statements be certified by independent auditors. These requirements have been underscored by amendments to the 1934 Act (enacted as part of the Foreign Corrupt Practices Act of 1977), which require that publicly-held corporations keep records which "in reasonable detail accurately and fairly reflect the transactions and dispositions" of their assets.[127] It further provided:

(i) that such corporations must devise and maintain a system of internal accounting controls sufficient to provide "reasonable assurances" that transactions are executed —and access to assets is allowed—only as authorized by management, and

(ii) that the execution of transactions and the use of assets is properly recorded so as to permit the preparation of financial statements in accordance with generally accepted accounting principles, including the periodic assessment of the accuracy of such records with respect to assets actually on hand.

Persons violating any of these provisions are subject to the civil and criminal penalties provided by the 1934 Act. These statutory requirements have prompted significant changes in the internal accounting practices of many public corporations,[128] and they have further diluted the freedom of corporate managers to vary bookkeeping practices in either undesirable or desirable ways.

The SEC has recently issued two additional rules:

(i) prohibiting the falsification of "any book, record or account" of any business enterprise subject to the accounting requirements of the Foreign Corrupt Practices Act,[129] and

(ii) prohibiting officers and directors from making fraudulent representations (including misleading omissions) to an accountant in connection with an audit of the financial statements of the issuer or any work by the accountant in preparation of any document filed with the SEC.[130]

Finally, there is the "omnibus" provision in the SEC's regulations that, "The information required with respect to any [financial] statement shall be furnished as a minimum requirement to which shall be added such further material information as is necessary to make the required statements, in the light of the circumstances under which they are made, not misleading." [131]

In combination, all of these rules have circumscribed the freedom of action of public corporations in respect of how they portray their financial performance. It does seem ironic, however, that the likelihood that possibly more meaningful accounting practices (e.g., rules reflecting the impact of inflation or the value of oil and gas reserves) will be adopted has been made highly uncertain in light of the enormous potential liability facing accountants for inaccuracies in a corporation's financial report. The accounting profession has been understandably reluctant to voluntarily adopt arguably more meaningful —but "softer"—accounting data if it is to remain liable to the same extent as under current law for inaccuracies in financial statements. Thus far, the tradeoff has generally been in favor of objectively verifiable "hard" data, as being less subject to manipulation.

3. Direct Regulation of Corporate Activities Connected with Securities Trading

In addition to the foregoing rules constraining corporate activities in connection with the acquisition and trading of securities, a further set of rules applies when individuals who are associated with a corporation trade in its securities. Still other rules prohibit all manner of market manipulation by corporations. Here again, the goal is to preserve the integrity of the capital market.

The practice of "insider trading" consists of transactions in the shares of a corporation based on information which is not available to the general public. Such trading is strictly forbidden by SEC Rule 10b-5. This prohibition is "based in policy on the justifiable expectation of the securities marketplace that all investors trading on impersonal exchanges have relatively equal access to material information," and that insiders trade only "on an equal footing with . . . outside investors." [132] Section 16(b) of the 1934 Act is similarly motivated. It prohibits officers, directors and principal shareholders of a corporation from purchasing and selling (or selling and purchasing) the securities of the corporation within a period of six months. Any profit realized from such transactions is considered a corporate asset and is recoverable by the corporation or by the shareholders acting in the corporation's behalf.

Closely connected in spirit with the ban on insider trading is the more general prohibition on misstatements or omissions of material information by corporate officials. Even where the purchase or sale of securities is not involved, an inaccurate or misleading material statement about a corporation's business by an official of the corporation (for example, a press release, a TV interview) or a failure timely to state known, material information may give rise to liability under Rule 10b-5. The premise here is that such activities may have a manipulative effect on trading in the securities of the corporation or of other corporations. [133]

Within the meaning of the securities laws, a misrepresentation includes not only false statements but also statements which are misleading because of incompleteness, and it includes statements which are not, strictly speaking, statements of fact. Thus, for example, a statement by management that earnings in the coming quarter will be high could constitute a Rule 10b-5 violation if made without a reasonable basis. Likewise, with respect to omissions, if the management of a publicly-traded corporation is aware of reasonably certain information material to the corporation's business, it may be obligated to make such information public within a reasonable time of becoming aware of it.[134] While exact requirements in this area vary with particular factual circumstances, the overall effect is to limit the ability of corporate managers to act in changing (material) circumstances, even for relatively short periods, without making public disclosure of the relevant events and thus enabling the market to assess—and reward or penalize—the actions involved. Moreover, corporate managers must be extremely careful that the information released, even though true, is not misleading either because too little or too much is said in the process. As discussed earlier, all these disclosure obligations serve to police corporate obedience to other laws, since disclosure may be required of corporate conduct which is in violation of such laws or which is simply of "questionable" legality (as in the case of the foreign payments scandals).

Securities trading is another of many areas where the institutions composing the market, such as the stock exchanges, play a major role in further constraining the corporation. The rules of the American Stock Exchange, for example, provide that a listed corporation "make prompt disclosures of any material developments in its affairs and operations, whether favorable or unfavorable, which might significantly affect the market for its securities or influence investment decisions."[135] In addition, the SEC has broad powers to suspend trading in a security when it determines that the interests of investor protection and the public interest so require.[136] It has done so frequently when it considers the information in circulation about an issuer of securities insufficient or misleading.[137]

It is difficult to exaggerate the importance of Rule 10b-5 and related disclosure requirements in light of the applicable penalties for violation. It is well established that a private cause of action for damages exists under Rule

10b-5, and some courts have held that one exists as well under the provisions of the 1933 Act.[138] As in the antitrust area, through these private causes of action aggrieved private citizens have time and again policed the securities markets against misconduct in the issuance and sale of securities.

Here also, however, an irony is apparent. While disclosures of material activities must be made, the language used must be carefully drafted because of the risks attendent to misstatements or omissions; consequently, corporate managers are constrained in publicly speaking out on corporate activities. Yet it seems that these very constraints on corporate communication have contributed to the popular notion of the corporation as possessing inordinate discretion—by "refusing" to talk openly about itself.

4. The Regulation of Corporate Takeovers

Corporate takeovers accomplished by merger or sale of assets have long been subject to the proxy solicitation or registration requirements of the securities laws, which are outlined above. In addition, corporate takeovers accomplished by tender offers have in recent years attracted special scrutiny under both federal and state securities laws, which prescribe substantial disclosures and restrictions in connection with such acquisitions. More recently, the Hart-Scott-Rodino Antitrust Improvements Act of 1976 has mandated additional substantial disclosures before any acquisition may take place. These developments are outlined below.

The Williams Act. A distinct set of laws under the so-called Williams Act[139] comprehensively regulates corporate acquisitions of stock through tender offers. The Act first requires disclosure of the owners of significant blocks of securities. Any person or group, once having acquired beneficial ownership of more than five percent of any class of SEC-registered equity securities, must disclose the size of its holdings to the issuer, to the exchanges on which such securities are traded, and to the SEC. Also required to be disclosed are the source and amount of the funds used in the acquisition of the securities, any agreements entered into respecting the securities, any plans to obtain control of the issuing company, and such other information as the SEC may by regulation require.[140] This information must be updated whenever any material change occurs.[141]

A second set of requirements pertains to disclosure of the terms of a tender offer. Anyone undertaking a tender offer who would thereby own more than 5% of any class of SEC-registered equity securities is required by the Williams Act to file with the SEC and distribute to security holders certain information prescribed by the SEC concerning the terms of the tender offer, the offeror's plans for the target company, any litigation or other legal problems (including tax and antitrust problems) existing or expected in connection with the offer, plus any other material information.[142] It is unlawful to undertake a tender offer until this filing is made. Where the tender offer involves an exchange of the offeror's stock, more extensive disclosures are required, similar to those required to register an issue of securities.

Additional regulations promulgated by the SEC under the Williams Act require that anyone accepting a tender offer be allowed to withdraw any securities deposited with the tender offeror for a period of at least 15 business days after definitive copies of the offers are made public or for a period of at least 10 business days in the event a competing offer is made public, whichever is later.[143] Moreover, the Williams Act contains a broad antifraud provision prohibiting materially misleading statements or omissions and fraudulent, deceptive or manipulative acts or practices "in connection with any tender offer or request or invitation for tenders, or any solicitation of security holders in opposition to or in favor of any such offer, request or invitation."[144] In addition to the SEC's broad enforcement powers, a private cause of action for damages has been recognized under this section.[145]

Another aspect of SEC regulation of takeover transactions, including tender offers, seeks to constrain corporate managers from undertaking unwarranted actions to protect themselves from hostile takeovers. The SEC's efforts in this area reflect the importance of takeover threats as a principal mechanism used by the market to discipline corporate managers to be efficient and innovative—conduct which by increasing the corporation's profitability should generally enhance the relative value of the corporation's stock and discourage attempts to replace management through a takeover. Thus, regulations recently issued by the SEC under the Williams Act require a company which is the target of a tender offer to issue, within 10 business days of commencement of the offer, a statement meeting certain disclosure requirements.[146] In addition, the SEC has indicated that it will examine with special care the adequacy of the disclosures made in proxy materials distributed to shareholders for the purpose of obtaining their approval of proposed corporate actions to avoid a takeover. Included in the corporate actions subject to such special review—whether or not intended to discourage takeovers—are employment contracts with management, staggered terms for officers and directors, issuance of a new class of stock or increase in the number of shares outstanding, supermajority voting requirements, and creation of employee stock ownership plans.[147]

State Tender Offer Statutes. As in most other areas of securities regulation, tender offers are regulated by the states as well as the federal government. Approximately thirty states have adopted statutes specifically governing both procedural and substantive aspects of tender offers. Unlike the federal regulatory scheme for tender offers which is addressed initially to the offering corporation, most of the state statutes are initially addressed to the target corporation. When the target corporation has a certain relationship to a state, the state's tender offer statute is brought into play, subject to certain exemptions. One or more of the following factors is usually required to trigger the applicability of the state statutes: the target must be incorporated in the state, have its principal place of business or substantial assets located in the state or a large percentage of its employees in the state, or be doing business within the state or have its securities registered under state securities laws. Significantly, under such criteria, a single tender offer may be subject to regulation by several states at the same time, in addition to the federal government. These state statutes thus impose additional safeguards against corporate actions inimical to the interests of shareholders and/or the public.[148]

Indeed, most states having tender offer statutes impose requirements going far beyond those imposed by the Williams Act. These are of three basic types:

(i) increased disclosure requirements, including, for example, descriptions of the organization and operations of the offeror, all its properties, and all of its business in the past three years;
(ii) different timing requirements, such as the requirement that disclosure be made weeks in advance of the effective date of the tender offer, that tender offers be kept open for periods ranging in various states from fifteen

70

days to sixty days, and that offerors be allowed to withdraw their tender of shares for periods varying in different states from seven days after the offer commences until three days after the termination of the offer; and

(iii) the requirement that a hearing must be held if requested by the administrator of the state's securities laws or if demanded by the target corporation or by ten percent of its shareholders. In general, the purpose of the hearing is to determine if all applicable laws and regulations have been complied with in connection with the tender offer. But in some cases tender offers may also be prohibited if found to be unfair or inequitable to the offerees. Furthermore, tender offers may be delayed during such hearings or prohibited if found not to comply with applicable laws.[149]

Premerger Notification to the FTC and Department of Justice. In addition to the Williams Act and state tender offer statutes, tender offers (and all other types of acquisitions) involving large corporations are also regulated by the Hart-Scott-Rodino Antitrust Improvements Act of 1976 ("H-S-R Act").[150] This statute is designed to ensure that the Federal Trade Commission and the Antitrust Division of the Department of Justice have sufficient data and sufficient opportunity to determine whether to seek to enjoin a proposed merger as in violation of Section 7 of the Clayton Act. The H-S-R Act applies (in accordance with criteria relative to the size of the transaction) to corporations and other business entities, to all types of acquisitions, as well as to the formation of joint ventures by existing businesses through the creation of a new corporation. Though the specific requirements of the H-S-R Act and the rules and regulations promulgated thereunder by its joint administrators—the FTC and Antitrust Division—are complicated, the law in essence imposes two types of requirements—(i) a disclosure requirement and (ii) a waiting period requirement.

The disclosure requirement imposed requires the submission of data reflecting the potential effect of a business combination on competition. When an acquisition or merger is covered by the H-S-R Act, both the acquiring and the acquired business (and sometimes other parties to a transaction) are required to file information and documentation concerning:

(i) the assets owned or controlled by both the acquired and acquiring businesses;

(ii) a history of both businesses, including descriptions of all previous acquisitions made by the acquiring business in the previous ten years;

(iii) a description by product line of each industry engaged in by both businesses and any entities under their control;

(iv) a description of the relationship between the acquired and acquiring businesses;

(v) the most recent annual reports and audited financial statements of both businesses, plus certain SEC reporting forms;

(vi) a description of the assets and/or securities to be acquired;

(vii) a description of the acquisition procedure and submission of the acquisition agreement and all nonprivileged documents prepared in connection with the acquisition; and

(viii) a description of the owners of both businesses.[151]

The competitively sensitive nature of these data, as well as the specialized purpose of their disclosure—limited to permitting informed determination by the government as to the legality of the transaction in question—is reflected by the fact that, unlike disclosures required under the securities laws, "H-S-R reports" are confidential and may not be released publicly by the FTC or Antitrust Division.

The H-S-R Act mandates a thirty day waiting period after the required filings are made before an acquisition covered by the H-S-R Act can be consummated. (An exception is made in the case of acquisitions by means of a cash tender offer, where the waiting period is fifteen days.) The waiting period will be automatically extended if, prior to its expiration, either the FTC or the Antitrust Division requests additional information from either the acquiring or target corporation.[152]

While a variety of specialized exemptions from the H-S-R Act are provided, in general its coverage is extremely broad. The regulations issued pursuant to the H-S-R Act elaborate on its coverage tests, define its terms, and set time periods and methods for determining its various criteria, such as the valuation of assets. Violators of the H-S-R Act are liable for penalties of $10,000 per day for each day of noncompliance and for such equitable relief as may be ordered by the courts. In addition, a waiting period or an extension period may be extended by court action until substantial compliance with the H-S-R Act's disclosure requirements is made. It is illegal to consummate a transaction subject to the H-S-R Act during the waiting period.

Withdrawal from the Public Capital Market

The fact that a public corporation is comprehensively regulated whichever way it turns to engage in capital market transactions is perhaps most graphically illustrated by the regulations which limit its discretion even to leave the public market—in other words, to become a private, closely held corporation. There are basically three ways in which a corporation may withdraw from the public capital market. First, a corporation may liquidate its assets and distribute the proceeds (or the assets themselves) to its shareholders. Second, a corporation may undergo reorganization into a new corporation

73

(through merger, acquisition, or otherwise) with or without the same name. Third, the number of shareholders of a corporation may be reduced so that it is subsequently operated as a closely-held corporation. All three of these ways of withdrawing from the public capital market are subject to regulation under the securities laws.[153]

First, where any of these methods requires shareholder approval, except in the case of certain bankruptcy proceedings, the proxy regulation provisions of the federal securities laws will apply, requiring disclosure of all material information. Second, where the transactions involve the purchase or sale of securities, the general prohibitions on fraudulent and manipulative trading practices, such as Rule 10b-5, will apply. Similarly, if a tender offer is involved, the above-described rules under the Williams Act and the various state laws will apply. These prohibitions, however, do not extend to the merits of withdrawal from the public capital market, but only to the manner by which it is carried out.[154]

Finally, the SEC is given certain limited powers with respect to the consequences to public security holders of corporate reorganizations under the bankruptcy laws.[155]

In recent years, the SEC has been predominantly concerned with "going-private" transactions—transactions whereby publicly-held corporations, usually listed on a stock exchange and subject to the periodic reporting, disclosure and other requirements of the 1934 Act, are delisted, become closely-held and no longer subject to a variety of legal requirements. Recently adopted SEC rules require, in essence, that, before any transaction or series of transactions is effected which has "either a reasonable likelihood or a purpose" of removing a corporation from the disclosure system of the securities laws, various disclosure materials must be filed with the SEC and disseminated to shareholders. The information which must be disclosed includes the purpose of "going private"; the alternatives considered; the effects of the transaction on the issuer and its security holders, including federal tax consequences; the corporation's belief as to the fairness of the transaction to its security holders and the basis therefor, including any reports or opinions of independent parties received in connection with the transaction; and a description of the negotiations leading to the transaction. The SEC's rules also include an antifraud provision specifically applicable to going private transactions. Such disclosures must be updated to account for any material changes in the accuracy of such information.[156] Compliance with the "going-private" rules is in addition to compliance with other rules, such as the tender offer rules, that may also be applicable to a going private transaction.

Notes

1. Although there are different "schools" of economic thought, there is general agreement among most economists on the ways in which the forces of supply and demand operate to constrain corporate behavior. *See, e.g.,* P. Samuelson, *Economics* (10th ed. 1976); A. Alchian & W. R. Allen, *Exchange and Production: Competition, Coordination and Control* (2d ed. 1977); F. M. Scherer, *Industrial Market Structure and Economic Performance* (2d ed. 1980); G. J. Stigler, *The Theory of Price* (3d ed. 1966). The discussion in this Chapter reflects such generally accepted economic principles.

2. A corporation's overall hiring policies will reflect a variety of factors. *See* pp. 147–62, 236–38, *infra.*

3. *Northern Pacific Railway Co. v. United States,* 356 U.S. 1, 4–5 (1958).

4. There are a limited number of statutory and judicially created exceptions to antitrust regulation. Some of the most important ones are for: agricultural cooperatives (15 U.S.C. §§13(b), 17; 7 U.S.C. §§291–92, 455); aspects of the business of insurance to the extent they are regulated by state law (15

U.S.C. §§1011–15); certain activities of labor unions (15 U.S.C. §17; 29 U.S.C. §§52, 101–113); rate fixing agreements among motor carriers and railroads approved by the Interstate Commerce Commission (49 U.S.C. §5b); mergers among railroads approved by the ICC (49 U.S.C. §5(11)); agreements among ocean carriers approved by the Federal Maritime Commission (46 U.S.C. §814); the activities of domestic export associations which do not restrain trade in the United States (15 U.S.C. §§61–66); certain energy agreements (42 U.S.C. §6272); actions engaged in or compelled by state governments (*e.g., Bates* v. *State Bar of Arizona,* 433 U.S. 350 (1977); *Parker* v. *Brown,* 317 U.S. 341 (1943)); actions engaged in or compelled by foreign governments (*e.g., Banco Nacional de Cuba* v. *Sabbatino,* 376 U.S. 398 (1964); *Interamerican Refining Co.* v. *Texaco Maracaibo, Inc.,* 307 F. Supp. 1291 (D. Del. 1970)); and actions engaged in to influence governmental policy (*e.g., Eastern Railroad Presidents Conference* v. *Noerr Motor Freight, Inc.,* 365 U.S. 127 (1961)).

5. *See, e.g., Radovich* v. *National Football League,* 352 U.S. 445 (1957).

6. *United States* v. *Trenton Potteries Co.,* 273 U.S. 392 (1927).

7. *See* 15 U.S.C. §§1 (the Sherman Act), 12 (the Clayton Act), 13 (the Robinson-Patman Act), 41 (the Federal Trade Commission Act).

8. 15 U.S.C. §1. The Sherman Act was enacted in 1890. Similar provisions, specifically making such a prohibition applicable to U.S. foreign commerce and import transactions, are contained in Section 3 of the Sherman Act and the Wilson Tariff Act, respectively. *See* 15 U.S.C. §§3, 8–11.

9. *See, e.g., Broadcast Music, Inc.* v. *Columbia Broadcasting System, Inc.,* 441 U.S. 1 (1979); *National Society of Professional Engineers* v. *United States,* 435 U.S. 679 (1978); *Continental T.V., Inc.* v. *GTE Sylvania, Inc.,* 433 U.S. 36 (1977); *Northern Pac. R. Co.* v. *United States, supra.*

10. *See, e.g., United States* v. *Socony Vacuum Oil Co.,* 310 U.S. 150 (1940); *United States* v. *Trenton Potteries Co., supra.*

11. *See, e.g., United States* v. *Topco Associates, Inc.,* 405 U.S. 596 (1972).

12. *See, e.g., Klor's, Inc.* v. *Broadway Hale Stores,* 359 U.S. 207 (1959); *Fashion Originators' Guild of America* v. *Federal Trade Commission,* 312 U.S. 457 (1941).

13. *See, e.g., Northern Pac. R. Co.* v. *United States, supra.* For a further discussion of tying arrangements, see pp. 40–41, *infra.*

14. *See, e.g., United States* v. *Socony Vacuum Oil Co., supra,* at 221, 224–26. The *per se* rule is applicable whether the price-fixing arrangement is between competitors or between customers and suppliers. *See, e.g., United States* v. *Parke, Davis & Co.,* 362 U.S. 29 (1960).

15. *United States* v. *Socony Vacuum Oil Co., supra* at 226 n. 59.

16. *United States* v. *General Motors Corp.,* 384 U.S. 127, 147–148 (1966). *But see Broadcast Music Inc.* v. *Columbia Broadcasting System, Inc., supra* at 23 (holding, in the context of blanket copyright licensing, that "not all arrangements among actual or potential competitors that have an impact on price are *per se* violations of the Sherman Act or even unreasonable restraints").

17. *United States* v. *Container Corp. of America,* 393 U.S. 333 (1969). While this decision did not condemn all exchanges of price information, it did use *per se* language to strike down the particular information exchange presented in the circumstances of that case.

18. *National Society of Professional Engineers* v. *United States, supra.*

19. *United States* v. *Socony Vacuum Oil Co., supra.*

20. *Chicago Board of Trade* v. *United States,* 246 U.S. 231, 238 (1918). *Accord, National Society of Professional Engineers* v. *United States, supra; Continental T.V. Inc.* v. *GTE Sylvania, Inc., supra.*

21. *See, e.g., Continental T.V., Inc.* v. *GTE Sylvania, Inc., supra.* In this decision, the Supreme Court reversed prior case law and held that territorial and customer limitations agreed upon by a supplier with its customers (so-called "vertical restraints") were to be judged under the rule of reason, rather than the *per se* standard.

22. *See, e.g., Mackey* v. *National Football League,* 543 F.2d 606 (8th Cir. 1976), *cert. dismissed,* 434 U.S. 801 (1977).

23. *See Eiberger* v. *Sony Corp. of America,* 459 F. Supp. 1276 (S.D.N.Y. 1978).

24. *See, e.g., United States* v. *Loew's Inc.,* 371 U.S. 38, 46 (1962); *Ethyl Gasoline Corp.* v. *United States,* 309 U.S. 436 (1940); *United States* v. *Associated Patents, Inc.,* 134 F. Supp. 74 (E.D. Mich. 1955), *aff'd per curiam,* 350 U.S. 960

(1956); *United States* v. *Krasnov*, 143 F. Supp. 184 (E.D. Pa. 1956), *aff'd per curiam*, 355 U.S. 5 (1957).

25. 15 U.S.C. §2.

26. *United States* v. *Grinnell Corp.*, 384 U.S. 563, 570–71 (1966).

27. *See, e.g., United States* v. *E. I. du Pont de Nemours & Co.*, 351 U.S. 377 (1956).

28. *See, e.g., United States* v. *United Shoe Machinery Corp.*, 110 F. Supp. 295, 342 (D. Mass. 1953), *aff'd per curiam*, 347 U.S. 521 (1954). *See also Telex Corp.* v. *International Business Machines Corp.*, 510 F.2d 894 (10th Cir. 1975), *cert. dismissed*, 423 U.S. 802 (1975); *United States* v. *Aluminum Co. of America*, 148 F.2d 416 (2d Cir. 1945).

29. *See United States* v. *United Shoe Machinery Corp.*, *supra*.

30. *Compare Berkey Photo, Inc.* v. *Eastman Kodak Co.*, 603 F.2d 263 (2d Cir. 1979), *cert. denied*, 100 S. Ct. 1061 (1980) (company with monopoly power may reap rewards attributable to its efficient size and engage in ordinary business conduct, such as the announcement of new products, without running afoul of Section 2), and *Telex Corp.* v. *International Business Machines Corp.*, *supra* (holding that a corporation can protect a market share acquired by technological superiority by "the adoption of legal and ordinary marketing methods already used by others in the market," including "price changes which are within a 'reasonable' range up or down"), *with Greyhound Computer Corp.* v. *International Business Machines Corp.*, 559 F.2d 488 (9th Cir. 1977), *cert. denied*, 434 U.S. 1040 (1978) (holding that a company could be found to have unlawfully maintained its monopoly power by engaging in normally lawful practices which "unnecessarily" excluded competition).

31. *United States* v. *Aluminum Co. of America*, *supra*.

32. *United States* v. *United Shoe Machinery Corp.*, *supra*.

33. *See, e.g., United States* v. *Griffith*, 334 U.S. 100 (1948).

34. *See, e.g., Berkey Photo, Inc.*, *supra; California Computer Products, Inc.* v. *International Business Machines Corp.*, 1979-1 Trade Cases ¶62,713 (9th Cir. 1979).

35. *See, e.g., Swift & Co.* v. *United States*, 196 U.S. 375 (1905); *Pacific Engineering & Production Co. of Nev.* v. *Kerr-McGee Corp.*, 551 F.2d 790 (10th Cir.), *cert. denied*, 434 U.S. 879 (1977); *FLM Collision Parts, Inc.* v. *Ford Motor Co.*, 543

F.2d 1019 (2d Cir. 1976), *cert. denied*, 429 U.S. 1097 (1977); *Yoder Bros.* v. *California-Florida Plant Corp.*, 537 F.2d 1347 (5th Cir. 1976), *cert. denied*, 429 U.S. 1094 (1977). *But see Marquis* v. *Chrysler Corp.*, 577 F.2d. 624 (9th Cir. 1978); *Lessig* v. *Tidewater Oil Co.*, 327 F.2d 459 (9th Cir.), *cert. denied*, 377 U.S. 933 (1964) (holding that independent proof of a dangerous probability of success may not be required where there is adequate proof of a specific intent to monopolize).

36. *Compare United States* v. *Consolidated Laundries Corp.*, 291 F.2d 563 (2d Cir. 1961) (proof of market power is not required because specific intent is the essential element of the offense), *with V & L. Cicione, Inc.* v. *C. Schmidt & Sons, Inc.*, 403 F. Supp. 643, 651–2 (E.D. Pa. 1975), *aff'd mem.*, 565 F.2d 154 (3d Cir. 1977) (holding dangerous probability of success to be an essential element of both the attempt and conspiracy to monopolize offenses).

37. *See, e.g.*, Memorandum on "Shared Monopolies" by John H. Shenefield, Assistant Attorney General in charge of the Antitrust Division, Dept. of Justice (May 28, 1978); Address by Alfred F. Dougherty, Jr., Director, FTC Bureau of Competition (June 19, 1979).

38. *See, e.g.*, H. J. Goldschmid, H. M. Mann, J. F. Weston (eds.), *Industrial Concentration: The New Learning* (1974).

39. *See In re Ethyl Corp.*, [1976-1979 Transfer Binder] Trade Reg. Rep. (CCH) ¶21, 579.

40. *E. I. du Pont de Nemours & Co.* v. *FTC*, 488 F. Supp. 747 (D. Del. 1980).

41. 15 U.S.C. §14.

42. *Standard Oil Co. of Cal.* v. *United States*, 337 U.S. 293 (1949).

43. *Standard Fashion Co.* v. *Magrane-Houston Co.*, 258 U.S. 346 (1922).

44. *Siegel* v. *Chicken Delight, Inc.*, 448 F.2d 43 (9th Cir. 1971), *cert. denied*, 405 U.S. 955 (1972).

45. *International Salt Co.* v. *United States*, 332 U.S. 392 (1947).

46. *United States* v. *Loew's Inc., supra.* Since the Clayton Act only applies to "goods, wares, merchandise, machinery, supplies or other commodities," the Sherman Act must be employed when noncommodities are involved.

A practice closely related to tying arrangements is reciprocal dealing, where company X agrees to purchase company Y's product on the condition that company Y will purchase company X's product. This practice has been held unlawful in circumstances where it unreasonably restrains competition. *See United States* v. *General Dynamics Corp.*, 258 F. Supp. 36 (S.D.N.Y. 1966).

47. 15 U.S.C. §18.

48. *See, e.g., United States* v. *Pabst Brewing Co.*, 384 U.S. 546, 551 (1966); *United States* v. *Von's Grocery Co.*, 384 U.S. 270 (1966); *United States* v. *Philadelphia National Bank*, 374 U.S. 321 (1963); *Brown Shoe Co.* v. *United States*, 370 U.S. 294 (1962).

49. *See United States* v. *Von's Grocery Co., supra.*

50. *See, e.g., Brown Shoe Co.* v. *United States, supra; United States* v. *E. I. du Pont de Nemours & Co.*, 353 U.S. 586 (1957).

51. *Id.*

52. *See, e.g., United States* v. *Marine Bancorporation, Inc.*, 418 U.S. 602 (1974); *United States* v. *Falstaff Brewery Corp.*, 410 U.S. 526 (1973); *FTC* v. *Proctor & Gamble Co.*, 386 U.S. 568 (1967).

53. 15 U.S.C. §19.

54. *Id.*

55. 15 U.S.C. §13, 13a–c, 21a. *See generally* F. M. Rowe, Price Discrimination Under the Robinson-Patman Act. (1962).

56. *Id.* at §13.

57. 15 U.S.C. §§13(a)–(b).

58. *See United States* v. *United States Gypsum Co.*, 438 U.S. 422 (1978).

59. *See, e.g., United States* v. *United States Gypsum Co., supra; Automatic Canteen Co.* v. *FTC*, 346 U.S. 61, 74 (1953).

60. *See, e.g., Utah Pie Co.* v. *Continental Baking Co.*, 386 U.S. 685 (1967); *Pacific Engineering & Prod. Co.* v. *Kerr-McGee Corp., supra; International Air Indus., Inc.* v. *American Excelsior Co.*, 517 F.2d 714 (5th Cir. 1975), *cert. denied*, 424 U.S. 943 (1976).

61. *See, e.g., Beatrice Foods Co.*, 76 F.T.C. 719 (1969), *aff'd sub nom. Kroger Co.* v. *FTC*, 438 F.2d 1372 (6th Cir.), *cert. denied*, 404 U.S. 871 (1971).

62. *See Fowler Manufacturing Co.* v. *Gorlick*, 415 F.2d 1248 (9th Cir. 1969), *cert. denied*, 396 U.S. 1012 (1970).

63. *See, e.g., Quaker Oats Co.*, 66 F.T.C. 1131 (1964); *American Oil Co.* v. *FTC*, 325 F.2d 101 (7th Cir. 1963), *cert. denied*, 377 U.S. 954 (1964).

64. *See Perkins* v. *Standard Oil Co.*, 395 U.S. 642 (1969).

65. 15 U.S.C. §13(c).

66. The provision has also been applied, however, to outlaw certain instances of commercial bribery. *See, e.g., Rangen, Inc.* v. *Sterling Nelson & Sons*, 351 F.2d 851, 851 (9th Cir. 1965), *cert. denied*, 383 U.S. 936 (1966).

67. *See* 15 U.S.C. §§13(d), (e).

68. 15 U.S.C. §41 *et seq.* The statute also prohibits "unfair and deceptive acts or practices in or affecting commerce," which prohibition is discussed in Chapter 4, at pp. 180–184, *infra.*

69. *See, e.g., FTC* v. *Sperry & Hutchinson Co.*, 405 U.S. 233 (1972); *FTC* v. *Texaco Inc.*, 393 U.S. 223 (1968); *FTC* v. *Brown Shoe Co.*, 384 U.S. 316 (1966); *Atlantic Refining Co.* v. *FTC.*, 318 U.S. 357 (1965); *FTC* v. *Motion Picture Advertising Service Co.*, 344 U.S. 392 (1953).

70. *See, e.g., FTC* v. *Texaco Inc., supra; FTC* v. *Brown Shoe Co., supra; Atlantic Refining Co.* v. *FTC, supra.*

71. *See, e.g., R. H. Macy & Co.* v. *FTC*, 326 F.2d 445 (2d Cir. 1964).

72. *See, e.g., Beatrice Foods Co.*, 67 F.T.C. 473 (1967), *modified by consent*, 1967 Trade Cases ¶72, 124 (9th Cir. 1967).

73. *See Boise Cascade Corp.* v. *FTC*, 1980-2 Trade Cases ¶63, 351 (9th Cir. 1980).

74. *See, e.g.,* Address by Michael Pertschuk, Chairman of the FTC, to the Annual Meeting of the Antitrust and Economic Regulation Section of the Association of American Law Schools (December 27, 1978).

75. *See* 15 U.S.C. §§1–3. The Clayton and Robinson-Patman Acts do not generally provide for criminal enforcement. A few minor provisions of these statutes, however, do contain either criminal or civil penalties. *See* 15 U.S.C. §§13a, 18a, 20.

76. *See* 15 U.S.C. §§4, 25.

77. *See* 15 U.S.C. §15a.

78. *See* 15 U.S.C. §§1311–14. Intentional evasion or obstruction of a civil investigative demand is punishable by criminal penalties of up to $5,000, or five years in jail, or both. 18 U.S.C. §1505.

79. The proposed budget for the Division for fiscal 1980 was $43,592,000, with a staff of 939 employees. See [BNA] 15 Daily Report for Executives, at D-29 (January 22, 1979).

80. *See* 15 U.S.C. §45(a).

81. *See* 15 U.S.C. §45(1).

82. *See* 15 U.S.C. §§46, 49.

83. *See* 15 U.S.C. §15.

84. Thus, for the twelve-month period ending June 30, 1979, there were 1,234 private antitrust cases instituted, as compared to 228 such cases instituted for a similar period ending June 30, 1960. *See* Annual Report of the Director of the Administrative Office of the United States Courts to the Judicial Conference of the United States (1979).

85. *See* Rule 23 of the Federal Rules of Civil Procedure.

86. *See* 15 U.S.C. §15c. In *parens patriae* suits in which the defendant is found to have fixed prices, damages may be proved and measured in the aggregate by sampling or other reasonable methods and there is no need to prove separately the individual claim of, or amount of damages suffered by, any individual on whose behalf the suit is brought. *Id.* at §15d.

87. *See generally*, 4 Trade Reg. Rep. (CCH) ¶30,000 (1978), for a comprehensive listing of both specialized federal legislation containing antitrust prohibitions (such as the Bank Holding Company Act, 12 U.S.C. §§1841–44; and the Capper-Volstead Act, 7 U.S.C. §§291–292) and state antitrust and "little FTC" acts.

88. *See, e.g., Karpinski* v. *Ingrasci*, 28 N.Y.2d 45 (1971); Blake, *Employee Covenants Not to Compete*, 73 Harv. L.Rev. 625 (1960).

89. *See generally*, J. O. Von Kalinowski, *Antitrust Laws and Trade Regulation* §1.03 (1979); Callman, *Unfair Competition Trademarks and Monopolies* (1967). The latter is different from the concept of "unfair methods of competition" as defined by the FTC Act and is being used here to refer generally to that body of law which regulates such aspects of "unfairness" in business behavior as the misappropriation of trademarks and trade secrets, interference with competitors' contractual relationships, the unlawful exploitation of a competitor's effort, and similar rules of law relating to what is "fair" conduct in the marketplace (whether or not that conduct has anticompetitive effects).

90. 1 L. Loss, *Securities Regulation* 3 (2d ed. 1961).

91. 15 U.S.C. §§77a–77aa, 78a–78bb.

92. L. D. Brandeis, *Other People's Money: How the Bankers Use It*, ch. 5 at 92 (1932); L. Loss, *supra* at 123.

93. *See* 1933 Act §2(1); 1934 Act §3(10); R. W. Jennings &

H. Marsh, Jr., *Securities Regulation: Cases and Materials* 218–269 (4th ed. 1977).

94.   1933 Act, §5. Section 5 is qualified in a number of ways. Certain kinds of securities, such as securities issued by government agencies or nonprofit organizations and securities of corporations in industries subject to special regulation, such as insurance or trucking, are exempted from the registration requirement of Section 5 by Section 3 of the 1933 Act. In addition, Section 4 of the 1933 Act exempts from the registration requirement certain transactions in securities, in general applying the requirement only to public offerings by issuers, underwriters (including certain controlling persons) and dealers.

95.   1933 Act §10; 17 C.F.R. §§230.153, 230.153a, 230.174 (1979).

96.   1933 Act, Schedule A(13).

97.   1933 Act, Schedule A(31), (32), (28).

98.   1933 Act, Schedule A(29).

99.   1933 Act, Schedule A(27).

100.   *Id.* Certain corporations are also subject to more extensive regulation of their accounting practices, in some cases including adherence to a uniform system of accounts, under requirements established either by the SEC, as in the case of public utilities, or by the ICC, FCC or CAB and adopted by the SEC for purposes of SEC filings by such corporations. *See* 17 C.F.R. Parts 210, 256 and 257 (1979).

101.   1933 Act, §7.

102.   *Jennings & Marsh, supra* at 106.

103.   *See Report of the Committee on the Judiciary, Bankruptcy Law Revision*, H. R. Rep. No. 95-595, 95th Cong., 1st Sess. 228 (1977). In light of the complexities and costs of registration, Section 3(b) of the 1933 Act authorizes the SEC to exempt from all or part of the registration requirements an issue of securities where the aggregate amount at which the issue is offered to the public is less than $2,000,000. The SEC has issued regulations allowing such issues upon the submission of certain filings with the SEC, including an offering circular containing certain basic information about the issuer. 17 C.F.R. §230.240, 601–610a (1979).

104.   1933 Act §8.

105.   See 1 L. Loss, *supra* at 272–277; 4 L. Loss, *supra* at 2332–2338 (Supp. 1969); F. M. Wheat & G. A. Blackstone,

Guideposts for a First Public Offering, 15 Bus. Law. 539, 555–558 (1960).

106. 1933 Act, §11(a).

107. 1933 Act, §§11(a), 19.

108. 1 *Blue Sky L. Rep.* (CCH) ¶511. *See* L. Loss & E. M. Cowett, *Blue Sky Law* (1958); Uniform Securities Act §306.

109. *See,* e.g., Calif. Corp. Code §25240 (West 1977); *id.* at ¶8171.

110. 1 *Blue Sky L. Rep.* (CCH) ¶514.

111. *See* 1934 Act, §§5–7, 11A, 15, 15A; *See generally* N. Wolfson, R. M. Phillips & T. A. Russo, *Regulation of Brokers, Dealers and Securities Markets* (1977, Supp. 1979); S. M. Jaffe, *Broker-Dealers and Securities Markets* (1977).

112. 1934 Act, §§7, 11.

113. 1933 Act, §11(a) (4), (b) (3).

114. *See* Exchange Act Release No. 9671 (July 26, 1972).

115. 1934 Act, §§15(b) (3), (c).

116. *See* 17 C.F.R. §240.15b10-2,-3,-4 (1979); Wolfson *et al., supra* at ¶2.08–2.11. The purchase of securities on credit ("margin") is also regulated by the Federal Reserve Board and its regulations are strictly administered by the SEC, mainly through brokers and dealers, who are liable for unlawful margin transactions. *See* 1934 Act, §7. The regulation of brokers and dealers also involves a mandatory insurance program for the benefit of their customers, through the Securities Investors Protection Corporation (the "SIPC"), a non-profit, nongovernmental corporation the membership of which, subject to certain exceptions, is composed of all registered brokers and dealers and all persons who are members of a national securities exchange. 15 U.S.C. §78ccc. The SIPC operates under the supervision of the SEC. The SIPC maintains a fund the purpose of which is to insure against losses occasioned by the financial inability of its members to meet their obligations to the securities investors who are their clients.

117. Investment Advisers Act of 1940, §3, 15 U.S.C. §80b-3.

118. *Id.* §4.

119. *Id.* §§5, 15.

120. *Id.* §§6, 7, 8.

121. *See* Investment Company Act of 1940, §§9–10, 15–17, 15 U.S.C. §§80a-9,-10,-15 to -17.

122. 1933 Act §19(a); 1934 Act §13(b).

123. 17 C.F.R. §210.2-02 (1979); SEC Accounting Series

Release No. 4 (April 25, 1938), 5 *Fed. Sec. L. Rep.* (CCH) ¶72,005.

124. SEC Accounting Series Release No. 150 (Dec. 20, 1973), 5 *Fed. Sec. L. Rep.* (CCH) ¶72,172.

125. SEC Accounting Series Release No. 253 (Aug. 31, 1978), 6 *Fed. Sec. L. Rep.* (CCH) ¶72,275.

126. This policy, which is reflected, *inter alia,* in a number of FASB statements and in the FASB's Proposed Statement of Financial Accounting Concepts, *Objectives of Financial Reporting and Elements of Financial Statements of Business Enterprises* (Dec. 1977), is the subject of considerable debate and controversy, given the substantial dissimilarities among corporate enterprises. *See, e.g.,* B. Horwitz, "Rule Two: Is Uniformity Necessarily Bad," address to the American Accounting Association, Hawaii, 1979; T. Murphy, "Setting Accounting Standards—A Suggestion from a Businessman," *Financial Executive* (Aug. 1979).

127. 1934 Act, §13(b) (2); P.L. 95-213 §102, 91 Stat. 1494 (Dec. 19, 1977).

128. *See, e.g.,* Arthur Andersen & Co., *An Analysis of the Foreign Corrupt Practices Act of 1977* (1978).

129. 17 C.F.R. §240.13b2-1 (1979).

130. 17 C.F.R. §240.13b2-2 (1979).

131. 17 C.F.R. §210.3-06 (1979).

132. *SEC* v. *Texas Gulf Sulphur Co.,* 401 F.2d 833, 848, 852 (2d Cir. 1968), *cert. denied,* 404 U.S. 1005 (1971).

133. *See* R. Bromberg & L. D. Lowenfels, *Securities Fraud & Commodities Fraud* §§7.2, .3(3), .4, .6 (1979).

134. *Id.* §7.4.

135. American Stock Exchange Listing Agreement §1, ¶3, 3 *Am. Stock Ex. Guide (CCH)* 8955. *See NYSE Guide (CCH)* A17; *NASD Manual (CCH)* 2073, ¶7.

136. 1934 Act, §§12(f) (3), (4), (k); 17 C.F.R. 240.12d2-1, 12f-3 (1979).

137. 5 Loss, *supra* at 2813–2815.

138. *See* 3 Bromberg & Lowenfels, *supra* §2.4.

139. 1934 Act, §§13 (d), (e), 14(d), (e), (f).

140. 1934 Act, §13(d) (1).

141. 1934 Act, §13(d) (2).

142. 1934 Act, §14(d).

143. Exchange Act Release No. 16384, 17 C.F.R. §§240.14d-7 (1980).

144. 1934 Act, §14(e).

145. *Smallwood* v. *Pearl Brewing Co.*, 489 F.2d 579 (5th Cir.), *cert. denied*, 419 U.S. 873 (1974).

146. Exchange Act Release No. 16384, 17 C.F.R. §§240.14d-9, 240.14d-101 (1980).

147. *See* Exchange Act Release No. 15230 (Oct. 13, 1978), [1978 Transfer Binder] *Fed. Sec. L. Rep.* (CCH) ¶81,748; Rose & Collins, *Porcupine Proposals*, 12 Rev. of Sec. Reg. 977 (Feb. 14, 1979).

148. The constitutionality of a number of these statutes has been challenged recently. *See, e.g., Leroy* v. *Great Western United Corp.*, 443 U.S. 173 (1979); *Televest, Inc.* v. *Bradshaw*, [Current] *Fed. Sec. L. Rep.* (CCH) ¶97,154 (E.D. Va. 1979); *City Investing Co.* v. *Simcox*, 476 F. Supp. 112 (S.D. Ind. 1979). In addition, rules recently promulgated by the SEC under the Williams Act respecting commencement of a tender offer and public dissemination of tender offer materials appear to conflict with the requirements of a number of such state statutes and, in the SEC's view, pre-empt the operation of such statutes. *See* Exchange Act Release No. 16384, 17 C.F.R. §240.14d-2, -3 (1980).

149. *See generally* E. R. Aranow, H. A. Einhorn & G. Bernstein, *Developments in Tender Offers for Corporate Control*, ch. 5 (1977).

150. 15 U.S.C. §18A.

151. 16 C.F.R. Parts 801–803 (1979).

152. 15 U.S.C. §18A (e) (2).

153. Such a change in basic corporate structure is also subject to regulation under organic state corporation laws. *See* p. 6 *supra*.

154. *Santa Fe Inds., Inc.* v. *Green*, 430 U.S. 462 (1977); Exchange Act Release No. 16075 (Aug. 18, 1979), 2 *Fed. Sec. L. Rep.* (CCH) ¶¶23,703A, 23,706, *to be codified as* 17 C.F.R. §240.13e-5.

155. *See* 11 U.S.C. §1109(a).

156. Exchange Act Release No. 16075 (Aug. 18, 1979), 2 *Fed. Sec. L. Rep.* (CCH) ¶¶23,703A, 23,706, *to be codified as* 17, C.F.R. §240.13e-5.

3

The Federal Tax System as a Constraint Upon Corporate Decision Making

THE Federal income tax system exerts a tremendous influence on corporate resource allocation. Decisions on capitalization, acquisitions, capital investment, employment, political activity and location of operations may all be substantially influenced by numerous tax incentives, as well as tax penalties, contained in the Internal Revenue Code of 1954, as amended ("Code"). This chapter will consider the forces exerted by the tax system; specifically, the ways in which it influences the discretionary powers of management.

While a tax "incentive" is not quite the same as a mandatory constraint, nevertheless, as discussed in Chapter 1, under organic state corporation laws managers owe their corporation a duty of loyalty and care, and are otherwise required by law to make the most advantageous and appropriate decisions for the corporation. Moreover, a manager's own personal advancement will depend on his performance. For these reasons, among others, tax incentives have long operated as *de facto* constraints upon corporate decision making. Indeed, these incentives seem so effective to some proponents of regulatory reform that they have been urged as substitutes for command-type controls in various regulatory areas; it is asserted that, in lieu of the manpower and other apparatus required by command-type regulation, tax constraints serve to utilize financial incentives to accomplish the same results. On the other hand, several commentators on the federal income tax system have urged total discontinuance of the practice of using the Code as a means of promoting social and economic goals unrelated to raising revenues,[1] and greater conformity to the oft-proclaimed goal of tax neutrality.[2]

Tax considerations presently influence some of the most critical areas of corporate decision making, and their constraining influence can have profound implications for the corporation and for the economy and society in general. This chapter will discuss *seriatim* the impact of the tax law on each of several important subject matters of corporate decision making:

   (i) the choice between debt and equity financing;
  (ii) how and whether to engage in an acquisition or merger;
 (iii) how and whether to allocate capital resources (e.g., investments in existing lines of business vs. new lines, depreciable property, real estate, and investments in special areas such as pollution control, energy, technology, transportation, and the like);
 (iv) what classes of employees to hire and what kinds of employment benefits and retirement policies to institute; and
  (v) whether and how to enter into international transactions.

Because enterprises such as banks, insurance companies, cooperatives, Real Estate Investment Trusts and Regulated Investment Companies are subject to specially tailored tax provisions,[3] they will not be accorded separate coverage herein.

Throughout this chapter, consideration is given to whether the particular tax provision under examination was or was not specifically intended to influence corporate decision making in the ways it does. It is noteworthy that, at this point in government regulatory evolution, it is open to argument that corporations are constrained to act in specific ways as much, if not more, by tax rules ostensibly not intended to elicit such behavior as by rules clearly designed to do so.

Capital Raising through Debt and Equity

Subject to certain exceptions,[4] the interest payable on debt is deductible in computing taxable income. By contrast, the corporation is allowed no deduction for dividends paid. Moreover, a debt repayment normally is not taxable to the creditor receiving it, while the proceeds of a stock redemption will be treated as dividend income to the shareholder in many circumstances.[5]

By allowing the deduction for interest on debt but not of dividends paid on equities, the tax law furnishes a reason for corporations to raise new capital through the issuance of debt, whether or not convertible, in preference to issuing preferred or common stock. Moreover, the ability of a creditor to recoup his investment tax free, plus the risk that a holder of redeemed shares will be held to have received dividend income, further encourage debt financing. There is no indication Congress intended the tax system to bias corporate capitalization decisions toward debt financing—a circumstance which is nothing short of remarkable[6] given the importance, in a number of areas and for a variety of reasons, of the relative amounts of money a corporation borrows from creditors or receives in return for stock. In general, the more highly dependent a corporation is on debt, the more vulnerable it becomes to pressures from creditors and to financial difficulties in periods when the economy is weak —when, for example, overhead costs increase as a result of such factors as capacity underutilization and high inventory carrying charges. A corporation which, in addition to such higher overhead costs, must pay out large sums in interest, may face a period of severe financial crisis (the Chrysler situation in 1979–1980 is a prime example). In all cases it will be placed at a disadvantage relative to a corporation that is not as heavily "leveraged." Additional problems are posed when such a corporation resorts to private lenders, such as banks, insurance companies, and other financing institutions. Private lenders typically insist on a variety of covenants in loan agreements with corporations to protect the lenders' investment (e.g., by allowing the entire loan to be called) in the event the corporation fails to satisfy certain financial criteria. Some covenants also restrict the kinds of investments the corporation can make and, in extreme cases, the covenants can give the lender substantial control over the corporation's operations.

Beyond these implications, moreover, the fact that corporations are encouraged by the tax laws to incur debt may mean that the equity market is in a sense artificially constricted, and investments which otherwise would have gone into stock are being allocated into other areas. While this is not the place to explore the separate ramifications of the economy's increasingly weak equity market, it is interesting to note that the stock value of many companies is today, and has been for a number of years, significantly below the value of the companies' assets. That this explains much of the increased merger activity in recent years has been well recognized.[7] The role played by the tax law in this area, however, has not been extensively explored with respect to public policy regarding acquisition activity.

Corporate Acquisitions

Tax law provisions influence both the manner of acquisition and the basic decision whether or not to engage in an acquisition. The impact of the tax law here is particularly uncoordinated—in those cases in which it achieves relative neutrality it quite often does so by cancelling out either its own directives or the influences of other disciplines (e.g., financial accounting considerations).

1. Use of Debt Versus Equity in Acquisitions

The tax provisions discussed above, allowing the corporation to deduct interest but not dividends paid, and allowing a creditor to recoup his investment tax free while a holder of redeemed shares may be held in receipt of dividend income, encourage debt financing of corporate acquisitions in the same way and for the same reasons they induce debt financing generally. Here again, however, there is no indication that Congress intended to influence in this fashion the method of corporate financing of acquisitions, particularly given the potential implications of over-reliance on debt financing discussed above.

91

But the debt financing of corporate acquisitions is encouraged by other provisions of the tax law as well. If an acquiring corporation purchases for debt or cash (which may be raised by debt issuance) the assets of another corporation (for convenience here called the "target corporation"), either directly or by purchasing the stock of the target and promptly liquidating it,[8] the assets in the hands of the acquiring corporation will have a "tax basis" (used, for example, to determine future depreciation) to be derived from the purchase price paid. This is so even though the tax basis of those assets in the hands of the target corporation, immediately prior to the acquisition, may have been low relative to economic value (for example, the replacement cost on the open market), and even though in many cases the difference between economic value and lower tax basis will not be taxed to the target corporation.[9] This nonrecognition concept, generically known in the tax law as the "General Utilities rule,"[10] encourages corporate combinations through purchase.

While nonrecognition at the target corporation level does not automatically avoid recognition of capital gain to its shareholders, other provisions of the tax law may lead to the result that little if any tax is paid. For example, if the shareholder dies, the stock of a corporation in the hands of his estate is "stepped up" and awarded a fair market value tax basis,[11] with the result that there may be no capital gains (amount received less tax basis). Alternatively, the holder of stock in the target corporation may sell the stock principally or entirely for debt obligations of the acquiring corporation, with the result that an election to defer reporting of gain, on the installment method, may be available.[12] The applicable rules are somewhat complex but, in general, the election will be available if the payment (for example, cash) in the year of sale does not exceed 30 percent of the total selling price, and the debt obligations received are promissory notes and are not bonds or debentures readily tradable in an established securities market. Neither the fresh-start-at-death basis nor the installment election was designed by Congress to favor the use of debt over equity in the financing of corporate acquisitions.

Paradoxically, while some of these Code provisions encourage debt-financed acquisitions, other provisions of the law furnish a contrary incentive under certain circumstances. Particularly relevant are the tax-free reorganization provisions. If one corporation, by voluntary transfer or merger, directly or through a controlled subsidiary, acquires the assets or controlling stock of a target corporation, in qualifying circumstances[13] the former shareholders of the target may exchange, tax free, their target shares for shares of the acquiring corporation.[14] No tax basis step-up is permitted in these circumstances. The former target shareholder holds shares of the acquiring corporation at his historic basis,[15] pregnant with future capital gains if, as normally is the case, the shares are worth more than that basis. The acquiring corporation or its subsidiary holds the assets of the target corporation at the same basis that these assets were held by the target corporation before the transaction.[16] Thus, unlike the situation that obtains when the acquisition is for cash or debt, gain potential is here retained at the corporate level. Nonetheless, the ability to combine corporations free of current tax burden, and to afford the shareholders of a closely-held target corporation the advantages of freely marketable shares, encourages equity-financed, as opposed to debt-financed, acquisitions in situations in which an exchange of shares is feasible. While Congress without question intended corporate combinations for share consideration to be tax free, it is less than clear that Congress, at least when the provisions were first enacted, focused upon reorganization exchanges using freely marketable shares.

In addition to the foregoing provisions which have a substantial impact on corporate debt/equity decisions, there exists at least one section of the Code which was intended by Congress to discourage corporations from making certain debt-financed acquisitions.[17] It denies a deduction for interest expense incurred by a corporation in narrowly specified debt-financed acquisitions of the stock or assets of another corporation. Designed to apply only to certain acquisition-minded "conglomerate" corporations using very large amounts of subordinated convertible debt and incurring annual interest expense in excess of $5 million, the provision is of extremely limited concern to the majority of corporations. In essence, it does little to alter the tax system's debt-over-equity tilt. It is ironic, however, that the tax law which, on the one hand, as discussed below (pp. 96–97), operates effectively but unintentionally to encourage cash mergers (which most often are of a conglomerate nature due to antitrust constraints on the acquisition of competitors, customers or suppliers) on the other hand ineffectually attempts directly to discourage conglomeration.

Finally, the impact of the tax law on the use of debt versus equity in acquisitions cannot be divorced from the relevant financial accounting rules. If in the corporate combination the shareholders of the target corporation received only voting common stock of the acquiring corporation, and other requirements are met, the combination will be accounted for as a pooling of interests.[18] Particularly if the target corporation is highly profitable, pooling treatment is likely to have a favorable impact on the reported earnings per share of the acquiring corporation. On the other hand, if the target corporation is acquired for cash or debt, the business combination will be accounted for as a purchase.[19] In many cases, the tax benefits inhering in purchase treatment may be viewed by management as outweighed by an adverse impact on balance sheet presentation and on reported earnings per share under the financial accounting rules. Moreover, there are circumstances—such as a tax-free exchange merger in which the acquiring corporation issues convertible preferred stock rather than voting common stock (or issues part stock and part cash)—in which the asset basis is not stepped up for tax purposes, but financial accounting requires purchase rather than pooling treatment.[20] Because a stockholder's subsequent exercise of the conversion privilege will not be treated as a taxable event [21]—a clear advantage to the former target corporation shareholder—the acquiring corporation is placed in a dilemma. It is encouraged on the one hand to issue convertible preferred stock in order to offer the target shareholders an advantageous transaction, but on the other hand choosing such an option is discouraged through the adverse tax and financial accounting impact upon the acquiring corporation.

In sum, the interacting provisions described above direct and in some cases impel corporate management decisions which, were the rules truly neutral in application, might not be made in the same way. Corporations are encouraged by the tax law to make debt-financed acquisitions, an encouragement that may be offset at least in part by financial accounting considerations and by the inability of target corporation shareholders to avoid at least deferred recognition of gain. On balance, however, corporation decisions are weighted toward incurring heavy debt burden—a circumstance which, as discussed above, can have a variety of adverse effects, particularly in times of recession.

2. Incentives to Corporate Combination

A number of the tax rules, moreover, directly serve to encourage corporate acquisitions. As discussed above, the General Utilities rule, which absolves a target corporation from recognizing gain inherent in its appreciated capital assets, and the income-tax-free step-up-of-share tax basis at the holder's death, separately and in combination encourage corporate acquisitions when the tax basis of assets in the hands of the target corporation is low relative to economic value. Were both concepts expunged from the tax law, there would likely be fewer purchases by large corporations of small corporations.

Paradoxically, the tax law encourages acquisitions not only when the tax basis of assets in the hands of the target corporation is low relative to economic value, but also in the converse situation, through what is known as a "leveraged buy-out." Since the tax law does not take cognizance of unrealized gain or loss on property,[22] a corporation with assets worth less than their tax basis is encouraged by the tax law to sell in order to recognize the loss at the corporate level. This is particularly true since the sale at a loss of property used in a taxpayer's trade or business generally produces fully deductible ordinary loss and not merely capital loss.[23] In addition, because it is generally desirable to sell assets used in a trade or business *en masse* in order to preserve goodwill or going concern value, the tax law effectively encourages a corporation to sell a division, or its entire business, when value is less than tax basis in order to recognize the loss and recoup taxes—either by loss carrybacks or by offset against the income of profitable divisions. To illustrate, assume a corporation has operated at a yearly after-tax profit of $1 million, that assets are valued at a multiple of 10 times earnings or $10 million, and that asset basis equals $12 million. If the corporation sells its assets for $10 million, it will receive an additional $1 million from the government through a tax loss carryback refund.[24] Thus, a business worth $10 million if retained—and worth only $10 million to the purchaser—is worth $11 million if sold. That this encourages sale of the business is obvious.

Moreover, the tax-free reorganization rules, which enable the shareholders in a close corporation to obtain marketable shares at no current tax cost, also encourage business combinations—in preference to liquidation or other ways of increasing the liquidity of owners' estates. Again, were the rules otherwise, and tax-free reorganizations limited, for example, to corporate combinations in which both corporate parties are public or neither corporate party is public, a reduction in the volume of reorganizations could be anticipated. However, such rules, in addition to raising a variety of administrative problems, would likely be considered unfair in a number of respects.

Finally, the two-tiered nature of the corporate tax, taxing the corporation on its earnings and again taxing distributions out of these earnings to individual shareholders, encourages corporate management to retain rather than distribute earnings, even when not needed in the corporation's current operations. A frequent channel for some of these accumulated earnings is the acquisition of other firms (mainly in unrelated industries due to antitrust restrictions). For closely held corporations, this impetus to acquire other firms is strengthened by the penalty tax provisions which, by levying additional tax on passive investments made with accumulated corporate earnings, effectively foreclose otherwise attractive alternatives.[25] There is no indication that the tax law was intended by Congress as a "policy" constraint to encourage business combinations. Yet this is precisely what it does.

Capital Investment and Special Expenditures

Depending on the exact situation involved, the tax law constitutes a major and in many cases determining factor in how management allocates corporate resources. This section will analyze Code provisions which determine the tax treatment to be afforded various kinds of business investment, including internal and acquisition expenditures, investments in depreciable property, real estate, research and development, energy, transportation, and other special classes of resources.

1. Internal Development through Advertising or R&D

In certain cases, the tax law favors and constrains internal investment over acquisitions. For example, consider a corporation that develops internally a new line of business expending $10 million in advertising (or R&D) to obtain 5 percent of the market. Because the $10 million investment will be fully deductible as an operating expense,[26] that company will then (at a 46 percent tax rate) have a net development cost of only approximately $5.4 million.[27] But if the same corporation had paid $10 million for the goodwill of an already established business occupying 5 percent of the market, it would have a net cost of the full $10 million. This is so because the good will of the established company, even if it is attributable to that company's prior advertising expenditures, is not deductible either immediately or over time.

In this respect, therefore, the tax law encourages internal development of a new business line where heavy advertising, R&D, or similar type expenditures may be involved, and discourages acquisition, at the same gross development cost, of a business operation established by another. Nothing suggests Congress either intended this result in fashioning the tax law or meant this as an exception to the general favoring of acquisitions (which itself was not intended). And nothing indicates that for new lines requiring advertising expenditures Congress wished to encourage original entry while for other types of development it wished to encourage acquisitions. Yet this is the result.

2. Investment in Depreciable Tangible Personal Property

Corporations are encouraged to invest in new depreciable tangible personal property, of all kinds, by means of the investment tax credit (ITC),[28] accelerated depreciation,[29] and the Asset Depreciation Range (ADR) system.[30]

In basic terms, the investment tax credit allows a corporation purchasing or producing or (in some cases) leasing depreciable tangible personal property with a useful life of three or more years, to reduce otherwise due taxes by up to 10 percent (depending upon the useful life)[31] of the production or purchase cost of the property. Although the rule generally reduces the corporation's tax in the amount of the credit, the corporate owner retains the full cost basis for all purposes, including calculating gain or loss on disposition and calculating depreciation deductions. Thus, unless the corporation has insufficient tax otherwise due[32] in the year of the production or purchase,[33] the investment credit provides a strong motivation to the corporation for producing or purchasing new depreciable tangible personal property, by in effect sub-

sidizing amounts up to 10 percent of the property's manufacture cost or purchase price. This investment credit
constrains corporations to invest currently in new tangible personal property "at the margin" which is to say that
without the credit the expenditure could not be justified
and would not be made. This credit is manifest and powerful, and was clearly intended by Congress.[34] The credit
also benefits corporations in the business of producing
capital equipment used by others in their trade or business or for the production of income. Corporate managers
are thus encouraged to enter into or expand operations to
produce such capital equipment.

Methods of accelerated depreciation also are available
for new depreciable tangible personal property. This allows the corporation to take depreciation deductions at
more rapid rates than the rate of physical deterioration or
economic obsolescence of the property. Assuming sufficient corporate income against which to take these deductions, accelerated depreciation leads to reduced taxes
in earlier years, and higher taxes in later years, than
would be payable if the property were depreciated on a
straight-line, physical deterioration, or economic obsolescence basis. Because of the time value of money, particularly in periods of inflation, this has the effect of
conferring a tax benefit in addition to investment credit
on corporations that invest in new depreciable tangible
personal property, and consequently, as Congress clearly
intended, provides an additional incentive for corporate
management to invest in such property.

The ADR system was designed "to minimize disputes
between taxpayers and the Internal Revenue Service as
to the useful life of property, and as to salvage value,
repairs, and other matters."[35] In practice, the election of
the ADR system frequently results in shorter useful
lives[36] and the availability of a favorable first year con-

vention for determining the date when assets are placed in service.[37] These in turn result in further accelerated depreciation for assets with respect to which the ADR system is available. The ADR system is available for most types of depreciable tangible personal property[38] and consequently corporate investment in the types of depreciable personal property covered by the ADR system is further encouraged, again because of the time value of money.

3. Investment in Real Property

The tax system also provides incentives for corporate investment in real property. Several provisions grant incentives for corporate investments in new real property of all kinds. While the ADR system is not available,[39] accelerated depreciation is allowed with respect to new real property.[40] Moreover, upon the sale or other disposition of real property, the owner of real property is able to avoid depreciation recapture by an amount equal to normal straight-line depreciation;[41] this enables the owner to convert ordinary income into capital gain, if the property is disposed of. At the margin, the knowledge of the availability of this potential benefit encourages investment in real property.

Finally, most corporations are exempt from the requirement that construction-period interest and taxes with respect to real property[42] be capitalized and deducted over a term of years. They are instead allowed to deduct these costs currently.[43] Thus, most corporations are particularly encouraged to construct real property since they are allowed to deduct these expenses immediately,[44] obtaining a consequent benefit measured by the time value of money.

In addition to generally encouraging investment in real estate, the tax system recently has created a special incentive—a new investment tax credit[45]—for the rehabilitation of older buildings. To qualify, the building to be rehabilitated must have been in use (by someone) for at least 20 years, and the improvements to be made must have a useful life of at least five years. This incentive was provided because of Congressional concern over deterioration in central cities and in other neighborhoods generally.[46] This provision is likely to be effective in inducing the rehabilitation of older buildings rather than the building of new ones.

4. Investment in Selected Types of Property: Pollution Control, Energy, Transportation, and Natural Resources

Provisions are periodically added to the tax law in order to channel corporate investments into areas of national priority.

Pollution Control

Investment in pollution control facilities is encouraged by the availability of unlimited amounts of financing through industrial development bonds, the interest on which is tax-free to the recipients.[47] The availability of funding through tax-free industrial development bonds leads to lower interest expense incurred by corporations investing in pollution control facilities, and consequently encourages corporations to make investments of this kind. In addition, corporate investment in pollution control facilities is encouraged by the availability of rapid amortization[48] for such facilities. Rapid amortization is another form of accelerated depreciation, and offers advantages due to the time value of money. An added inducement is that the full 10 percent investment tax credit is available for pollution control facilities with useful lives of over five years.[49]

Energy

Investment in certain types of energy property is induced by the addition of an extra 10 percent energy tax credit to the 10 percent investment tax credit already available for tangible personal property,[50] plus the provision of a 10 percent energy tax credit even if the acquired asset is not tangible personal property.[51] Also, corporate investment in facilities for the local furnishing of electricity or gas is encouraged by the availability of unlimited amounts of tax-free industrial development bonds.[52]

Transportation

Corporate investment in selected forms of transportation property also is encouraged by the tax law. Investment in new real property (except a building and its structural components) used in the furnishing of transportation of any kind is influenced by the availability of an investment tax credit.[53] Investment in airports, docks, wharves, mass commuting facilities, parking facilities, or related storage or training facilities is aided by the availability of unlimited amounts of tax-free industrial development bond financing.[54] Railroad investment is encouraged by allowing rapid amortization of railroad grading, tunnel bores[55] and railroad rolling stock[56] (although, if rapid amortization of the rolling stock is elected, the investment credit must be foregone).[57] In addition, certain expenditures in connection with the rehabilitation of railroad rolling stock are currently deductible and are not required to be capitalized.[58]

Natural Resources

Investment in the extraction of natural resources is encouraged by a number of provisions which lower the effective tax rate on gain from such activities. The primary advantage afforded such investment is provided by the percentage depletion deduction.[59] This allows for deduction of a specified proportion, depending on the resource,[60] of the gross income from the property each year. In general, percentage depletion in the case of a successful venture leads to recovery of the original investment at an accelerated rate, and may produce deductions totaling far more than the original investment in the property. In addition, development expenses of a mine or other natural resource deposit (other than an oil or gas well), which otherwise would be nondepreciable capital expenditures, are allowed as a deduction against ordinary income when incurred.[61] Current deduction against ordinary income also is allowed for certain otherwise nondeductible mining exploration expenditures.[62] Finally, under specified conditions coal and timber royalties are taxable at capital gain rates, and not at the higher rates normally applicable to ordinary income.[63]

All of the incentives to corporate investment in specific types of property discussed in this section were intended as such by Congress.

5. Investment in the Creation of New Technology

The tax system provides substantial incentives for corporate investment in the creation of new technology. This is done by allowing the current deduction of research and experimental expenditures,[64] or, if more advantageous (presumably because there are no current profits), amortization over a five-year or longer period.[65] These expenditures would otherwise be chargeable to the capital account, and would be recouped only through depreciation deductions or possibly not until sale or disposition of the business in which they are incurred. This tax incentive was intended by Congress.

6. Relation to Antitrust Policy

One of the expenditures least favored by corporate managers is the payment of antitrust damages; and the tax law does little, if anything, to alleviate the deterrent effect of antitrust penalties, discussed in Chapter 2 above.

If in a criminal proceeding a taxpayer is convicted of a violation of the antitrust laws or pleads guilty or *nolo contendere* to a charge, no deduction is allowed for two-thirds (i.e., the punitive portion) of damages paid in a private civil action based on the same violation.[66] The clear Congressional purpose of this rule was to leave the deterrent effect of punitive damage awards in private antitrust actions undiluted by the federal income tax law.

Combined with the collateral estoppel effect of a criminal conviction on subsequent civil proceedings,[67] the denial of a deduction places enormous pressure on corporate management to forestall criminal proceedings by some means other than a plea of guilty or *nolo con-*

tendere. On the other hand, if it is impossible to persuade the government not to seek less than a criminal conviction, then corporate management is induced to seek acquittal even more vigorously than the direct penalties imposed for conviction and the resulting adverse publicity would suggest, because of the potentially enormous additional and *nondeductible* costs of resulting civil liability.[68]

7. Donations to Charities and Political Candidates, and Expenses to Influence Public Opinion

Corporations are encouraged to make donations to charities by the allowance of a deduction in the amount of their charitable contributions, so long as the contributions do not exceed 5 percent of the corporation's taxable income.[69] Corporations, however, are given no deductions for contributions to political candidates,[70] or for expenses incurred in connection with attempts to influence public opinion, even if the contribution or expenditure is otherwise an ordinary and necessary business expense.[71] A corporation is not denied a deduction, however, for the ordinary and necessary business expenses[72] of establishing or supporting a political action committee,[73] or incurred in lawful lobbying efforts.[74]

All of this channeling of corporate activity by the tax system was intended by Congress.

Employment

1. Hiring of Selected Types of Employees

Congress designed provisions in the tax system to induce corporations to hire certain new employees[75] and to participate in the work-incentive program.[76] Employers can receive a tax credit for 50 percent of the first-year wages, and 25 percent of the second-year wages,[77] paid to new employees who are members of certain targeted groups,[78] including economically disadvantaged youths, Vietnam-era veterans, ex-convicts and participants in certain work incentive programs.[79]

2. Providing Selected Types of Benefits to Employees

The employer is influenced by the tax system, as intended by Congress, to provide certain types of benefits to its employees. This is done indirectly by deducting an employer's contributions to certain plans from its income and by excluding them from income of benefited employees. This allows the employer to convey the full benefit of its contributions to the employees undiluted by current (or in some cases, any) taxes imposed on the recipients. Among the programs encouraged in this way are group term insurance,[80] group medical insurance plans,[81] group legal services,[82] educational assistance,[83] and transportation between an employee's residence and his place of employment in a commuter highway vehicle.[84]

3. Retirement Arrangements

From the employee viewpoint, perhaps the most important monetary consideration next to wages in selecting an employer is the type of retirement program available. In the tax law and related legislation, such as the Social Security system, Congress has created a maze of mandatory requirements and incentives to influence corporations to adopt various types of retirement programs. As with other provisions of the tax law, the rules and incentives frequently give mixed signals to the corporation, urging it in contradictory directions. As elsewhere, these various incentives also have unintended effects on seemingly unrelated corporate actions, such as the closing of a plant or the undertaking of an acquisition. Described below are the Social Security system, tax law incentives, and the Employee Retirement Income Security Act of 1974 (commonly referred to as "ERISA"), all of which influence substantially the corporation's ultimate decision on the kind of retirement benefits to provide (or not to provide).

Social Security

Except for federal, state and local government employees, and employees of nonprofit organizations, Social Security is universal in the United States, with mandatory coverage and contributions required of all employers, employees and self-employed individuals. The Social Security system operates principally on a pay-as-you-go basis with current contributions used to fund current benefits. There is a trust fund which increases in surplus years, but operates mostly as a cushion to offset deficits in the system in lean years. As a result of financing problems, the Social Security Act of 1977 was enacted which made major changes in the Social Security law. In order to reduce immediate and projected deficits in the Social Security system, contributions of employers, employees and self-employed individuals will substantially increase by reason of an increase in the percentage contribution rates and the taxable wage base. At the same time, benefits projected to be paid in future years will increase at a slower rate. Notwithstanding the changes made by the Social Security Act of 1977, there is continued uncertainty about funding the Social Security system over the long term. Currently, there are over three persons contributing to the system for each person receiving a benefit. Based on present demographic trends, it is predicted that in the year 2035 there will only be approximately two persons contributing to the system for each person receiving a benefit.[85] The increase in the taxable wage base, coupled with the increase in the contribution rate under Social Security has resulted in a substantial increase in employment costs as a percentage of payroll. These costs, characterized by the Social Security system as employment taxes, can be more accurately described as transfer payments from the employed and their employers to the retired. This financing system taxes labor-intensive industries more than capital-intensive industries regardless of the profit levels of either, and thus represents a substantial incentive for employers to make labor-saving expenditures.

The Social Security system represents a compromise between a system that is strictly wage-related and a system which provides benefits based upon need. As a result, while the benefit schedule is based upon wages earned during a person's working lifetime, the system is weighted towards low income workers by providing certain minimum benefit levels.

One effect of Social Security being weighted towards lower-paid employees is that those employees can have aggregate retirement benefits (including Social Security and private pension fund benefits) equal to or even greater than their pre-retirement wages. Where this does happen there is a strong incentive for such employees to retire and not continue to work, especially as Social Security benefits are not subject to tax, while wages are.

This in turn affects corporate hiring and benefit practices—employers must replace through private retirement plans a greater percentage of earnings for higher paid employees to place such employees when they retire in a position in which their standard of living will not be materially decreased as a result of retiring. As a consequence of the dual problem to the corporations of not providing too much in retirement benefits for low-paid employees and providing a greater percentage of benefits for high-paid employees, they often have no practical alternative but to design private retirement plans to provide an offset for Social Security benefits, which is permitted within certain limitations under the Code and Treasury Department regulations.[86]

Employer-Sponsored Programs

The regulation of employer-sponsored retirement benefits by the government has evolved through two important phases. First, the Revenue Act of 1942 contained provisions (retained in the Internal Revenue Code of 1954) encouraging employers to provide pension and profit-sharing benefits.[87] Second, in 1974, ERISA made significant changes in those laws to insure that promised employee retirement benefits would be realized. As a result of ERISA, employers now shoulder new substantial administrative burdens. Additionally, serious new problems have been created by Title IV of ERISA, which established a new government agency, the Pension Benefit Guaranty Corporation ("PBGC"), and established employer liability upon termination of pension plans.

1. Phase I: Provision of Tax Incentives for the Implementation of Pension and Profit-Sharing Plans

No legislation has been adopted in this country which requires private employers to provide employees with retirement benefits in addition to Social Security benefits. Union representatives, similarly, are free to seek retirement benefits or not, as they deem them to be in the best interests of union members, pursuant to collective bargaining agreements. For competitive and social reasons, however, most corporate employers choose to provide benefits for employees upon retirement.

In this connection, the tax system provides a powerful incentive for the adoption of retirement plans. Under the tax provisions applicable to retirement plans, contributions by employers to plans that satisfy designated standards—especially, that a plan not discriminate in favor of high-paid employees, officers, or shareholders—are immediately deductible by the employer.[88] Moreover, the employee is not taxed on employer contributions to and earnings from the plan until benefits are distributed upon termination of employment, retirement or death.[89] Under the tax law, many different types of plans can be adopted to best suit an employer's needs, including plans pursuant to which contributions are based on profits, stock of the employer is contributed, or a defined benefit (which may be based on age, service and earnings) is promised at retirement. By 1974, an estimated $175 billion in assets had been set aside in such plans covering over 30 million participants.[90]

2. Phase II: ERISA

In 1974, ERISA, a law as voluminous as it is complex, was enacted. Addressing itself to several perceived shortcomings, ERISA set minimum vesting standards,[91] minimum funding standards[92] and a system to guarantee benefits on termination for private employee benefit plans.[93] Provisions were also enacted to protect plan assets from tampering.[94] Generally, a prophylactic rule was established prohibiting persons associated with a plan (e.g., employer or trustees) from inducing or influencing plan investments in enterprises which they own or with which they are connected. The detailed provisions are commonly referred to as the prohibited transaction rules. In addition, ERISA established numerous reporting and disclosure standards to control, through the threat of publicity, activities believed to be inimical to employee interests.[95] It also tightened the pre-existing requirements that plans not discriminate in favor of high-paid employees, and it set maximum benefit levels for tax qualified plans[96] and minimum requirements for the accrual of benefits and vesting of benefits over the period of employment.[97] As a result, under ERISA plan benefits do not arise predominately by reason of retirement, but rather by reason of continued employment over a given period of years. Thus, plan benefits more nearly resemble deferred wages than classic retirement protection.

Many of the requirements of ERISA were extended to non-tax-qualified plans. All of these matters were thus effectively removed from the ambit of corporate discretion for those corporations maintaining retirement plans.

While ERISA's goals have generally been achieved, in the process there has developed a morass of detailed regulation of and paperwork for employers, greatly increasing the cost and time associated with plan administration. One initial effect was that many small employers terminated their plans.

Another significant change made by ERISA in the regulation of pension plans was its setting of minimum funding standards for employers contributing to defined benefit plans.[98] No longer could employers adopt a pension plan promising a fixed or defined benefit at retirement and fail to set aside adequate funds each year to satisfy the liabilities accruing, based upon minimum funding levels. Nevertheless, Congress recognized that certain plans would still not have sufficient funds upon termination or partial termination to meet promised benefits. This would occur if there were adverse investment experience, actuarial error in funding benefits,[99] or a premature termination or partial termination of the plan prior to the funding of all liabilities. Accordingly, there was created the PBGC which guarantees (to a certain extent) the payment of vested pension benefits from tax-qualified defined benefit plans to employees.[100] This quasi-governmental agency behaves like a private insurance company and collects premiums from the qualified defined benefit plans, based upon the number of participants in such plans, to cover its expected liabilities. As discussed below, however, this arrangement may have very important ramifications on corporate choices in areas unrelated to the provision of retirement benefits.

Most serious is the effect of potential employer liability to the PBGC by reason of termination of an under-funded plan. While the purposes of the PBGC are praiseworthy —to insure that employees in fact receive plan benefits —the potential cost of insuring these benefits is stagger-

113

ing.[101] In 1977, the unfunded vested benefits of one hundred of the largest corporations aggregated $18.5 billion dollars.[102] For some companies, the contingent liability exceeded a billion dollars.[103] A company cannot make an acquisition, sell a part of its business, close a plant or obtain a loan without considering the effect of this contingent liability to the PBGC on its financial situation.

So threatening is the risk of liability that corporations have had to make decisions that would otherwise be unjustified in light of underlying economic realities. This can best be illustrated by example. Assume a steel manufacturer has three plants. One plant is outmoded, highly reliant on manual labor, and unable to produce an end product that can be sold at a competitive price in the marketplace. The company is considering closing the plant, which will result in the discharge of 30 percent of its total employees, and expanding its most modern facility to employ new workers. However, after it is informed that the closing of the plant will result in a termination of the pension plan for the plant workers and the imposition of a very substantial liability to the PBGC because of the unfunded status of the plan, the company may be forced to continue operating the inefficient plant.

Termination liability coverage for multi-employer (union) plans augurs additional substantial problems for the PBGC and industry, particularly in declining industries where the possibility of termination of plans is greatest and where, under the original ERISA legislation, contingent liability may be imposed upon the few remaining healthy companies in an industry, in turn weakening them. It is estimated that imposition of PBGC coverage for multi-employer plans would create potential liabilities of $4.8 billion and require an annual premium of $80 per plan participant to cover this liability.[104]

To limit to some extent fiduciary liability in connection

114

with the holding of employer securities and in order to encourage adoption of plans, even by cash-poor companies, Congress has authorized creation of employee stock ownership plans (commonly referred to as ESOPs), which qualify for the favorable tax benefits described above. In lieu of cash contributions, employers may contribute their own stock (including stock purchased on the open market) to a plan. The employer is entitled to a tax deduction for the value of the stock contributed to the plan. The plan affords employees, who now own part of the company through the vehicle of the ESOP, a greater stake in the firm's success.

A form of ESOP generally known as TRASOP (Tax Reduction Act Stock Ownership Plan) further encourages the use of employer stock in tax qualified plans. Under a TRASOP, a contributing employer is entitled to an extra 1 percent investment credit with respect to qualifying investment credit property, provided an equivalent amount of employer stock is contributed to the TRASOP.[105] The additional investment credit can be further increased by one-half of 1 percent if employees contribute to the TRASOP.[106] All contributions to a TRASOP are nonforfeitable by participating employees.[107] TRASOPS in effect generate capital for a contributing employer equivalent to the sale of stock to the public while at the same time providing an important benefit for participating employees.

In the Revenue Act of 1978, a new type of tax-qualified plan was created, giving employers yet another incentive to provide for employee retirement: Qualified simplified employee pension plans (commonly referred to as SEPs), under which an employer may contribute to Individual Retirement Accounts of employees up to the lesser of 15 percent of compensation or $7,500, with an offset permitted for the employer's Social Security contributions on behalf of participating employees. Contributions must be made on a nondiscriminatory basis and are 100 percent vested. This type of plan permits simplified record keeping and, therefore, appears attractive to employers wary of the ERISA administration burden.

In sum, in a characteristically schizophrenic way, the tax law system and ERISA have placed corporate managers in a quandary with respect to whether and how to provide retirement benefits to employees. The net effect, however, is clearly to promote adoption of retirement plans.

International Operations

1. Foreign Versus Domestic Investment

The oft-proclaimed goal of tax neutrality, and in particular capital-export neutrality,[108] has not prevented the United States from employing its tax system to discourage foreign direct investment by American business and to reward investment in the United States. Indeed, any choice between foreign and domestic investment necessarily is tax-directed to a significant degree, and in many cases tax differentials will be a deciding factor.

While not all of the varied tax techniques employed to influence these corporate decisions were introduced into the law as a conscious exercise of governmental regulatory power, an overall regulatory pattern is clearly discernible:

1. The United States no longer fully honors the principle that income earned abroad should not bear double taxation. The foreign tax credit[109]—the mechanism designed to avoid additive burdens by reducing U.S. income

tax to the extent income tax is paid to a foreign country —has been diluted in recent years by congressional amendments restricting its scope of operation,[110] by Treasury regulations which employ a system of allocating deductions to ensure in many circumstances that less than full credit will be given for foreign income taxes paid,[111] and by a series of Internal Revenue Service rulings concluding that many foreign income taxes should not give rise to any foreign tax credit at all.[112] The cumulative effect of these changes often is to make the total tax cost of foreign operation greater, sometimes prohibitively greater, than the cost of domestic operation.

2. Because, alone among developed nations, the United States taxes its nationals who are resident in any location abroad, the cost of posting American executives, engineers and other employees to foreign locations often is much higher than the cost to companies of other countries of posting personnel to the same locations. Recent changes to the limited tax relief that is granted U.S. citizens abroad have, in many circumstances, exacerbated the situation.[113]

3. The United States offers significant tax incentives to companies that locate business activity in the United States or in U.S. possessions (for example, the investment tax credit,[114] the reduction in taxes on export income afforded by the DISC (Domestic International Sales Corporation) provisions,[115] and the tax credit for income earned in Puerto Rico and in U.S. possessions).[116] An American corporation owning and operating property and business abroad does not receive these benefits, and is thus influenced to invest domestically.

By and large, this system of penalties and rewards was formulated for the express purpose of encouraging investment in the United States even where free market forces would have favored an overseas investment.

In recent years, moreover, there have been further and recurrent proposals to "drive business onshore" by increasing the penalties for offshore operation to the point where they no longer could be accepted or avoided—proposals to repeal the foreign tax credit entirely and to "end deferral."[117] Inevitably, the risk that such punitive measures may be adopted in midcourse acts as a further deterrent to direct overseas investment.

2. Regulation of Offshore Activity through the Tax System

The U.S. has employed its tax system to regulate overseas activity of U.S. taxpayers for many years. An early example was adoption in 1937 of the foreign personal holding company provisions for the purpose of preventing U.S. taxpayers from transferring portfolio investments to offshore entities as a means to avoid U.S. taxes.[118] In 1962, the system was greatly expanded by the adoption of subpart F of the Code, provisions designed in part to prevent U.S. persons from using offshore companies as a means to avoid foreign, as distinguished from U.S., taxes.[119] Under the 1937 and 1962 enactments, because the foreign entity was beyond the reach of the U.S. taxing power, the restraining technique employed was to tax U.S. shareholders currently on the undistributed income of the foreign company.

The trend toward restrictive and restraining regulation in this area has continued, and more recent legislation imposes further tax penalties on specified types of foreign activity. The Tax Reform Act of 1976 imposes penalties on U.S. companies which themselves, or through domestic or foreign subsidiaries, participate in or cooperate with an international boycott.[120] The same Act imposes further tax penalties on U.S. companies which directly or through foreign subsidiaries make unlawful payments to foreign government officials.[121] These provisions are notable in that they penalize activity, undertaken by foreign entities, that may be perfectly legal in the countries in which they are located. For example, the penalties on foreign bribes apply if the payment was unlawful under the laws of the country in which made or, even though legal under the laws of the country in which it was made, if it would have been unlawful if the laws of the U.S. were applicable.

A more general tax penalty is imposed on illegal bribes or kickbacks to officials of any government, whether domestic or foreign, by the denial of a deduction for the payments.[122] In testing the legality of a payment to a foreign official, U.S. law is applied.[123]

Notes

1. *See, e.g.*, Surrey, *Federal Income Tax Reform: The Varied Approaches Necessary to Replace Tax Expenditures with Direct Governmental Assistance*, 84 Harv. L. Rev. 352 (1970); McDaniel, *Alternatives to Utilization of the Federal Income Tax System to Meet Social Problems*, 11 B.C. Indus. & Com. L. Rev. 867 (1970).

2. The goal of tax neutrality is achieved when business decisions are not motivated by tax considerations.

3. Sections 581–596 (banks); Sections 801–844 (insurance companies); Sections 1381–1383 (Cooperatives); Sections 856–860 (Real Estate Investment Trusts); Sections 851–855 (Regulated Investment Companies). Except as otherwise specified, references to "Section" in this Chapter are to sections of the Internal Revenue Code of 1954, as amended, 26 U.S.C. §1 *et seq.*

4. *See, e.g.*, Sections 163(d), 265, 279.

5. *See* Section 302.

6. Perhaps reflecting this, the tax law has reacted to the disparate treatment of debt and equity by not unquestioningly accepting the corporate label placed on an instrument as "debt" or "stock." *See* Section 385; Plumb, *The Federal In-*

come Tax Significance of Corporate Debt: A Critical Analysis and a Proposal, 26 Tax L. Rev. 369 (1971). Particularly when stock and denominated-debt are held by the same person, the debt may be recharacterized as stock for tax purposes, resulting in the denial of an interest deduction to the corporation and dividend tax consequences to the creditor. This "debt–equity" characterization problem has plagued the tax law for perhaps half a century, producing an enormous volume of litigation but, to date, no clear line of demarcation. Recently, however, more than ten years after the enactment of Section 385, regulations thereunder have been proposed. Proposed U.S. Treas. Reg. §§1.385-1 through 1.385-12. This likely signals the initiation of a period of comment and revision which ultimately will result in the promulgation of final regulations under Section 385 that, in addition to adding significantly greater certainty to the "debt-equity" characterization problem, will themselves have substantial impact on future corporate decision-making.

7.   *See* G. J. Benston, *Conglomerate Mergers: Causes, Consequences and Remedies* (1980).

8.   *See* Section 334(b) (2).

9.   *Compare* Sections 336, 337, *with* 1245 and 1250.

10.   *See General Utilities & Operating Co.* v. *Helvering,* 296 U.S. 200 (1935).

11.   Section 1014.

12.   Section 453(b).

13.   Section 368(a).

14.   Section 354.

15.   Section 358(a)(1).

16.   Section 362(b).

17.   Section 279.

18.   APB Opinion No. 16, *Business Combinations,* ¶¶45–48 (1970).

19.   *Id.* at ¶44.

20.   *Id.* at ¶44, 47b.

21.   *See* Sections 354, 368(a) (1) (E).

22.   *See* Section 1001; *see also Eisner* v. *Macomber,* 252 U.S. 189 (1920).

23.   Section 1231.

24.   The $1 million figure is an approximation based on an assumed 50 percent combined marginal federal, state and local tax rate.

25.   In point are the accumulated earnings tax, Sections

531–537 and the personal holding company penalty tax, Sections 541–547.

26. R&D expenditures are currently deductible at the taxpayer's election. Section 174; *see* text accompanying notes 64 and 65 *infra*.

27. Realistically, the corporation has a net cost of approximately $5 million since it saves approximately $5 million (50 percent of $10 million) in federal, state and local taxes as a result of its advertising deductions.

28. Sections 38, 46, 48.

29. Section 167(b), (c).

30. Section 167(m); U.S. Treas. Regs., §1.167(a)-11.

31. If the property has a useful life of between 3 and 5 years the credit is 3.33 percent; if the useful life is between 5 and 7 years the credit is 6.67 percent; if the useful life is 7 or more years, the credit is a full 10 percent.

32. Section 46(a) (3) places limits on how much tax can be offset by the investment tax credit in a given year, so that if the tax due exceeds $25,000 it cannot be fully offset by the credit.

33. Section 46(b) provides for the carryback and carryover of unused credits, so that a corporation may obtain the benefit of the credit even if it has insufficient income in the year of production or purchase.

34. The investment tax credit was made permanent as of November 6, 1978. Revenue Act of 1978, §311(a) amending Section 46(a) (2) (B). Prior to this amendment the impetus to immediate corporate investment in new depreciable tangible personal property was even more powerful, as there was always the possibility the credit would be discontinued shortly.

35. U.S. Treas. Regs., §1.167(a)-11(a) (1).

36. *See* Section 167(m); U.S. Treas. Regs., §1.167(a)-11(b) (4); Rev. Proc. 77-10, 1977-1 C.B. 548.

37. U.S. Treas. Regs., §1.167(a)–11(c) (2).

38. *See* Rev. Proc. 77-10, 1977-1 C.B. 548.

39. *Id.*

40. *See* Section 167(b), (c) and (j).

41. Section 1250; *compare* Section 1245.

42. There is no corresponding requirement that such expenses with respect to personal property be capitalized.

43. Section 189. Subchapter S corporations, personal holding companies, and foreign personal holding companies—all closely-held entities—are denied this benefit.

44. Section 189(a).

45. Revenue Act of 1978, §315 *adding* Section 48(g).
46. *See General Explanation of the Revenue Act of 1978,* H.R. Rep. No. 13511, 95th Cong., 2d Sess. (1979).
47. Section 103(b) (4) (F).
48. Section 169.
49. Section 46(c) (5); *compare* note 31 *supra.*
50. *See* text accompanying notes 31–34 *supra.*
51. Section 46(a) (2).
52. Section 103(b) (4) (E).
53. Section 48(a) (1) (B).
54. Section 103(b) (4) (D).
55. Section 185.
56. Section 184.
57. Section 48(a) (8).
58. Section 263(d).
59. Section 613.
60. Sections 613(a) & (b).
61. Section 616.
62. Section 617.
63. Section 631.
64. Section 174(a).
65. Section 174(b).
66. Section 162(g); U.S. Treas. Regs., §1.162-22.
67. *See Local 167* v. *United States,* 291 U.S. 293, 298 (1934). The extent of damages would be the only issue open in subsequent civil litigation, the illegality of the corporation's actions being collaterally estopped.
68. The cost would be roughly equal to five-sixths of any subsequent civil damages; this would reflect application of a 50 percent marginal tax rate on one-third of the total damages (the remaining two-thirds portion, which is punitive, not being deductible).
69. Section 170.
70. Section 41, granting a tax credit, is limited to contributions by individuals.
71. Section 162(e) (2).
72. Section 162(a).
73. Section 162(e) (1) (B).
74. Section 162(e) (1) (A).
75. Sections 44B, 51, 52 & 53.
76. Sections 40, 50A, 50B; Social Security Act, §432(b) (1).
77. Section 51(a).
78. Section 51(d).

79. Sections 51(d) (1) (A), (B), (C) & (G), 50A(a) (1) and 50B(a) (4).

80. Section 79.

81. Section 106.

82. Section 120.

83. Section 127.

84. Section 124.

85. "Propping Up Social Security," *Business Week*, July 19, 1976, at 36.

86. Section 401(a) (5); Revenue Ruling 71-446, 1971-2 C.B. 187.

87. Sections 401 *et seq.*

88. Section 404.

89. Sections 402 and 501.

90. D. McGill, *Fundamentals of Private Pensions* 29 (1975).

91. Section 411; ERISA §203.

92. Section 412; ERISA §302.

93. ERISA, Title IV.

94. Section 4975; ERISA, Title I, Part 4.

95. ERISA, Title I.

96. Section 415.

97. Section 411, ERISA §§203 and 204.

98. Section 412; ERISA §302.

99. Examples of actuarial errors are incorrect earnings, salary growth, employee turnover and mortality projections.

100. ERISA, Title IV.

101. A corporation (and its affiliates) that contributed to an underfunded terminated plan will be liable to the PBGC for the amount of the underfunding with respect to vested benefits guaranteed by the PBGC or 30 percent of its net worth, whichever is less.

102. *See* "Unfunded Pension Liabilities: A Continuing Burden" *Business Week*, August 14, 1978, at 60.

103. *Id.*

104. PBGC, *Summary of Study of Multiemployer Plan Coverage By Termination Program Under Title IV of ERISA*, BNA Pension Rep., No. 195 (July 1, 1978). Because of the many problems with multi-employer plans, Congress debated for many months changes in PBGC coverage for such plans. On August 26, 1980 the House and Senate finally agreed on most provisions of a bill, the Multiemployer Pension Plan Amendments Act of 1980 (H.R. 3904), which would change

PBGC coverage applicable to multi-employer plans to ameliorate the main problem of the original legislation of imposing contingent liability on remaining healthy companies in a declining industry. In lieu thereof, the bill imposes potential liability on employers withdrawing from multi-employers' plans as part of a complicated and detailed new set of laws under ERISA. Clearly we have not seen the end of legislation affecting employer liability under Title IV of ERISA.

105. Sections 46(a) and 409A.

106. Section 46(a).

107. Section 409A.

108. *See* note 2 *supra.* Capital-export neutrality is achieved when capital employed abroad is taxed neither more nor less heavily than capital employed at home.

109. Sections 901–908.

110. *See, e.g.,* Tax Reform Act of 1976, §1032 *amending* Sections 904(f), 907.

111. U.S. Treas. Regs., §1.861-8.

112. *See, e.g.* Revenue Rulings 78-61, 78-62, 78-63, 1978-1 C.B. 221, 226, 228.

113. Foreign Earned Income Act of 1978, §202, *amending* Sections 911, 217, 119, 1034 and *adding* Section 913.

114. *See* Section 48(a) (2). With limited exceptions (enumerated in Section 48(a) (2) (B)), the investment credit is not available for property "used predominantly outside the United States."

115. Sections 991–997.

116. Section 936.

117. Message on Taxes from President Carter to the Congress, January 21, 1978, providing that "deferral" was to be phased out in stages between 1979 and 1981. Thereafter, U.S. parent companies would be taxed currently on the undistributed income of their foreign subsidiaries.

118. These provisions currently are found in Sections 551–558.

119. Sections 951–964.

120. Tax Reform Act of 1976, §§1061–1067, *amending* Sections 952–995 and *adding* Sections 908, 999.

121. Tax Reform Act of 1976, §1065, *amending* Sections 952, 964, 995.

122. Section 162(c) (1); U.S. Treas. Regs., §1.162-18.

123. U.S. Treas. Regs., §1.162-18.

4

The Constraining Effect of Direct Regulation on the Corporate Decision-Making Process

THIS chapter discusses the systems of government regulation that supplement and frequently overrule market forces.[1] These government requirements, which constitute direct legal limitations on corporate discretionary powers, are imposed in enormously diverse circumstances and for a wide variety of reasons—ranging, for example, from the control of prices charged for electricity and gasoline, to the protection of the public from unsafe products, and on to defining the physical characteristics of ladders in factories.

Regulation has been with us since the founding of the Republic. Some industries, such as the railroads, have been heavily regulated for nearly a century, and a large growth in regulation took place during the 1930's. But as is illustrated on pp. 127–31, a virtual explosion of federal regulation took place beginning in the mid-1960's.

Government regulation affects corporate discretion in several ways. Foremost, perhaps, is the direct level of obedience to the command itself—e.g., placing a care-label on garments, renovating an old plant to meet new requirements. Regulation has indirect effects, too. A firm may choose not to make the garment or revitalize an aging plant because of the costs which would be imposed by regulatory requirements. Regulation can also raise the price—in terms of money and time—for a corporation to embark on new undertakings by requiring permits, licenses, and a plethora of government approvals. Moreover, because of changes or additions to regulations which would affect a particular activity, if undertaken, the corporation may find it is better to do nothing until the regulatory environment has stabilized, lest it be necessary to spend large amounts to reverse course. Thus, as will become evident from the discussion below of various specific regulatory programs, government regulation can constrain corporate managers from such actions as producing and offering various kinds of goods and services, from opening new plants, hiring particular kinds of employees, or even from lowering prices.

The effects of government regulation cannot be assessed solely in terms of federal programs. Almost all state and local governments impose their own regulatory requirements on corporations doing business within their jurisdictions. Some of these programs address questions also regulated at the federal level. For example, a trucking firm must not only comply with the Department of Transportation's rules and the regulations of the Interstate Commerce Commission, but also with state and local safety regulations. The Clean Air Act requires states to devise a series of plans that provide the specific

Indices of Regulation

I: PAGES IN THE FEDERAL REGISTER
(Thousands of pages)

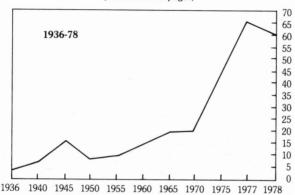

II: FEDERAL REPORTING BURDEN
(In millions of work hours; unaudited data from Office of Management and Budget and General Accounting Office inventories of reports.)

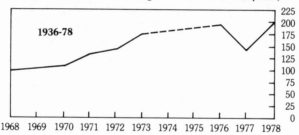

SOURCE: *Regulatory Eye,* June, 1979.

regulatory details for achieving federally-promulgated air quality standards.[2] In this case, even though the goals are the same from state to state, the actual regulatory requirements vary. In other contexts, state and local regulations address issues not the subject of federal control. While this web of state and local regulation may not be as visible as its federal counterpart precisely because it is so dispersed, it does nonetheless impose additional layers of legal restrictions and obligations on the corporation and can often result in the corporation's being confronted with inconsistent regulatory requirements.

127

Growth Chart of Federal Regulatory Agencies

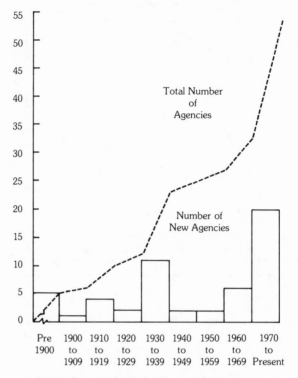

SOURCE: Center for the Study of American Business.

The federal government as a commercial entity imposes still further regulatory controls on business, particularly large corporations. The government is the nation's single largest purchaser and it conditions doing business with a corporation on that firm's agreeing to be bound by many regulatory-like obligations. For example, before entering a contract for more than $5,000,000, the contracting corporation must certify that it is in compliance with the federal "voluntary" anti-inflation wage-price guidelines.[3] Similarly, the Walsh-Healey Act requires any corporation doing more than $10,000 worth of business with the federal government to certify that its employees are

128

paid at least the prevailing minimum wage for persons engaged in similar work, are not required to work more than eight hours per day, and are not subjected to hazardous working conditions.[4] Indeed, special occupational safety and health standards have been developed to implement the latter requirement. Also, government contractors are required by Executive Order to take affirmative action to overcome discriminatory practices.[5] In these and many other ways, the government can and does use its vast purchasing power to influence corporate decisions. While a corporation could avoid these dictates by not doing business with the government, that is not a realistic option today for most companies of significant size.

This chapter is divided into two sections. The first describes the various regulatory theories which generally explain most of the command-type regulations imposed by the federal government. The second section describes several of the more important regulatory programs to illustrate concretely the scope of government regulation. The General Accounting Office has identified one hundred and sixteen federal agencies with regulatory responsibilities, and simply cataloging the myriad different programs takes hundreds of pages.[6] For illustrative purposes, we have selected only the following significant areas of government regulation: labor relations; environment; consumer protection; the political process; and energy.

Theories of Regulation

This section describes the principal theories of government regulation—why government has in certain circumstances chosen to supplement or replace the free

TABLE 1
EXPENDITURES ON FEDERAL REGULATORY ACTIVITIES
(FISCAL YEARS, MILLIONS OF DOLLARS)

AREA OF REGULATION	1970	1971	1972	1973	1974	1975	1976	1977	1978	(ESTIMATED) 1979	GROWTH FACTOR (1979 & 1970)
Consumer Safety and Health	$ 435	$ 655	$ 842	$1113	$1331	$1424	$1554	$1860	$2425	$2530	5.8
Job Safety and Other Working Conditions	62	104	124	227	310	379	447	492	550	620	10.0
Environment and Energy	94	154	47	213	370	445	628	826	1002	1105	11.8
Financial Reporting and Other Financial	22	23	27	31	36	45	52	56	68	67	3.0
Industry-Specific Regulation	125	151	166	140	203	220	251	286	290	293	2.3
General Business	73	81	92	100	115	122	145	166	186	190	2.6
Total	$ 811	$1168	$1298	$1824	$2365	$2635	$3077	$3686	$4521	$4805	5.9
Annual % Increase		44%	11%	41%	30%	11%	17%	20%	23%	6%	

TABLE 2
STAFFING OF FEDERAL REGULATORY AGENCIES
(FISCAL YEARS, PERMANENT FULL-TIME POSITIONS)

AREA OF REGULATION	1970	1971	1972	1973	1974	1975	1976	1977	1978	(ESTIMATED) 1979	GROWTH FACTOR (1979 & 1970)
Consumer Safety and Health	5768	6212	21543	27567	27991	27943	29010	32618	32110	32699	5.7
Job Safety and Other Working Conditions	3921	4337	5100	9946	10820	11857	12563	13278	13578	14883	3.8
Environment and Energy	N/A	54	5119	5138	7055	7421	7834	8899	9114	9863	N/A
Financial Reporting and Other Financial	7635	8073	8388	8703	9006	9599	10429	10890	11387	11813	1.5
Industry-Specific Regulation	5874	5771	5798	6112	6583	7215	7538	6140	6179	6275	1.1
General Business	4445	4472	1675	1852	4951	5094	5282	5236	5275	5293	1.2
Total	27643	28919	47623	59318	66406	69129	72656	77061	77643	80826	2.9
Annual % Increase		5%	65%	25%	12%	4%	5%	6%	1%	4%	

Source of Tables 1 and 2: M. Weidenbaum, Director, Center for the Study of American Business, Washington University, "Analyzing the Benefits and Costs of Regulation," printed in *Government Regulation of Business: The New Outlook, The New Realities* 101–102 (1978).

market with direct, command-type requirements on corporations as a means of achieving public policy objectives.[7] It should be emphasized here that since the actual decisions creating new regulatory programs are political choices representing compromises among people with differing interests and views, many specific regulatory programs reflect a number of different theoretical bases.

1. Economic Regulation

A frequent political response to those situations where it is believed that competition is ineffective in constraining corporate price behavior is to impose a regulatory scheme that controls prices directly. These situations arise for several reasons, and the precise nature of the regulatory program depends on the particular kind of perceived competitive failure.

Natural Monopoly

Historically, the most common justification for detailed control of a corporation's prices is that the company enjoys a "natural monopoly." Technically speaking, a natural monopoly occurs when it is impractical for several companies to compete in serving the same customers, a situation which exists when the capital costs involved in providing adequate service are so large that the marginal costs of the service are decreasing throughout the expected demand. Examples are street railways, electricity distribution, and telephone switching.

Because the costs are decreasing, lower overall prices can be obtained by granting one firm—or a small number of firms—a monopoly. To ensure that the favored company does not earn monopoly profits, a governmental regulatory program is created which controls its operations —to the point where its rates will be governmentally determined (generally by comparing the return on investment for price-regulated corporations with the return for comparable corporations whose prices are not directly regulated, taking account of such factors as comparative risk and the need to raise capital).

Sometimes the regulatory theory contemplates that some who receive the service will be required to pay more than the actual cost of providing it to them, while others will pay less than would be justified on an allocated cost basis. This process is called cross-subsidization. Regulations providing for cross-subsidization typically require a corporation to undertake less profitable services (e.g., air service to low density areas) as a condition to being permitted to provide more profitable services (e.g., the New York-Miami run). In this situation, corporate discretion is constrained to undertake activities which, absent regulation, the market would discourage. The goal of cross-subsidization, moreover, has been used to justify regulation of businesses which are not, technically speaking, natural monopolists; and it is the main argument for the postal monopoly.

Because a consumer will have no alternative but to deal with the monopoly corporation, another aspect of the regulatory program is to limit the corporation's traditional "free trader" discretion to deal with whom it pleases. In many regulated areas, therefore, the corporation *must* provide service on a nondiscriminatory basis to all who request it. These are the so-called "common-carrier obligations."

This entire complex of regulations dealing with the natural monopoly situation falls within the category of so-called "economic regulation." A company subjected to this type of economic regulation must seek approval of a government agency for virtually all of its major decisions —including the prices it charges and services it provides. The company is in essence only one step away from government ownership.

Examples of agencies exercising this kind of economic regulation include the Interstate Commerce Commission —which has tightly regulated the railroads; the Federal Communications Commission (interstate telephone, telegraph, broadcast services); the Federal Energy Regulatory Commission (oil and gas pipelines); and State Public Utility Commissions.

Economic regulation can create many problems of its own. Even though such regulation may at one time have been justified in a particular industry, the historical reasons for it may change or disappear over time. For example, after years of full economic regulation, tight controls on airlines have been reduced, allowing the free market to function more than in the past. While some dislocations resulted in the short run, with large carriers leaving smaller (cross-subsidized) markets, many believe that the long-term response will be significantly beneficial. In these cases, control over corporate discretion is in effect handed back to the market by the government, on the theory that competitive market strictures will lead to greater overall efficiency and responsiveness to consumer demand.

"Destructive" Competition

Economic regulation has also been justified as necessary to protect against so-called "destructive" competition. One form of this occurs where excess capacity exists in an industry with a high ratio of fixed costs to total costs and where production capacity is relatively immobile and therefore slow to adjust to changing circumstances. Because of the excess capacity, not all firms in the market will be able to cover their total costs, so each has an incentive to charge any price above variable costs which will attract patronage. The argument runs that eventually such pricing will weaken many participants to the point where they must leave the market. Then, when demand grows, those few who remain in the market will have the unrestrained discretion to charge monopoly rates because of the long time it would take for new firms to enter. Economic regulation is proposed to protect against this by keeping prices up during slack times. As an example, the railroads suffered damaging price wars before the creation of the ICC, and one of the primary purposes of regulating them was to end this destructive competition.[8] This argument has also been put forward to justify shipping conferences, pooling agreements, and certain international trade restrictions in the United States and abroad.

Excess Profits

A corporation may own a product that increases in price far beyond that which the corporation paid for it. Usually, the benefits thus realized (higher profits) represent rewards bestowed by the market for the corporation's foresight. But, when the differential becomes very large and competitors do not have access to the lower priced product, the political response in some cases is to curb such asserted "windfall" gains by imposing a form of economic regulation.[9]

For example, with the increases in the price of imported oil, those who owned domestic oil suddenly received a large benefit, since the value of domestic oil jumped relative to what they paid for it. Unlike economic regulation in the natural monopoly situation, in which the governmentally fixed prices are based on the cost of production plus a "fair" rate of return, the prices imposed by the government to guard against "excess profits" are more likely to be based either on the historical price of the commodity (e.g., the price of "old" crude oil is based on what used to be charged) or on estimates of that price which will induce increased production of the commodity and thereby reduce the shortages which have driven prices up (e.g., "new" crude oil is priced higher to encourage production).

Emergencies

Types of economic regulation are also used during national emergencies. The political response to shortages caused either by war or sudden changes in supply, such as the disruptions of oil imports, is sometimes to impose price controls on the commodities rather than let prices rise to reflect their supply and demand. Wage and price controls have also been used in an attempt to curb inflationary pressures in the economy. For example, the current "voluntary" guidelines for wages and prices are a form of this type of regulation, differing only in the manner of enforcement.[10] Like the regulation designed to control excess profits, this form of economic regulation is generally based on the historical prices charged for the product—it freezes the prices for a time. But many adjustments have to be made: corporations are generally allowed to pass on at least a portion of their own cost increases; prices must be devised for new entrants in the market; special cases always arise, such as where one

136

competitor had not yet put into effect a general price increase that others in the industry had adopted; and terms of sale may change. Further, this form of regulation can distort the market by constraining firms to cut back on the production of products that are no longer profitable at the controlled price and by inducing these firms to shift resources into areas that are currently more lucrative, even though such resource allocations would not be dictated by demand shifts and would not be justified in the long run with controls discontinued.[11]

Examples of Economic Regulatory Programs

Civil Aeronautics Board (CAB)	Regulation of air transportation routes, air fares, airline accounting and business practices, including mergers, consolidations, etc. (Phased decontrol of these regulations is mandated under the Deregulation Act of 1978, with termination of the CAB scheduled for December 1984.)
Council on Wage and Price Stability (COWPS) and Office of Federal Procurement Policy (OFPP)	Regulation of all business by "voluntary" standards governing levels of wage and price increases.
Department of Energy (DOE)	Allocation and price regulation of crude oil and other petroleum products; emergency allocations of natural gas under Emergency Natural Gas Act of 1977.
Federal Communications Commission (FCC)	Regulation of interstate and foreign communication by radio, television, wire, cable, and satellite, including rates, allocation of broadcast channels, business

	management and operation, and construction and operation of communications facilities.
Federal Energy Regulatory Commission (FERC)	Licensing of hydroelectric projects, regulation of interstate transmission and wholesale price of electricity, regulation of wellhead and transportation prices for natural gas, and regulation of oil and gas pipline construction and rates.
Federal Maritime Commission (FMC)	Regulation of rates, contracts, and financial responsibility for companies providing domestic offshore and international water transportation.
Interstate Commerce Commission (ICC)	Regulation of rates, route entry and exit for railroads, trucking companies, bus lines, domestic water carriers, freight forwarders and transportation brokers.
State Agencies	Quotas for oil production under Connally Hot Oil Act.

2. Regulation of "Externalities"

A corporation may, without some form of regulation, shift certain costs to society at large without providing compensation. For example, without regulation, a corporation might not have to pay for dumping industrial wastes into a river or for discharging chemicals from its stack. Indeed, in a competitive environment where corporations labor to reduce costs, the economic (market) incentives would be against corporate efforts to pay for these "external" costs—because of the fear that the corporation's competitors would not do likewise and that it would consequently be placed at a significant competitive disadvantage. Regulation in these areas is imposed to "internalize" these costs to all of the corporations involved, on the premise that they are in fact—or at least should be—a cost of doing business. The theory holds that by initially requiring the companies to pay for these costs, they will eventually absorb some of them (i.e., returns to stockholders and managers will be less) and will pass on the rest to the consumers who buy the product or service involved—thus spreading out the costs over all who benefit from the economic activities in question.

One way for the government to internalize these costs would be to charge the corporations an appropriate price for the "externality" in the form of a tax. For example, the corporation could be charged a fee for discharging chemicals into the air or water. In that case, the corporation would have an incentive to reduce the pollution to the point where the marginal cost of doing so equals the fine or tax imposed. But by far the most common way of dealing with this situation has been for an agency to prescribe a definite, objectively measurable, physical standard which the corporation is required to meet if it engages in a specified activity. For example, the amount of a specific chemical which may be discharged into the air or water has been limited by a standard; the maximum noise level of a plant has been controlled for worker safety; and minimum safety features which must be included in an automobile have been established.

Environmental regulations provide a prevalent example of these standards. As will be described below, direct controls presently predominate environmental regulation, and most frequently consist of emission or effluent requirements, or outright bans of specific pollutants. A company must conform to each of these constraints in its production processes if it wishes to do business in areas so regulated.

Worker safety is another example, at the federal level, of a legislative decision that the otherwise (and historically) external costs of maintaining a safe working environment should be shared by employers and consumers. Other examples of such "internalizing" standards are automobile safety standards imposed by the National Highway Traffic Safety Administration; product standards set by the Consumer Product Safety Commission; Truth-in-Lending Act requirements imposed upon lenders; and nuclear power standards imposed by the Nuclear Regulatory Commission. In all of these areas, the corporation is directly commanded to meet nonmarket requirements. And, because the cost of doing business in these areas thereby increases, the standards inevitably, if more subtly, influence basic resource allocation decisions. The added costs of complying with the Occupational Safety and Health Act must be taken into account in weighing entry into a labor-intensive industry, for example.

Regulation in these areas also can have an adverse effect on competition—as in the automobile industry where the government has required that all car manufacturers meet specific fuel efficiency standards. Because domestic producers have historically manufactured large cars, while foreign producers have traditionally focused on smaller, fuel efficient cars (gas having always been relatively dear in Europe and Japan), the foreign companies have been effectively assisted by this government regulatory program.

EXAMPLES OF EXTERNALITY REGULATIONS

Consumer Product Safety Commission (CPSC)	Establishes mandatory product safety standards

	governing such factors as product design, packaging, labeling.
Department of Agriculture, Food Safety and Quality Service (FSQS)	Establishes and enforces safety and health regulations pertaining to production, importation, and distribution of certain plant, poultry, and meat products.
Department of Energy (DOE)	Establishes energy efficiency targets for consumer products.
Department of Health and Human Services (formerly HEW), Food and Drug Administration (FDA)	Develops and enforces purity, safety, and labeling requirements for foods, drugs, and medical devices.
Department of Housing and Urban Development (HUD)	Establishes standards for mobile home construction, and participation in federally sponsored insurance programs.
Department of Labor, Mine Safety and Health Administration (MSHA)	Sets and enforces mine safety and health standards.
Department of Labor, Occupational Safety and Health Administration (OSHA)	Develops and enforces job-related safety and health standards, including equipment and record-keeping requirements.
Department of Transportation (DOT)	Prescribes and enforces safety standards for ships (Coast Guard); airplanes, airports, and aviation personnel (FAA); commercial interstate motor carriers (FHA); railroads (FRA); trucks and cars (NHTSA); pipelines and hazardous materials in transportation (MTB).
Environmental Protection Agency (EPA)	Develops and enforces environmental quality and

	performance standards in areas of air, water, noise, waste disposal, pesticides and toxic substances.
Nuclear Regulatory Commission (NRC)	Establishes standards and issues licenses, covers all aspects of design, construction, and operation of nuclear facilities.

3. Preclearance

In this type of regulation, a firm must receive the permission of an agency before marketing its products.[12] This form of regulation, like the externality standards described above, controls the characteristics of a product; but it also requires specific agency preclearance because of the potential for great or widespread harm if the standards are not met. For example, pesticides and pharmaceuticals must be certified as safe and effective before they may be marketed; agencies must determine that the design of an aircraft or ship is safe before it is used; and nuclear reactors must be certified as meeting safety and environmental standards in advance of start-up. (In the case of other standards, as in the environmental area, compliance is generally enforced after the fact through civil and/or criminal sanctions.)

This form of regulation is usually characterized by agency approval standards which are subjective—e.g., "safe" or "effective." This is because the technology which is to be controlled is sufficiently new that objective standards cannot yet be defined. Frequently, the administrative standards issued under a statute imposing certification requirements are guidelines for information to be supplied by the company and used by the agency in making the ultimate value judgment. In such areas, considerable discretionary power is effectively transferred from the corporations to the government regulators.

4. Licenses and Allocations

This type of regulation requires a corporation to receive permission from a government agency before engaging in either a specified line of business or a particular business transaction. There are three main types of licenses as used in this context.

Qualification

The theory underlying this type of license is much the same as that underlying product and service preclearance: if the person or corporation is not qualified, great harm could result. The licensing of airline pilots is one example at the federal level. The same theory applies to state licensing of physicians, pharmacists, attorneys and insurance companies.

Allocation

This second type of licensing allocates scarce resources. The regulation of radio and television stations is an example.[13] By limiting broadcasting corporations to specific electromagnetic frequencies, locations, power, and sometimes time of day, the Federal Communications Commission lessens signal interference.[14] Historically, state and federal regulation of crude oil and natural gas production is another example of direct resource allocation by the government. Oil or gas leases and wells held by competing firms frequently draw from the same pool. Lack of restrictions on the amount of oil or gas a lessee could produce in a month could induce owners to pump each claim rapidly until it is exhausted. To prevent this, the major oil producing states limited production by a proration schedule of oil and gas allocation.

A similar form of regulation allocates the supply of a product at a controlled price to meet demand. For example, during the fuel shortages in the spring of 1979, corporations were ordered to allocate a certain portion of diesel fuel to farmers; similarly, gasoline was allocated among the individual service stations.[15] Although under this form of allocation individual suppliers or purchasers may not have to deal directly with an agency for permission to buy or sell the product, the sale is nevertheless controlled by regulations issued by the agency. That is, the sale must be "sanctioned" under the regulations, which has the same effect as if a license were required.

Allocations may be based on a broad "public interest" standard, entailing a large amount of subjective judgment on the part of the agency involved. Another form of allocation apportions resources according to past use. For example, the amount of gasoline a filling station received during the summer of 1979 depended on how much it received during a "base period" prior to that time.[16] Yet another form of allocation takes place when a scarce resource owned by the government is sold to the highest bidder. This is done, for example, with respect to timber from the National Forests.[17]

Enforcement

A third use of licenses is for regulatory enforcement. In this case, before the firm can obtain a required license, it must demonstrate its compliance with applicable regulatory requirements. For example, as will be described in more detail below, a corporation wishing to build a new plant must obtain a permit from the Environmental Protection Agency; and to do so, it must demonstrate the plant will meet applicable air quality regulations.[18]

5. Disclosures

In addition to the area of securities regulation discussed in Chapter 2, a number of other regulatory programs rest on the premise that consumers often require data and information which would not be furnished as the result of the operation of market forces. One response to this situation is to treat the absence of such information as an externality and to require the company and consumers to bear the costs of disclosure. For example, labels on foods must by law disclose the ingredients; lenders are required to inform loan applicants of the annual interest rate on loans; and appliances must be labeled as to their energy efficiency. The Occupational Safety and Health Act provides that the Secretary of Labor may require "the use of labels or other appropriate forms of warning as are necessary to insure that employees are apprised of all hazards to which they are exposed," and to that end, recent OSHA standards concerning the regulation of cancer-causing chemicals require that employees be warned of their danger.[19] All of these requirements impose controls and constraints on corporations which would not otherwise be imposed by the market.

Another type of information-centered regulation consists of the numerous government regulations which require companies to develop and retain enormous numbers of records and reports (some for the use of consumers and some for law enforcement purposes). These duties range from the requirement that employers maintain a log of all occupational injuries and illnesses,[20] to record keeping requirements for tax purposes, and on to such obligations as the duty of the proprietor of a vinegar factory to keep daily records of its operation.[21] Merely listing all the record retention requirements making up this "paperwork jungle" takes more than 85 pages of fine type,[22] and compliance is estimated to require in excess of 780 million man-hours per year.[23]

6. Social Regulation

This type of regulation is not based on perceived market failures, but rather on a governmental disagreement with the solution provided by the market. Social security, federal regulation of labor relations, and more recently, civil rights, are examples of essentially social regulation. Thus, the Wagner Act and its successor, the Taft-Hartley Act, were enacted more from considerations of equity and fair play and a political decision to redistribute income than from a perceived economic need to permit collective bargaining and unionization. Similarly, in enacting the Civil Rights Act of 1964, the Equal Employment Opportunity Act of 1972, and the Age Discrimination in Employment Act of 1967, Congress's concern focused more on offering special protection to classes of individuals believed to be in need of that protection—minority individuals, women, individuals between the ages of 40 and 65—than, for example, on the economic consequences of the historic underrepresentation of these classes in the work force.

Illustrative Regulatory Programs

A number of different regulatory programs which illustrate the current scope of government regulation are considered below. The areas covered are: labor; environment; consumer protection; the political process; and energy. In each case, the underlying statutes and administrative regulations are outlined with a view to assessing the program's overall impact—both directly in commanding the corporation's obedience, and indirectly in constraining other corporate decisions.

1. Regulation of Labor Relations, Equal Employment Opportunity, and Employee Working Conditions

Reflecting the "social" theory of regulation, the federal government has comprehensively regulated how business corporations deal with their employees—by requiring collective bargaining, outlawing unfair labor practices, and guaranteeing equal employment opportunities. Moreover, in passing the Occupational Health and Safety Act, Congress imposed pervasive and specific employee health and safety standards on corporations—reflecting the "externalities" basis for government regulation.

Labor Relations

In 1935, at the depths of the Great Depression, with more than 10 million Americans unemployed and with labor strife severely limiting the ability of industry to produce necessary goods, Congress passed the National Labor Relations Act, also known as the Wagner Act. Congress stated:

The inequality of bargaining power between employees who do not possess full freedom of association or actual liberty of contract, and employers who are organized in the corporate or other forms of ownership association substantially burdens and affects the flow of commerce, and tends to aggravate recurrent business depressions, by depressing wage rates and the purchasing power of wage earners in industry and by preventing the stabilization of competitive wage rates and working conditions within and between industries. . . . It is hereby declared to be the policy of the United States to eliminate the causes of certain substantial obstructions to the free flow of commerce and to mitigate and eliminate these obstructions when they have occurred by encouraging the practice and procedure of collective bargaining. . . .

More than 40 years later, and after two major amendments to our labor laws,[24] the basic philosophy and thrust of the Act remain intact: that it is desirable to regulate certain corporate policies in the area of wages, hours, and other terms and conditions of employment.

1. The Basic Structure of the Act

The primary purpose of the Act is set forth in Section 7:

Employees shall have the right to self-organization, to form, join or assist labor organizations, to bargain collectively through representatives of their own choosing, and to engage in other concerted activities for the purpose of collective bargaining or other mutual aid or protection, and shall also have the right to refrain from any or all of such activities except to the extent that such right may be affected by an agreement requiring membership in a labor organization as a condition of employment. . . .

In considering the effect of these rights on the corporation, it is well to keep in mind the following three aspects of labor relations, each of which finds its genesis in Section 7: (i) the right of employees to be represented by a union; (ii) the obligation of a union and an employer to bargain in good faith; and (iii) the right of each employee to engage or not to engage in activities on behalf of a union without any interference from either union or management.

The Right of Employees to Select a Collective Bargaining Representative. The Act establishes a basic framework for determining whether a majority of an employee unit that is appropriate for purposes of collective bargaining wishes to be represented by a union. Although employers may voluntarily recognize a union as the collective bargaining representative for a group of employees—based on objective evidence of majority support for the union among those employees—it is far more often the case that the employer refuses to recognize the union unless a majority of the employees in question vote for such representation in a secret ballot election conducted by the National Labor Relations Board ("NLRB").

Over the years, the NLRB has established and refined a set of rules governing the conduct of both employers and unions in representation elections—rules which permit unions great latitude as to what they may say or promise to employees in return for a pro-union vote in an election but which severely circumscribe what employers may say and do in such an election.[25]

The Duty to Bargain in Good Faith. When a union wins a representation election, or is voluntarily recognized by an employer pursuant to some other objective evidence of majority status, the union and the employer are under a duty to bargain with each other. The NLRB is often called upon to determine whether the parties in a collective bargaining relationship have lived up to their mutual obligations to bargain collectively, or, as the question is usually framed, whether the parties have bargained in

149

good faith. In practice, NLRB determinations as to whether specific conduct at the bargaining table constitutes a refusal to bargain in good faith most often reflect a concern to equalize the relative bargaining strength of the parties.[26]

Conduct That Constitutes an Unfair Labor Practice. Another major area of regulation by the NLRB concerns a wide range of conduct denominated as "unfair labor practices." Corporations are prohibited from interfering with, restraining or coercing employees in the exercise of any of the rights guaranteed to them by Section 7 of the Wagner Act. Thus, a corporate employer may not discharge an employee or change his working conditions when the corporation's actions are motivated by the employee's present or past activities on behalf of a union.[27] Similarly, it is an unfair labor practice for the corporation to recognize and bargain with a union which does not enjoy majority support of the employees in an appropriate unit.[28]

The responsibility for enforcement of the Act is divided between a five-member Board, which in practice has interpreted the Act through case-by-case adjudication rather than by rulemaking processes (though it has rulemaking power), and the Office of the General Counsel, which has absolute authority over whether to issue and prosecute a complaint when someone has charged that the Act has been violated. Decisions of the NLRB in unfair labor practice cases are subject to review in federal appellate courts.

2. Assessment of the Wagner Act's Impact

It is beyond dispute that unionized workers generally have greater economic muscle when dealing with their employers than do unorganized workers. Indeed, one of the principal purposes of the Wagner Act was to increase employee bargaining power through collective bargaining. What was perhaps not foreseen was that this increased bargaining power would, in some instances, become largely unrestrained by market factors, and that, as a result, unionized workers would sometimes obtain wage settlements and other contract terms that ultimately placed the employer in a noncompetitive position. As an extreme case, for example, this inflexibility contributed to General Motors' decision to dispose of its Frigidaire Division. Frigidaire had for too long been in a difficult competitive position because it was locked into United Automobile Workers wage rates and benefit levels, while the rest of the appliance industry operated under less costly International Brotherhood of Electrical Workers' wage and benefit packages.

The potential for economic disruption is heightened when corporations face multiplant or even multicompany bargaining, which tends to increase union bargaining power. Even where corporations resist the creation of such bargaining units, organized labor has been successful in establishing *de facto* multiplant or multicompany bargaining by insisting that a bargaining settlement at one plant or company serve as a model for other plants or even whole industries. Moreover, the process of collective bargaining itself tends to sharply diminish corporate flexibility. The simple fact is that collective bargaining agreements lock employers into work rules and wage and benefit levels that cannot easily be changed, even where market factors otherwise might warrant such change. Most collective bargaining in the United States, particularly in highly organized heavy industries, such as steel, oil, rubber, automobiles, etc., produces multiyear agreements, with a three-year agreement being the most common. These agreements not only establish the rules for dealing with organized employees, but often—because they become, in effect, long-term fixed costs for the corporation—bear directly on corporate management's operational flexibility in such matters as subcontracting, plant and department relocations, and automation, and indirectly on corporate marketing and capital allocation decisions.

The constraining force of the collective bargaining process on managerial flexibility has been heightened by the continuing need of union leaders to demonstrate that they can wield power on behalf of their constituencies. To an increasing extent, unions are seeking to bargain about items that were once regarded as exclusively within the prerogatives of management. In this effort the unions have been aided by the NLRB, which has taken a consistently broad view of what is encompassed within the phrase "wages, hours and other terms and conditions of employment."[29]

Further, our labor laws have had a major impact on a corporation's flexibility in making basic employment decisions in the areas of hiring, dismissal, discipline, promotions, etc. Where there are no unions involved (leaving aside the constraints provided by equal employment legislation, discussed below), the corporation's discretion will be subject to market considerations, and its decision will be based on its own objective analysis of the merits of a given situation. But where a union is involved, the situation is entirely different. Labor agreements may call for all hiring to be done exclusively through a union-run hiring hall. Similarly, a decision to discharge (or otherwise discipline) an employee is likely to be subject to review pursuant to a grievance and arbitration procedure, where the propriety of the decision must be established by the employer through objective evidence under defined standards.

Equal Employment Opportunity Regulation

Although chattel slavery was abolished in the United States in 1865, and some antidiscrimination laws have been on the books since Reconstruction days, it was not until the New Deal period that an attempt was made directly to regulate corporate employment practices to further equal employment objectives. By and large, however, these efforts involved little more than expressions of government policy, and it was not until the 1960's that laws and regulations with some real teeth in them were adopted in relatively quick succession. As described below, these laws and the enforcement activities of the Equal Employment Opportunity Commission (EEOC) have had a profound impact on corporate hiring practices.

1. Title VII of the Civil Rights Act of 1964

Title VII prohibits employment discrimination on the basis of race, color, religion, sex or national origin. The Act restricts all corporations (and all other employers with 15 or more employees) in all industries affecting commerce. The Act's constraints extend to all employment decisions, including hiring, discharge, promotions, pay rates and fringe benefits.

The Act has been interpreted to bar not only intentional discrimination, but any employment practice which has a disproportionate adverse effect on a protected class of persons unless the practice can be shown by the employer to be a "business necessity."[30] Thus, for example, the use of personality tests which screen out a disproportionate percentage of minority group candidates is unlawful, unless the particular test can be shown to be a valid indicator of successful performance on the job for which the test is administered.

The enforcement scheme mandated by Title VII may be summarized as follows: Proceedings are initiated by the filing of a charge by or on behalf of an aggrieved person with the EEOC, the agency established by the Act to administer its provisions. If a state or local anti-discrimination agency also has jurisdiction of the matter, the EEOC ordinarily refers the charge to that agency for initial processing. If the matter is not finally disposed of by the state or local agency, the EEOC itself will proceed to investigate the charge. If the EEOC finds probable cause to support the charge, it first attempts to resolve the matter through informal and voluntary conciliation efforts. When successful, these efforts typically lead to the execution by all parties of a conciliation agreement, which may include various nondiscrimination commitments, monetary remedies and monitoring provisions. If conciliation fails, the Act authorizes suit either by the EEOC or the aggrieved party or parties. Even if the charge is dismissed by the EEOC as nonmeritorious, the private right of action is preserved for the charging party. Provision is made in the Act for the appointment of counsel for the aggrieved party in appropriate cases, and for an award of attorneys' fees, in the discretion of the court, to the prevailing party.

The EEOC has never been granted either cease and desist powers or substantive rulemaking authority. Nevertheless, soon after it was established, the EEOC began issuing substantive "guidelines" delineating the agency's interpretations of the Act's requirements.[31] More often than not, the courts have sustained these guidelines,[32] and they have come to constitute *de facto* rules restricting employer conduct.

Perhaps the most significant of the guidelines are those

governing employee selection procedures. They were first issued by the EEOC in 1970, and were then reissued in 1978 in revised form by the EEOC and four other Federal agencies with enforcement responsibility for federal equal employment laws (the Departments of Justice, Labor and Treasury, and the Office of Personnel Management). These guidelines purport to impose affirmative obligations upon employers to analyze each and every employee selection practice or procedure with respect to whether it has an adverse impact upon a protected class, and, if so, to establish standards for the validation of the practice or procedure.[33] The EEOC validation requirements include not only steps which are generally accepted in the testing profession, but also other steps which go far beyond professionally accepted norms— such as an obligation to consider available alternative selection procedures having lesser adverse effects.

In addition to its substantive guidelines, the EEOC has issued procedural regulations requiring employers with 100 employees or more to file annual reports providing aggregate data by certain broad job categories on the racial and sexual composition of their workforce.[34] Employers also are required to maintain all records pertaining to employment matters for at least six months.

2. Affirmative Action Obligations of Government Contractors

Executive Order 11246 is the most recent of a series of orders promulgated to ensure nondiscrimination in employment by federal government contractors. The Order parallels Title VII in prohibiting employment discrimination on the basis of race, color, religion, sex or national origin. However, it imposes additional obligations upon contractors with 50 or more employees having government contracts in excess of $50,000. Specifically, such employers—generally large corporations—are required to develop and implement written affirmative action programs designed to achieve a more racially and sexually balanced workforce in all their establishments. Government contractors also are under a statutory obligation to take affirmative action in the employment of the mentally and physically handicapped, as well as disabled veterans and veterans of the Vietnam war.

Detailed regulations issued by the Department of Labor pursuant to Executive Order 11246 define the content and methodology to be used by contractors in preparing their affirmative action programs.[35] Through analysis of the workforce and the relevant labor market, contractors must identify job categories in which there is "underutilization" of minorities and women. Then, on the basis of these data and projected employment turnover, these corporations must define specific goals as well as timetables to correct the existing underutilization. Although the regulations state that the goals are not meant to be rigid and inflexible quotas, as a practical matter they constrain many corporations to treat the goals as quota requirements.

Between 1966 and 1979, responsibility for the administration and enforcement of Executive Order 11246 was in the hands of 11 different federal agencies. In late 1978, pursuant to Executive Order 12086, this responsibility was consolidated in the Department of Labor's Office of Federal Contract Compliance Programs (OFCCP). The OFCCP is now directly responsible for performing the actual office and field audits of the affirmative action programs of government contractors, in order to ensure that the contractors are meeting their affirmative action obligations. This consolidation should serve to increase the effectiveness of the affirmative action enforcement effort.

Executive Order 11246 furnishes the government with a variety of sanctions which may be employed for non-compliance with the terms of the Order and the implementing regulations. These include barring future contracts, cancelling existing contracts, conditioning continuation of contracts upon compliance with revised programs, and recommending civil litigation by the Department of Justice or the EEOC.

3. Equal Pay Act

The Equal Pay Act makes it unlawful for any employer covered by the Fair Labor Standards Act to pay wages "at a rate less than the rate at which [the employer] pays wages to employees of the opposite sex . . . for equal work on jobs the performance of which requires equal skill, efforts, and responsibility, and which are performed under similar working conditions." The jobs being compared need not be identical, but only need be "substantially equal" for the requirement of equal pay to be applicable.[36] "Pay" includes not only salaries and wages, but all fringe benefits provided by the employer.

Assuming two jobs being compared are substantially equal, the employer may not be held liable if it can be demonstrated that any wage differential which exists is based upon a seniority system, merit system, piece rate system, or any other factor other than sex. The last defense has caused a considerable amount of litigation. It has been held, for example, that a pay differential for substantially equal jobs may be justified on the basis of the higher profitability to the employer of the higher paid job.[37] On the other hand, the fact that the labor market may place a higher price on the services of males than on the services of females is not a permissible defense.

Between 1963 and 1979, the Equal Pay Act was enforced primarily by civil actions brought by the Secretary of Labor. The Act also provides a private right of action for aggrieved employees. In a successful action back pay plus an equal amount in punitive damages may be awarded by the court for a period going back up to three years from the date of commencement of the action. In addition, attorneys' fees may be awarded to the successful public or private plaintiff.

The Federal Wage and Hour Administrator, pursuant to a delegation of authority from the Secretary of Labor, has issued interpretive bulletins defining what constitutes equal skill, effort, responsibility, and similar working conditions; what kinds of pay plans meet the statutory defenses, and what constitutes unequal pay.[38] The views of the Administrator, as set forth in the interpretative bulletins, have not always coincided with those of the EEOC in interpreting the overlapping sex discrimination ban contained in Title VII. For example, in considering fringe benefits for which the average costs were higher for women than for men, the Administrator took the position that either equal employer contributions or equal benefits would satisfy the Equal Pay Act, while the EEOC held to the view that only equal benefits would be lawful under Title VII.

Primary enforcement authority under the Equal Pay Act passed in 1979 from the Secretary of Labor to the EEOC. The consolidation of this authority with the existing authority of the EEOC to enforce compliance with the Title VII prohibition against sex discrimination is likely to eliminate previous inconsistencies in government positions and enhance the government's overall effectiveness in enforcing legal constraints outlawing sex discrimination.

4. Age Discrimination in Employment Act

The ADEA prohibits discrimination in employment on the basis of age for individuals between the ages of 40 and 70 years. It reaches all employers of 20 or more persons and, jurisdictionally, is almost as broad as Title VII and the Equal Pay Act. Although the Act bars discrimination on the basis of age in all employment decisions, its most significant impact is in preventing employers from enforcing mandatory retirement rules for employees under 70.

Only a few exceptions are permitted by the Act. Certain high-paid executives may be mandatorily retired at age 65, provided they will receive pension benefits from the employer in excess of $27,000 per year. And age may be a factor in employment decisions where it is a *bona fide* occupational qualification, such as for retirement of commercial airline pilots.

The enforcement mechanism under the ADEA is similar to that under the Equal Pay Act, with both public and private rights of action to enforce the Act through suit in federal court. However, some significant differences exist. Private plaintiffs suing under the ADEA are entitled to a jury trial, whereas no right to a jury trial exists under the Equal Pay Act or Title VII. Private plaintiffs suing on age discrimination claims also may be able to recover consequential and punitive damages (in addition to reinstatement and back pay) based on the psychic harm of age discrimination; such relief is not available under the Equal Pay Act or Title VII.

With the transfer of primary enforcement authority under the ADEA from the Secretary of Labor to the EEOC in 1979, the EEOC is in a position to move against employers on a wide spectrum of fronts in regulating their employment decision-making processes.

5. Assessment of EEO Regulation

The controversy which surrounded equal employment opportunity at the time of the Congressional debates on Title VII in 1964 has not diminished over time. Indeed, it is quite likely that the true dimensions of the policy issues and dilemmas posed by EEO regulation, and its profound impact, are only now beginning to be appreciated.

Beyond the fact that EEO regulation has constrained all employers to avoid acts of intentional discrimination, for most large corporations (which invariably are government contractors) EEO considerations may now: constitute an influential factor in a majority of employment decisions; have a significant direct and indirect cost impact on the corporation; create labor relations problems with unions; and bear heavily on overall and individual employee morale.

As a result of broad-based governmental enforcement efforts, some of the nation's biggest companies—including AT&T, General Electric, and the major steel companies—have undertaken massive commitments in consent decrees to attempt to correct alleged underutilization of minorities and women in their workforces and to compensate alleged victims of discrimination. For AT&T, the nation's largest private employer and the first major corporation to enter into a consent decree, the costs of settling were substantial. The company made $18 million in compensatory payments to 20,000 asserted victims of unequal pay, and granted pay increases for 72,000 employees at an annual cost estimated at $53 million. More significantly, however, the company undertook a massive overhaul of its employment decision-making procedures to implement a system of goals and timetables for improving the racial and sexual balance of its workforce within 15 broad job classes.

160

Simply to implement these affirmative action objectives, AT&T employs an estimated 750 employees on a full-time basis, and incurs additional recruiting and training costs. Perhaps of greatest significance to the long-term performance of such a company, it has retreated from its standard of hiring and promoting the "best qualified" candidates. In doing so, it has created labor relations problems for itself in dealing with its unions and those of its employees who believe they have been the victims of reverse discrimination.

Indeed, given the proliferation of proscribed forms of discrimination, the suggestion has been made that we are reaching a point where many corporations will lack any meaningful discretion in making employment decisions. Moreover, changes in the government's own policies affecting EEO matters often make compliance by corporations difficult, if not impossible.

To cite a case in point, it was because the government itself had quotas that discriminated against blacks and females that the veterans of World War II were disproportionately white males. These veterans, who were preferentially hired under federal legislation and educated at federal government expense, rose to become the present senior management of our major corporations. Now, these white males are the major beneficiaries of more recent federal legislation banning mandatory retirement prior to age 70. A corporation subject to such inflexible government-mandated rules preserving the predominantly white male character of senior management faces an obvious dilemma in satisfying other governmental requirements to correct the underutilization of minorities and women in these same positions.

Perhaps one virtue of the consolidation of federal enforcement activities in the EEOC will be the necessity for a single government agency to face up to conflicting priorities established by various antidiscrimination laws protecting minorities, women, and handicapped, veterans, the aged, and whatever other categories may be added in the future.

Occupational Safety and Health

Workplace safety has been regulated, directly or indirectly, for over a hundred years.[39] Prior to the passage of the Occupational Safety and Health ("OSH") Act, however, there was no comprehensive regulatory program at any level of government. Following a sharp rise in the reported injury rate among workers in the 1960's, a pervasive federal regulatory program long advocated by the unions was developed.

The program reflected a number of political compromises: The Occupational Safety and Health Administration ("OSHA") itself was placed in the Labor Department and given the responsibility for promulgating safety and health standards, and enforcing the standards by means of inspecting workplaces and issuing citations and proposed fines against employers for violations.[40] The Occupational Safety and Health Review Commission (OSHRC) was established as an independent agency to hear appeals from OSHA-issued citations and fines.[41] The National Institute for Occupational Safety and Health (NIOSH) was placed in the Department of Health and Human Services and assigned research functions with respect to both specific standards proposed by OSHA and more general issues of workplace safety and health.[42] The National Advisory Commission on Safety and Health (NACOSH) was created as an official forum for business and labor representatives to discuss policy issues.[43] NACOSH was also supposed to assist in coordination of the activities of the three government agencies.

With respect to worker safety, Section 5(a) of the OSH Act imposes a "general duty" on an employer to "furnish to each of his employees employment and a place of employment which are free from recognized hazards that are causing or are likely to cause death or serious physical harm to his employees."[44] Although the Act directed OSHA to develop and issue occupational safety and health standards that are "reasonably necessary or appropriate to provide safe or healthful employment and places of employment",[45] Congress—to ensure that OSHA began operations soon after its creation—directed it to adopt, as enforceable mandatory standards, all existing safety health standards which had been imposed by the federal government or which had been adopted by industry "consensus."[46] Within months of its creation, therefore, OSHA issued more than five hundred pages of finely printed regulations that were derived from varying sources. Because of their diverse parentage, no coherent theme ran through these initial standards: some were hopelessly out of date, such as the one that prohibited workers from using ice in drinking water (a throwback to the days when ice was cut from ponds which might be polluted). Some were irrelevant, such as requiring split toilet seats or describing the Latin names of the kinds of wood that can be used to make ladders. Some were excessively detailed, such as the one which specified the number of rivets that must be in a particular guard or that workrests must be precisely $\frac{1}{8}$-inch from a grinding wheel. Still others were excessively vague and gave little guidance as to what was required, such as the single most important standard dealing with machinery, which provided simply:

One or more methods of machine guarding shall be provided to protect the operator and other employees in the machine area from hazards such as those created by point of operation, ingoing nip points, rotating parts, flying chips and sparks. Examples of guarding methods are—barrier guards, two-hand tripping devices, electronic safety devices, *etc.*[47]

As early as 1972, only a year after the initial standards were issued, OSHA undertook to reduce the problems stemming from this collage of rules. The most dramatic effort was the repeal of many of these standards in 1978.[48] But even this action addressed only the obvious absurdities and did not resolve the general problems of over-specificity and inconsistency; nor did OSHA extend the safety standards into areas left uncovered by the hasty adoption of the initial safety standards.

In the area of health standards, the OSH Act requires OSHA to issue standards dealing with toxic materials and to set the standard "which most adequately assures that to the extent feasible . . . no employee will suffer material impairment of health" even if the employee is exposed to the hazard daily throughout his working life.[49] OSHA has steadfastly held the view that it is not generally sufficient to rely on personal protective equipment —such as respirators—to protect workers from toxic materials. Rather, OSHA health standards require that engineering controls be developed. These new health-related standards have had and will continue to have a significant effect on all corporations that use any of the more than one thousand target chemicals in their production processes.

OSHA's direct impact on manufacturing corporations lies in the requirement that they comply with its numerous standards in the safety and health areas. In this connection, the position taken by OSHA that cost/benefit analyses are simply irrelevant—except to the extent a standard would bankrupt an entire industry—has resulted in regulations imposing enormous costs. For example, OSHA imposed a regulation controlling exposure to benzene that OSHA itself estimated would cost $500,000,000 to comply with, even though it made no estimate as to the magnitude of the benefits that would result. On review of this action, the Supreme Court, in a sharply divided opinion, stated that OSHA must demonstrate that significant benefits will flow from a new standard, and it held that OSHA had failed to do so in the case of its benzene rule. However, although the Court remanded the matter back to OSHA, it did not fully resolve the long-standing dispute over the precise extent of the agency's duty to weigh costs against benefits.

Beyond the costs of complying with OSHA regulations —very often requiring corporations to engineer substantial changes in production processes—the impact of federal worker safety regulations on corporations is magnified by the fact that OSHA sends in its inspectors unannounced. In response to a constitutional challenge to this practice, the Supreme Court ruled that OSHA inspectors must obtain a search warrant or its equivalent in order to inspect the premises when an employer objects to that inspection.[51] However, the Court held that OSHA need *not* show reasonable cause to believe a violation is occurring to obtain a warrant, but simply that the business "has been chosen for an OSHA search on the basis of a general administrative plan for the enforcement of the Act derived from neutral sources. . . ."[52]

Finally, corporations have been required by OSHA to maintain a vast number of records. For example, OSHA requires firms to maintain a log of all occupational injuries and illnesses for each plant and the employer must compile an annual summary of the injuries and illnesses. All fatalities and all accidents requiring hospitalization for five or more employees must be reported directly to OSHA.[53] All of these and the other costs of worker protection are, as in other areas of externalities' regulation, partly absorbed by the corporation affected and partly passed on to the consumers of the corporations' output.

2. Federal Environmental Regulation

In another classic example of government regulation of market externalities, federal laws and regulations seeking to achieve environmental goals have over the past ten years mandated an enormous allocation of capital resources to the protection and enhancement of the environment. Many companies have been forced to spend as much as 20 percent of their capital and 10 percent of their operating budgets for pollution control.[54] The Census Bureau estimates that total manufacturing expenditures for pollution control were $9.1 billion in 1977.[55] Arthur Andersen & Co.'s study of the incremental cost to business of federal regulations found the Environmental Protection Agency's programs to be the most expensive by far, causing $2 billion in accelerating expenditures that would not otherwise have occurred.[56] Environmental controls play a major role in determining plant location and the utilization of existing plants. They clearly constrain the discretion of corporations with respect to the processes they use and where they will locate their activities. Because of the large amounts of money involved, corporate management must always consider the effects of these regulations in connection with major plant decisions.

This section will focus principally on the Clean Air Act and the Federal Water Pollution Control Act—the two most significant aspects of a comprehensive panoply of environmental statutes which includes: the National Environmental Policy Act of 1969;[57] Reorganization Plan Number 3 of 1970, creating the Environmental Protection Agency (EPA);[58] the Resource Recovery Act of 1970;[59] the Noise Control Act of 1972;[60] the Federal Environmental Pesticide Control Act of 1972, amending the Federal Insecticide, Fungicide and Rodenticide Act;[61] and the Coastal Zone Management Act of 1972.[62] A more recent—and potentially very significant—addition to this list is the Toxic Substances Control Act of 1976.[63]

Air Pollution

Although originally passed in 1963, the Clean Air Act did not become truly effective until after 1970, when Congress passed a series of significant amendments. The most important features of the regulatory program created pursuant to the Act are as follows:

1. National Ambient Air Quality Standards and State Plans (NAAQS)

Under the Clean Air Act, the Administrator of the Environmental Protection Agency must publish a list of pollutants and issue standards for each pollutant listed, setting forth the permissible quantities of the pollutant which may exist (per part of atmosphere).[64] While these air quality standards are uniform throughout the country, the strategies to achieve them are developed on a state and substate basis. The EPA Administrator is required to divide the country into Air Quality Control Regions, which the states are to use in developing their plans.[65] A corporation doing business in more than one

167

state must therefore comply with the potentially different standards of the various states in which it operates.

Two sets of standards have been promulgated by EPA for each of seven pollutants. The "primary" standards are those which are deemed necessary to protect human life and health. These are the principal goals toward which state plans must move. The "secondary" standards are those necessary to protect the "public welfare." Both types of standards were set in 1971 for six pollutants—carbon monoxide, hydrocarbons, nitrogen oxides, particulate matter, sulfur oxides, and photochemical oxidants (changed to ozone in 1979)—and in 1976 for one additional pollutant—lead.[66] Three pollutants—hydrocarbons, particulate matter, and ozone—actually cover more than one chemical element or compound, effectively expanding the coverage of the pollutant list. Further, hazardous pollutants such as mercury and asbestos are separately regulated through direct EPA emission controls.[67] Since most industrialized manufacturing operations yield one or more of these pollutants, these standards have wide applicability.

2. Nonattainment

When the deadlines for attaining the primary air quality standards passed in 1975 and 1976, it became apparent that virtually every industrialized area of the country had not in fact achieved these goals. At that point, the EPA administratively adopted a policy prohibiting new industrial construction, including expansion of an existing plant, unless it could be shown that pollution from the new source would be "offset" by a reduction in pollution from existing sources within the same geographical area, whether or not such sources were owned by the firm seeking to initiate the construction.[68]

The 1977 Amendments to the Clean Air Act recognized both the failure to attain the standards and the cumbersome nature of EPA's solution to the problem, and officially granted delays in the required attainment dates. States were given until 1982 to attain all the standards, and could apply for additional five-year extensions for the automotive-related pollutants carbon monoxide and ozone. In order to receive these extensions, states were required to submit "nonattainment plans"—a new subplan within a state implementation plan. There are several statutory sanctions against states which do not submit an approvable nonattainment plan, the most Draconian of which is a prohibition on construction of new or modified major industrial facilities.[69]

3. Prevention of Significant Deterioration

The industrial corporation is not merely affected by clean air standards in states which presently have air pollution levels exceeding the standards. A policy known as the "prevention of significant deterioration" (PSD or nondeterioration) has been adopted for areas of the country with air significantly cleaner than that required by either the primary or secondary standards to prevent the air in such areas from becoming as dirty as those standards would allow.

Application of clean air standards to prevent deterioration in air quality represents a substantial expansion in the impact of Clean Air Act requirements and broadly affects the activities and resource allocation decisions of corporations doing business or planning to do business in areas which do not presently have pollution problems. The 1977 statutory approach directs the states to divide nondeterioration areas into three categories, with most national parks and wilderness areas automatically placed in Class I, the "purest" category. Virtually no additional pollution is allowed in Class I areas, with increasing amounts allowed for Class II and III areas, as specified in the statute.[70]

To insure that there is not a race to begin construction in Class II and III areas, to the point where the maximum amounts of allowable pollution are reached, several additional restrictions are placed on new industrial development. States must adopt a permit system prohibiting corporations from undertaking new construction unless:

(i) the facility uses the best available control technology for all pollutants;

(ii) the state has held a public hearing at which EPA representatives are present and the corporation involved affirmatively demonstrates both that the nondeterioriation standards will not be violated and that the transportation of pollution from the facility will not cause a violation of any pollution standard in another area;

(iii) the corporation provides an air quality impact analysis based on the area's general economic growth; and

(iv) the corporation agrees to conduct monitoring to determine the actual effect of emissions from the facility once it is operating.

In terms of the underlying externality theory for this type of regulation, the government has, in effect, made the air an aspect of public property which is leased to corporations subject to the condition that the air be returned relatively undamaged.

4. Direct EPA Authority

In addition to promulgating the NAAQS and supervising state regulatory activity, EPA has direct regulatory responsibilities. One of the most important of these—adding an entire tier of mandatory constraints on the corporation—is the authority to establish new source performance standards for each type of major polluting industry.[71] Enforced by civil and criminal sanctions, these requirements must be met by every builder and operator of a new or substantially modified industrial facility. (They thus represent another indirect governmental factor tending to favor expansion through acquisition, rather than *de novo* investment.) In addition, the 1977 Amendments give EPA added authority with respect to controlling pollution from existing facilities by allowing federal penalties to be imposed on corporations which fail to meet state-imposed pollution standards.

Several major regulatory and public policy issues have emerged from the Clean Air Act and its implementation which are pertinent to the question of how the major corporation has been affected. One of the most important of these is the conflict between clean air and energy goals. This has been especially acute in two areas: burning coal in electric power plants and reducing emissions from automobiles. For example, developing the technology to reduce emissions affects the ability of the automotive corporations to increase fuel economy. This is exacerbated by the EPA limitations on the use of fuel additives and the phase-out of leaded gasoline. These problems led former Secretary of Transportation Brock Adams to call for a major government-industry effort to "reinvent the car." In the meantime, the deadlines remain for both sets of standards—effectively creating new markets (and new sets of market constraints) for the development of automobile technology, design and parts which will be useful in meeting these requirements. The automobile companies estimate that compliance with these regulations will cost many billions of dollars and result in automobiles significantly different from those traditionally preferred by the American market.

Another issue is the extent to which economic incentives and penalties should be relied upon to reduce pollution emissions. The 1977 Amendments provide for a noncompliance penalty equal to the cost which the corporation would have incurred to achieve the emission reductions.[72] If this monetary penalty proves successful, it may push the concept into other areas of environmental regulation. Its potential advantage is that it focuses on the achievement of antipollution goals rather than spelling out the specific means of reducing pollution in complex regulations. In other words, it seeks to achieve defined objectives by influencing corporate discretion through a system of rewards and penalties, as the market does and as the tax law does.

Water Pollution

Corporations with manufacturing operations on lakes and waterways (or which seek to build facilities there) are subject to another set of environmental constraints. Control of pollution of "navigable waters" is governed by the Federal Water Pollution Control Act (FWPCA).[73] The FWPCA was enacted in 1948 and amended twelve times between then and October 1972, when the 1972 Amendments were passed. Prior to 1972, the program for water pollution control focused primarily on providing federal funds for municipal waste treatment plants and on state-established water quality standards (levels of pollution in a particular body of water). With no deadlines for achieving the water quality standards, and no specific discharge regulations, the progress in controlling water pollution made by the FWPCA prior to the 1972 Amendments was minimal. With the 1972 Amendments to FWPCA, however, the government commenced a significant effort to change industrial manufacturing operations which result in water pollution. Essentially, the corporation is given the option of cleaning up the pollution or of discontinuing the manufacturing operations which cause it. In terms of the regulatory theory involved here, the government has attempted to internalize within the corporation some of the costs of water pollution.

As amended in 1972, the FWPCA set two ambitious goals: first, making all navigable waters "fishable and swimmable" by July 1, 1983; and second, eliminating *all* discharges of pollutants into navigable waters by 1985.[74] In order to achieve these goals, the 1972 Amendments empowered EPA to establish and implement water pollution permit programs governing facilities discharging waste into water. In contrast to the Clean Air Act, the initial responsibilities were placed on EPA, with supplemental responsibilities given to the states. The final permit providing for the allowable pollution from a given facility is issued by EPA; however, in each case the state's interest is taken into account in determining the amount of pollution which will be allowed. The permit is the basic enforcement tool in the FWPCA. The process leading to the issuance of a specific permit is as follows:

1. Effluent Guidelines

For each category, and in many cases subcategory, of major sources of industrial pollution, EPA is required to establish two sets of guidelines which specify the maximum amount of pollutant per unit of production which may be discharged during a given period of time. One set is based on levels of control attainable by using the "best practicable technology currently available" (BPT), and the other set is based on levels attainable by using the "best available technology economically achievable"

173

(BAT).[75] The BPT guidelines were to be used prior to 1977, and the BAT by 1983. The BPT incorporates a cost/benefit approach, giving consideration to the cost to the industry involved and the availability of both the technology and the money to pay for it. The BAT standards are somewhat tighter, giving greater weight to benefits than costs on the assumption that corporations will be motivated to develop new technology which will achieve greater efficiencies in pollution control (and ultimately lower costs).

2. State Water Quality Standards

The 1965 Water Quality Act, one of the series of changes made in the 1948 FWPCA leading to the 1972 Amendments, required each state to adopt "water quality" standards for all "interstate waters." The "water quality" levels were to be expressed in terms of pollutant concentrations and established according to designated uses for the portion of the body of water involved. That is, water to be used for swimming was to be given substantially stricter water quality standards than water solely designated for industrial use. Prior to passage of the 1972 Amendments, each state had submitted, and received EPA approval for, its set of standards. The amendments sought to implement the standards through use of the effluent guidelines, industrial permit program, and municipal waste treatment grant and permit programs. In addition, the 1972 Amendments extended standards coverage from "interstate waters" (defined as waters which, at some point, touch more than one state) to "navigable waters" (a much broader definition covering virtually all moving and many still bodies of water in the country). Moreover, the 1972 Amendments required states to identify bodies of water within their boundaries for which the effluent guidelines would be insufficient to allow the water quality standards to be met. For these waters, the states were required to establish additional plans for achieving the standards, and EPA is required to tighten the allowable discharge levels on permits issued in those areas.

3. NPDES Permit Program

The National Pollution Discharge Elimination System (NPDES) permit program is the heart of the FWPCA.[76] Each corporate facility which discharges pollutants into water must have an NPDES permit issued by EPA or the relevant state (if a state has been delegated NPDES authority by EPA). The discharges allowed by the permit are the effluent limitations contained in EPA's industry and subindustry guidelines, modified as necessary to meet the state water quality standards. Permits are valid for up to five years, with this time period corresponding, at the time the 1972 Amendments were passed, to the 1977 and 1983 implementation dates for BPT and BAT. As in the case of the Clean Air Act, 1977 amendments to the FWPCA eased standards and extended deadlines.

When most businesses were unable to meet the required discharge levels in the initial round of permits, EPA developed an "administrative order" procedure by which firms agreed to a specific compliance schedule. Because of the way the appeal provisions of the 1972 Amendments were structured, the corporations which entered into these agreements were precluded from later appealing the reasonableness of the final permit conditions. They in effect agreed to the imposition of substantial sanctions if they violated their permit. The sanctions can include an order to close the facility until a permit is obtained, imposition of fines up to $10,000 per day, and criminal penalties for willful violations.

Like the Clean Air Act, the FWPCA requires EPA to establish higher standards for new sources of pollution, on the assumption that it is easier for corporations to put in better pollution control equipment in the first instance than it is for them to replace equipment already paid for and in place. A corporation must therefore obtain an NPDES permit for any new facility which emits water pollutants, and the requirements which must be met before that permit is granted are much higher than for existing sources.[77] (Again, a clear if unintended regulatory deterrent to *de novo* expansion and construction may be observed.)

4. Toxic Substances

The 1972 and 1977 amendments to the FWPCA gave special attention to toxic pollutants. In the 1972 version, the focus was on the discharge into either navigable waters or municipal waste systems. EPA was required to identify toxic pollutants and establish standards for their discharge which provide a margin of safety. In 1977 standards were modified to require corporations, by July 1, 1984, to use the best available control technology for identified toxic pollutants (and, for any new toxic pollutants, by three years from the date of their identification). Further, the 1977 Amendments addressed the problem of "leaching" from land dumps by requiring corporations to use the "best management practices" in the "ancillary" (e.g., land dumping) activities related to toxic pollutants.[78]

Although the foregoing programs and requirements have had the most direct and costly impact on corporate

practices and planning, three additional FWPCA programs serve broadly, if indirectly, to constrain corporate
operations. First, the grant and regulatory programs for
local municipal waste treatment plants have a substantial impact on those industrial and commercial facilities
which discharge into municipal systems rather than
nearby waters. Most important are the requirements that
certain kinds of industrial and commercial waste be "pre-
treated" before discharge into the sewer systems and that
municipalities and other waste treatment plant operators
develop user charges based on the volume of discharges
into the system.[79] The pretreatment criteria generally require substantial elimination of wastes, such as heavy
metals, which are not treatable by the municipal plants.
The user fees are substantial so that corporations will be
induced economically to clean up "their portion" of pollution cost to the general tax base. Both of these requirements have been controversial but are now becoming
generally applicable. Minor changes were made by the
1977 Amendments which eased some of the problems,
allowing, for example, the use of *ad valorem* taxes in
place of user fees in limited circumstances.

Second, the major program of the 1972 Amendments,
which is only now beginning to be felt, is the areawide
planning process.[80] The slow start is due in large part to
the nature of the contemplated process—metropolitan
area sewage and "nonpoint" source regulatory strategies. In many ways, this requires "intercommunity"
agreements on land use. Nonpoint source water pollution
is that which is not generated from identifiable discharge
pipes. In general, the main source of nonpoint source pollution is storm water runoff from streets and parking lots
which then flows into bodies of water either through
storm sewer systems or over land, and its impact is substantial. In the Washington, D.C., area, for example, the

local Council of Governments has found that the major sources of pollution now in the Potomac River are non-point sources. The regulation of this is very difficult and generally involves slowing economic growth or prohibiting the use of certain chemicals on land areas which generate runoffs. The process of remedying nonpoint pollution this way imposes relatively tougher and more costly standards on affected corporations, and otherwise available land sites may become off limits. Similarly, planning areawide sewage treatment has usually led to debates about how much economic and residential growth will be allowed and where it will occur.

The third program is the "dredge and fill" permit program.[81] This is run by the Army Corps of Engineers, which, as a result of lawsuits, has established fairly strict antipollution terms for these permits and has extended the program to nearly every pond, stream, and swamp in the country. The scope of the 1972 Amendments covers all "navigable waters," which has been interpreted to mean both *potentially* navigable waters and waters connected to navigable waters. Since much of this country's industrial development occurs in areas where some small amount of water is diverted or filled in, the extension of this program has meant that developers of virtually every type of industrial facility must obtain permits—a process which not only is costly but which inevitably occasions substantial delays in the completion of projects.

3. Consumer Protection Regulation

It is no exaggeration to suggest that in the past two decades the nation has witnessed a revolutionary change in the traditional relationship between business and the

178

consumer. Historically, at common law, the Latin phrase *caveat emptor*—let the buyer beware—reflected the legal relationship; but today, even the incautious buyer will find himself armed with numerous rights and resources against a seller—so that the maxim *caveat venditor* is at least equally applicable if not of controlling significance.

Beginning with the passage of the Federal Trade Commission Act,[82] which (as amended in 1938) prohibits "unfair or deceptive acts or practices in or affecting commerce," the government has enacted a series of laws specifically designed to benefit consumers. Many of these laws reflect the "market externality" theory of regulation as well as social objectives. And they all act as direct constraints on a corporation's discretion to engage in a wide range of practices affecting consumer interests. In general, these constraints have significantly raised the cost of doing business in the consumer product and service sector of the economy—both directly in terms of costs required for compliance with government standards (e.g., percentage and weight of down required in down-labeled garments, size and print type standards for consumer credit agreements) and indirectly in terms of the liability risks for law violations and the substantial legal and other expenses incurred to avoid them.

So-called " consumer protection" legislation is pervasive at all levels of government. Some statutes, such as the Federal Trade Commission Act, affect the practices of all kinds of businesses everywhere in the country. Others—such as the Consumer Product Safety Act and Truth-in-Lending Act—apply to particular sectors of economic activity (manufacturing, consumer financing)—while others, such as the Food, Drug & Cosmetic Act, the Federal Insecticide, Fungicide & Rodenticide Act, and the Hobby Protection Act—are limited in application to particular products (or, as in the case of the postal laws and the Federal Communications Act, to particular means of communication). Moreover, almost all states and many localities have adopted their own consumer protection statutes.[83] A corporation doing business in different geographical areas invariably will have to abide by a multiplicity of consumer protection requirements.

The following discussion outlines the jurisdiction of the Federal Trade Commission and Consumer Product Safety Commission, and the nature of consumer credit regulation. While a complete analysis of consumer protection requirements is beyond the scope of this book, a cursory outline of these three areas will illustrate their extent and impact.

FTC Jurisdiction and Enforcement

1. The Federal Trade Commission Act

The Federal Trade Commission Act,[84] as discussed in Chapter 2, broadly prohibits antitrust violations and any other "unfair methods of competition." But this antitrust-oriented mandate of the FTC represents only one half of its statutory jurisdiction under the Act. In its additional proscription of all "unfair or deceptive acts or practices in or affecting commerce," Section 5 of the FTC Act[85] is by far today's most wide-ranging consumer protection law. It applies virtually to all packaging, labeling and advertising (radio, television, newspapers, magazines, billboards, showroom displays, catalogs, trade advertisements, point-of-sale material). And it also applies to a host of other trade activities unrelated to advertising— such as the collection of past-due accounts, the offering of negative option plans for book clubs, the sale of used cars, and the conduct of sweepstakes and games of chance, to name but a few.

If any corporation is found to have violated the "unfairness" standard of Section 5, whether or not it intended to do so, it may be subjected to a cease and desist order which in many cases prohibits not only the specific practices in question but also—under the so-called "fencing-in doctrine"—related practices in which the corporation may never have engaged. Cease and desist orders have also imposed affirmative requirements, such as the mandatory running of "corrective ads" worded, according to strict specifications set by the FTC, to dispel or mitigate asserted misimpressions created by deceptive statements in previous ads. (The advertisements noting that "Listerine will not cure colds" are a recent example of an affirmative requirement imposed by an FTC cease and desist order.) Violation of a cease and desist order may result in civil penalties of up to $10,000 per day per violation. In addition, if consumers have suffered monetary loss by reason of an illegal practice, the offending company may be required to make restitution.

Beyond this kind of case-by-case enforcement approach, the Magnuson-Moss Federal Trade Commission Improvements Act of 1975[86] specifically empowers the FTC to adopt industry-wide rules specifying what constitute unfair or deceptive acts and practices within the meaning of Section 5 of the FTC Act. Once a legislative-type rule of this kind is adopted (for example, a rule requiring companies to post octane ratings or put care labels on garments), a company faces fines of up to $10,000 per day for each violation. A company alleged to have violated one of these "trade regulation rules" is not generally free to defend against liability by challenging its substantive content. It is as though Congress itself had legislated the standard.

In implementing its authority under Section 5 of the FTC Act[87] to prohibit "deception" and "unfairness," the Commission has challenged an ever-changing and constantly expanding range of business practices. Historically, the Commission concentrated its efforts in the area of deceptive advertising. Any advertisement which has the capacity or tendency to deceive—through explicit or implicit representations—is unlawful regardless of whether anyone actually has been deceived. So is any advertisement which is misleading in any respect (even though not totally false), or which fails to disclose a "material" fact. The FTC serves as the primary judge of the meaning of an ad, of whether an ad has a tendency to deceive, and of what facts are material.

In recent years, moreover, the Commission has construed as illegal under Section 5 advertisements which lacked adequate substantiation at the time they were made—even if the claims made were perfectly true and subsequently were substantiated.[88] This recent expansion of Commission activity has added a new layer of constraints on corporate advertisers—requiring them to ensure that each ad they make is not only true, but "proven" true in advance and to retain adequate proof to that effect.

While the Commission has most frequently challenged deceptive advertising through cease and desist order proceedings against individual companies, the Commission recently initiated a proceeding aimed at formulating an industry-wide trade regulation rule which would ban advertising to children.[89] This proposal, like other similar rules,[90] has been the subject of considerable controversy and has been criticized on the grounds that the Commission, consisting of five unelected Presidential appointees, should leave "social policy" decisions of this kind to Congress. The Commission has responded that aspects of the issues involved raise questions of fact requiring the exercise of agency expertise. Regardless of the merits of this dispute, the nature of this and similar FTC actions and the controversies they have engendered illustrate the breadth of the Commission's jurisdiction in interpreting and implementing the amorphous "unfairness" standard.*

Through both rulemaking and individual company cease and desist order proceedings, the FTC has comprehensively regulated a wide variety of other business practices outside the area of advertising, including the following: endorsements and testimonials; product demonstrations; the conduct of "sales"; stakes and games of chance; door-to-door and mail order sales; negative option plans; references to "tests," "surveys," and the like; product composition; care labeling; nutritional claims; foreign origin disclosures; pyramid sales; and use of the word "new." In each of these areas, corporations must conform to specific requirements laid down by the FTC's rules and decisions. Even in areas where the FTC has not adopted an industry-wide rule, a new provision in the Magnuson-Moss Act has substantially broadened the effect of FTC decisions in individual company cease and desist order proceedings. Thus any corporation with knowledge that the FTC has ruled, in an individual cease and desist order case, that a particular trade practice is "unfair or deceptive," can itself be bound by that ruling and subjected to stiff penalties for engaging in the same or similar practices, even though it is precluded from contesting, and was not itself a party to, the first case.

---

* It should be noted that Congress in 1980 prohibited the FTC for 3 years from basing *any* commercial advertising rule on the "unfairness" doctrine alone, and permanently prohibited FTC adoption of a children's advertising rule based on that doctrine. *See* Pub. L. 96-252, §11, 94 Stat. 374, 379.

2. Special Warranty Requirements Mandated by FTC Act

For many years, the Federal Trade Commission dealt with warranties and guarantees under the general provisions of Section 5 of the FTC Act.[91] In 1960, for example, it issued Guides Against Deceptive Advertising of Guarantees,[92] which laid down basic rules for all guarantees and made specific provision for certain variants such as "lifetime" guarantees.

In 1975, the Magnuson-Moss Act[93] became law and provided a new framework for regulating warranties for consumer products (that is, products normally used for personal, family or household purposes). The Act, which has had a major impact in the warranties area, applies to written promises that a product will be defect free or meet a certain level of performance for a specific time period, or that a warrantor will take some specified remedial action if the product fails to live up to the warrantor's promises about it.

Under the Act, written warranties may not ordinarily be conditioned on the consumer's using a brand named or trademarked product or service. Nor may a written warranty disclaim or modify any implied warranty (e.g., the product is fit for ordinary use), beyond limiting its duration to that of the written warranty itself if that warranty is of a "reasonable" duration. Exclusions or limitations of "consequential damages" must appear "conspicuously" on the face of the warranty. The broad reach of the Act and the FTC's implementing rules is perhaps best illustrated by the fact that requirements imposed on companies vary substantially, depending on even small changes in the retail sales price of a product which is warrantied and the extent of warranty coverage the manufacturer or seller wishes to provide. Thus, the warranty of any product selling for more than $10 must be designated as a "Full [Statement of Duration] Warranty" or a "Limited Warranty." When a "Full Warranty" is offered, the warrantor, in addition to satisfying the conditions noted above, *must* (i) remedy the problem within a reasonable time without charge, (ii) offer the consumer a choice of a refund or replacement if a remedy is unattainable after a "reasonable" number of attempts, and (iii) impose no duty on the consumer other than notification (unless such duty is "reasonable"). A "Limited Warranty," on the other hand, simply is defined as one which does not meet all of the aforementioned requirements (as, for example, where the warrantor does not wish to make available a refund under all circumstances). But if it is at all ambiguous whether a full or limited warranty is being offered, the warrantor will be held responsible by the FTC for complying with the full warranty requirements. In such instances (e.g., where the warrantor offers a "*Full* Year *Limited* Warranty"), the FTC is inclined to require the "offending" warrantor to mail purchasers a notification spelling out their retroactive "full warranty" rights. For products costing more than $15, the FTC rules require that the written warranty disclose nine specific items, including, among other things, identification of what parts are covered, what has to be done and what costs have to be paid by each party to have a defect corrected, and the effective period of the warranty.

In addition to all of the foregoing warranty requirements, the FTC has adopted numerous rules pertaining to the advertising of warranties and to making warranties available for consumer inspection in advance of sale. A "money back" guarantee or warranty still must be backed by product performance substantiation. For example, an advertiser of a battery guaranteed for "36 months or your money back" may be held liable if he lacks actual proof that the battery could indeed be expected to last 36 months, irrespective of whether the expectation is borne out in fact or of whether the advertiser freely provides refunds to those purchasers returning defective batteries within the 36-month period.

3. FTC Enforcement of Other Laws

In addition to Section 5 of the FTC Act, the Commission has been directed to enforce a number of other consumer protection statutes covering specific areas. Examples include: the Federal Fair Packaging and Labeling Act,[94] which generally requires packages to indicate the products contained in the package, who is selling the products, and how much or how many of the products are included; the Wool Products Labeling Act,[95] and the Textile Fiber Products Identification Act[96] both of which require wearing apparel and home furnishings such as blankets to carry labels specifying their composition; the Hobby Protection Act,[97] requiring sellers of imitation coins to make appropriate disclosures; and the Energy Policy and Conservation Act,[98] which authorizes the FTC to impose energy information disclosure requirements on sellers of household appliances.

Jurisdiction of Consumer Product Safety Commission

1. Consumer Product Safety Act

The federal government enforces at least ten laws which govern the safety of products sold to customers. Because it applies to more different products than any of the other statutes, and because its provisions are so comprehensive, the Consumer Product Safety Act ("CPSA") is by far the most important.

Since its passage in 1972, the CPSA has established a regulatory scheme of significant reach and impact on corporate decision making. A recent study by The Conference Board found that the CPSA ranks third in corporate impact, behind only the Occupational Safety and Health Act and the Environmental Protection Act. The Federal Hazardous Substances Act, the Flammable Fabrics Act, the Poison Prevention Packaging Act, and the Refrigerator Safety Act, each of which is also administered by the CPSC, were ranked 5th, 8th, 10th, and 14th, respectively.[99]

The Consumer Product Safety Commission ("CPSC") is invested with a wide variety of powers, ranging from research through standards making, seizures, and consumer education. The Commission's use of the available regulatory options varies according to the degree of risk which a consumer product is believed to present. Commission action will also often depend upon a manufacturer's, distributor's, or retailer's willingness to undertake voluntary remedial action either to render harmless an allegedly unsafe product or to remove the product from the marketplace.

Standards, Regulations, and Bans. The Commission's basic regulatory tool is the power to issue standards and regulations which are "reasonably necessary to prevent or reduce an unreasonable risk of injury"[100] associated with a consumer product. A standard issued under the Consumer Product Safety Act is in many ways 'similar to standards issued by private standards making bodies such as the Underwriters' Laboratory, the American Society for Testing and Materials, or the American National Standards Institute. There is one important difference, however: standards issued by the CPSC are legally binding, and importing or selling a product which fails to conform with a CPSC standard can subject the importer or seller to heavy civil fines and, in some cases, criminal penalties. To date, the CPSC has promulgated standards applicable to matchbooks, swimming pool slides, architectural glass and glazing materials, walk-behind power lawnmowers, small parts in children's toys, and cellulose insulation,[101] and it is now considering standards for upholstered furniture and other products.[102]

When the CPSC finds that standards and regulations are inadequate to protect the public from an unreasonable risk of injury, it may seek to ban the offending product entirely from the marketplace. The CPSC has taken this action against unstable refuse bins, certain flammable contact adhesives, paints containing lead, patching compounds containing asbestos and "emberizing materials."[103] Moreover, although bans are generally prospective in effect, the Commission may in certain circumstances require that products already distributed in commerce be refitted or otherwise repaired to avoid inclusion in the banned category. For example, when the Commission announced its ban of unstable refuse bins, it stated that the ban would take effect in twelve months, reasoning that this lead time would induce businesses to modify existing bins.[104] This situation represents a clearcut example of government reallocating resources to overcome factors external to the market.

Substantial Product Hazards. In addition to its authority to establish standards, regulations, and bans, the CPSC may, under Section 15 of the CPSA, order a recall of products already distributed when it finds they constitute a "substantial product hazard."[105] Among the products the CPSC has dealt with in this manner are arc welders, architectural glass and glazing materials, aluminized kites, certain smoke detectors, hot pots, and cross-bows.

Generally speaking, Section 15 has two parts. First, it imposes a disclosure requirement—that manufacturers, importers, distributors, and retailers report to the Commission the fact that their products may be dangerous. Second, it allows the Commission to order public notification that a product is hazardous, and a recall program involving repair, replacement, or refund.[106] Under certain circumstances, the Commission can also ask a court to enjoin the further sale of products which constitute a substantial product hazard.

Imminent Hazards. When a product is believed to be so dangerous that it constitutes an "imminent hazard," which means that the risk of injury is both immediate and severe,[107] the CPSC is authorized to proceed directly for a court order to protect the public. In essence, the imminent hazard procedure is a speeded-up version of the substantial product hazard procedure. The court may order notification of the risk to purchasers of the product, including advertisements and press releases. The court may also require a recall involving the repair or replacement of the product or order a refund. The court may also require a general public notification program to inform potential consumers of the danger, and may also order a *total* recall program to get the dangerous product entirely out of the channels of commerce. While no court has yet ordered such far-reaching action, the Commission has sought it against certain amusement rides, aluminum wiring systems, trouble lights, and baseball-pitching machines.

2. Other Laws Administered by CPSC

The CPSC, like the FTC, has been empowered to administer and enforce a number of other statutes related to its primary area of jurisdiction. Thus, the CPSC has been authorized to enforce the Flammable Fabrics Act, which covers wearing apparel and interior furnishings and the fabrics used therein. Under it, the Commission may promulgate binding safety standards to prevent the unreasonable risk of fire leading to death, injury, or significant property damage. Existing standards under this statute cover all wearing apparel, children's sleepwear, carpets and rugs, and mattresses. The Commission also administers the Federal Hazardous Substances Act, dealing with household substances and toys;[108] the Poison Prevention Packaging Act, authorizing the Commission to require special packaging for substances which would be harmful to children;[109] and the Lead-Based Paint Poisoning Prevention Act, authorizing the Commission to determine safe levels of lead in paint used in residential construction or on toys or furniture.[110]

Consumer Credit

The regulation of the terms and conditions in the granting of credit to consumers reflects primarily social considerations, but uses a variety of regulatory strategies: disclosure requirements; directives requiring credit grantors to consider or not to consider certain factors; and a type of economic regulation which imposes ceilings on credit charges.

Federal regulation of consumer credit governs many areas, including discrimination in granting credit,[111] the collection, maintenance and use of consumer financial information,[112] the disclosure of credit terms,[113] debt collection practices,[114] the correction of billing errors,[115] and the chartering, rates, and practices of certain financial institutions.[116] Moreover, Congress has not preempted state laws except to the extent they are inconsistent with federal statutes or provide less protection to the consumer.[117] Thus, in addition to the federal system of regulation, there is pervasive state regulation as well. The duties imposed on credit-extending corporations by local law vary from state to state, both in terms of substance and in terms of the issues addressed. As a result of this lack of uniformity, a company that does business in several states—which of course would include all national companies—must comply with a welter of varying credit requirements.

The following overview of federal and state law in this area will highlight the nature and scope of government regulation of credit practices.

1. Antidiscrimination Statutes

Three federal statutes prohibit discrimination against certain specified protected classes of applicants: First, the Equal Credit Opportunity Act[118] prohibits discrimination by creditors on the basis of sex, marital status, race, color, religion, national origin, age, income derived from public assistance programs, or the exercise of any right under the Consumer Credit Protection Act. Creditors must also, upon request, provide the applicant the reason for terminating or denying credit. Second, the Federal Home Loan Mortgage Disclosure Act[119] seeks to discourage the practice of "redlining" by requiring institutions which lend home mortgage funds to disclose the details of their loan practices. They are required to make available mortgage loan data itemizing the terms, number, geographical location, and total dollar amounts of all mortgage loans. Third, the Fair Housing Act[120] prohibits, subject to minor exemptions, discrimination on grounds of race, color, religion, sex, and national origin in the terms and conditions of sale, rental, advertising, or financing of housing.

A corporation is therefore not free to use any of the

191

factors prohibited by these laws in determining whether to grant credit, even if these factors would predict or have, in the past, reliably predicted credit-worthiness. Regulation has supplanted corporate discretion in this regard.

2. Consumer Reporting Laws

The Federal Fair Credit Reporting Act[121] regulates the use, content, and disclosure of credit bureau and investigatory reports which may be used in the consideration of credit, insurance, or employment applications. When an application is rejected, the law gives the consumer a number of rights, such as the right to obtain the nature and substance as well as the sources of information in his credit file and the right to have disputed entries reinvestigated. Thus, among other restrictions, a company is precluded from obtaining information from obsolete or irrelevant sources in making credit decisions.

3. Disclosure Requirements

Subject to narrow exceptions, the Truth in Lending Act[122] applies to all consumer credit transactions irrespective of the type of creditor involved. It requires the uniform disclosure of credit terms in connection with consumer credit sales and consumer loans. The Act also regulates consumer leases, provides a three-day cooling-off period for certain transactions secured by real property and regulates the advertising of credit so as to insure that all terms are fairly and uniformly disclosed. The Act also prohibits creditors from sending unsolicited credit cards to consumers.

With regard to revolving charge accounts, the Act requires that, before the first transaction takes place, the corporation give the customer notice of all essential terms of the account, including the method of computation of finance charges. The customer also must periodically receive a billing statement which sets forth a number of items such as the balance in the account, any payments and credits made, the finance charges and their annual percentage rate. When the terms of the account are subsequently changed, both federal and many state laws mandate the timing and type of notice which must be given to customers.

Corporations are thus obligated by regulations to provide information beyond that which would be made available solely through the operation of free market forces. Indeed, unlike most disclosure requirements where the consumer is provided information only *before* undertaking the transaction, here the corporation is required to send out information periodically to make sure the consumer is continually informed of his rights and duties.

The Federal Fair Credit Billing Act[123] amendments to the Truth in Lending Act establish a procedure for resolving billing disputes in revolving charge accounts and other credit card accounts. With regard to disputed charges, creditors must respond to consumer inquiries within a given time and may not impose finance charges on that portion of the balance until the dispute is resolved. Creditors must also provide summaries of the dispute settlement procedure to the customer at the time the account is opened and, in most cases, again every six months.

4. The Cost of Credit

State usury statutes typically place low limits on interest rates which may be charged on a debt (averaging in

1980, between 10–12 percent). Since many modern, large scale consumer credit transactions would not be feasible with the low ceilings set by these statutes, exceptions to the low rates set by general usury statutes have been carved out for such transactions as small loans, revolving credit sales, vehicle sales, and industrial loans. This *ad hoc* process has resulted in a confusing range of rate ceilings which vary from state to state and which apply to different lenders and different transactions in each state.

Almost all states and some federal agencies regulate the delinquency and collection charges which may be imposed after the borrower has defaulted on one or more installments. The charges may include reasonable attorney's fees incurred in collection, the expenses of repossession, and court costs.[124]

Various state laws permit the imposition of additional charges on installment loan contracts. The most common charges, especially with regard to installment sales of motor vehicles, are fees which must be paid to public agencies for registering or releasing the lender's security interest, referred to as "filing fees" or "official fees." Additional costs such as maintaining escrow funds for taxes, assessments, and insurance, or other "closing costs" are authorized in a few states.

5. Creditor Remedies

Recent federal and state enactments have sought to afford greater protection to consumers by restricting, and in many cases eliminating, creditor corporations' remedies for nonpayment of debts and by increasing the rights of consumers to avoid undesired transactions or contractual provisions. On the federal level, the agency most active in the area has been the Federal Trade Commission, using its powers to prohibit "unfair or deceptive acts and practices."

A detailed FTC Trade Regulation Rule permits buyers to cancel a door-to-door contract within three days of signing and to receive full refund from the seller.[125] Additional state laws also govern the format and content of door-to-door sales contracts, including the disclosure of the buyer's rights under the law.[126]

In 1976, in a landmark step, the FTC effectively abolished the holder-in-due-course doctrine with regard to consumer transactions, by subjecting any subsequent holder of a consumer obligation to any claim or defense which the buyer would have had against the seller.[127] The FTC Rule requires consumer contracts to provide notice of the customer's rights, and it permits the consumer to recover any amounts paid under the contract.[128]

Most states also regulate the methods a creditor can use to secure payment for a debt. Contracts which waive a right to defend a law suit are prohibited, and a creditor may not seize certain forms of property to satisfy the debt. Further, the ability of a creditor to go after a debtor's wages is also strictly limited.

Repossession of collateral is extensively regulated by state law.[129] Generally, a creditor may repossess goods without resort to judicial proceedings, if it can be done without breach of the peace. After the goods have been repossessed, the creditor must comply with procedures for the time, place, and manner of sale of the items seized. The proceeds of any sale of the goods by the creditor must be applied to the amount owed by the debtor, although the creditor may deduct the costs of retaking, storing, and selling the goods.

Moreover, most states regulate the means used in debt collection. Some states specifically regulate collection agencies and have licensing requirements aimed at excluding those who may engage in illegal or unconscionable business practices.[130] The Federal Fair Debt Collection Practices Act regulates the collection of debts by third parties.[131] Many state statutes proscribe the use of deceptive or unfair debt collection practices.[132]

In sum, it can be seen that pervasive federal and state regulations have substantially bolstered the rights and interests of consumers while at the same time curtailing the rights and remedies of corporations which offer goods and services for general consumption and use.

4. Regulation of Political Activities

The Supreme Court has recognized the First Amendment right of corporations to participate in political debate regarding public issues.[133] Nonetheless, the manner in which corporations may engage in political activities remains subject to extensive regulation on both the state and federal level. Corporate political contributions are prohibited by federal law and by the majority of states, and corporate lobbying efforts are subject to comprehensive federal and state disclosure requirements. The right of corporations to enter the political arena has been recognized, but the means of access are strewn with regulatory constraints.

The government also restricts corporate activities that may affect the political process less directly. The federal government may prohibit companies from trading with countries with which the United States has political differences, and it likewise may restrict them from complying with the demands of other countries not to trade with nations which the United States does wish to support. The federal government also has prohibited payments by domestic corporations to officials of a foreign country as a means of obtaining business even if such payments are routine and customary in that country. Absent these regulatory restrictions, a firm would be free to respond to the market by making judgments for itself as to where *its* best interests lie. Instead, those interests are subordinated to the political goals of the United States and the discretion of the corporation is thereby diminished.

Corporate Political Contributions

1. The Federal Election Campaign Act

As described below, the federal election laws which regulate campaigns for federal elective offices impose substantial restrictions on corporate participation in the political process.

Political Action Committees. As amended in 1976, the Federal Election Campaign Act (FECA)[134] prohibits corporations and labor organizations from contributing money directly to candidates for federal office. The Act does, however, permit corporations to establish political action committees (PACs) to: solicit, administer, and allocate voluntary political contributions made by employees and stockholders; communicate with stockholders, executives, and administrative personnel on any subject, including partisan politics; and conduct nonpartisan "get-out-the-vote" drives.

Because corporations are not permitted to make contributions or expenditures in connection with a federal election, a corporation must form a political action committee if it is to participate in the federal political process. PACs are extensively regulated under the Act, and they must comply with detailed record keeping and filing requirements. While a corporation may exercise

197

control over the daily operations of its PAC, funds must be segregated from corporate assets. PACs must file a statement of organization with the Federal Election Commission setting forth the identity of affiliated organizations, the custodian of books and accounts, all bank accounts, the principal officers, and, if known at the time, the candidates it will support. Detailed records of all contributions must be maintained and reports must be filed for public inspection which identify all assets, each contributor of more than $100, and each recipient of a contribution from the fund. Although a corporation need not routinely disclose costs of administering the PAC, nor the PACs correspondence, it may be required to submit "such other information as shall be required by the Commission."

It is unlawful for a PAC to solicit or receive a prohibited contribution, such as from any corporation or foreign national, a cash donation in excess of $100, or donations from an individual which total more than $5,000 in any calendar year. All fund-raising materials must include a prescribed notice informing recipients that contributions are strictly voluntary and will be used for a political purpose, and that a refusal to contribute will not be met with reprisals of any kind. While contribution guidelines may be suggested, solicitations must make it clear that no person will be disadvantaged because of the amount of his or her contribution or a decision not to contribute at all.

The corporation is also restricted in soliciting contributions. The company or its PAC may solicit only from its stockholders and their families and the corporation's "executive or administrative personnel" and their families. The term "executive or administrative personnel" includes "individuals employed by a corporation who are paid on a salary rather than hourly basis and who have policy-making, managerial, professional, or supervisory responsibilities."[135] Similarly, while a corporation may also direct partisan political communications to its stockholders and executive or administrative personnel and their families, it may not do so to other employees.

FECA also restricts solicitations by the political action committees of trade associations to the stockholders and executive or administrative personnel of member corporations. While there is no limit on the number of solicitations which a trade association PAC may make, a member corporation must first authorize in writing the solicitation of its stockholders or personnel, the authorization is valid for only one calendar year, and only one trade association may be authorized to solicit a corporation's stockholders or personnel during a calendar year.

The 1976 amendments to the Act placed a $5,000 ceiling on the total contributions which a PAC may make to a single candidate in any election. For the purposes of the maximum contribution restriction, all committees established by a corporation and its subsidiaries are regarded as a single PAC.

Other Permissible Corporation Activity. Under FECA and the implementing regulations issued by the Federal Election Commission, the direct expenses a corporation may incur related to the election process which are not prohibited "contributions" or "expenditures" are extremely limited. For example, the regulations limit corporate participation in nonpartisan activities to those which urge employees to register and vote. And while corporations are permitted to administer "employee participation plans" under which a bank account may be established for employee contributions through payroll deduction plans, employees must exercise complete control over the disbursements of funds contributed through such plans. Moreover, employee participation must be wholly voluntary, and contributions forwarded to candidates may not reveal the name of the corporation which established the plan.

Further, while the Act provides that honorariums are not considered "contributions," no single honorarium to a federal officeholder may exceed $2,000 and such persons may not collect more than $25,000 for honorariums per year. Similarly, although legal or accounting services rendered "solely for the purpose of insuring compliance with [the Act]" are not deemed to be expenditures or contributions, such services must be reported by the candidate or the political committee.

Finally, Commission regulations severely limit the use of corporate facilities for political purposes to the "incidental" volunteer work of individual stockholders, executives, or administrative personnel, and only to the extent such use does not increase the corporation's operating costs. Corporate facilities normally available to community groups may also be made available to candidates on a nonpartisan basis; however, while candidates may be allowed, on an equal basis, to address employees on corporate premises, contributions may not be solicited during such appearances, nor may the corporation endorse a candidate during such an appearance.

Enforcement. The Federal Election Commission may conduct investigations of alleged violations of the Act, and it is empowered to correct violations by a conciliation process. Where such efforts fail, the Commission may initiate civil enforcement proceedings or refer criminal violations to the Justice Department. Civil penalties include fines up to the greater of $5,000 or the amount of the illegal contribution or, in the case of knowing and willful violations, fines of $10,000 or 200 times the amount of the contribution. Criminal penalties may be imposed for "knowing and willful" violations involving amounts in excess of $1,000.[136]

2. State Regulation

In addition to federal regulation, approximately one-half of the states and Puerto Rico prohibit campaign contributions by corporations or specified types of corporations (such as public utilities) to candidates for state elective office.[137] Several of these states, however, permit the establishment of political action committees similar to those envisioned by the federal election law.[138] Ten other states place a ceiling on the aggregate contributions which a corporation may make per year.[139]

Corporate Lobbying Activities

1. The Federal Lobby Act

The Federal Regulation of Lobbying Act[140] is essentially a disclosure statute. It requires that corporate activities designed to influence the passage of legislation must be disclosed. This alone can serve to diminish the flexibility available to the corporation since it may decide it would prefer not going on record with respect to a particular issue.

The Act applies to all "persons," including associations, partnerships, and corporations, which have solicited, collected, or received contributions for the "principal purpose" of influencing legislation through direct communication with members of Congress.[141] The "principal purpose" requirement is intended to exclude those persons and contributions who have only an incidental involvement with legislative activities. The Act specifically exempts persons who merely appear before Congress in support of or in opposition to legislation, public officials acting in their official capacity, and newspapers or periodicals which merely publish editorials or advertisements with respect to legislation, but do not pursue the passage or defeat of legislation.[142]

All persons to whom the Act applies must register with the Clerk of the House of Representatives and the Secretary of the Senate by filing reports setting forth personal information, the identity of the interests represented, the amount of their compensation and by whom paid, and the length of their employment.[143] Persons covered by the Act are also required to report on a quarterly basis—among other items—the amounts received or expended in lobbying efforts, to whom paid, the purpose of such payments, and the proposed legislation the person has been employed to support or oppose.[144] The reports must also list each person who has made a contribution of $500 or more, the total contributions of such persons, and the name and address of recipients of contributions of $10 or more.[145]

2. State Regulation of Lobbying

Lobbying activities at the state level are also subject to extensive regulation. For example, the New York Regulation of Lobbying Act[146] applies not only to attempts to influence legislation but to activities before the governor and ratemaking and rulemaking matters before state agencies. The New York law has been construed very strictly and includes both formal and informal (but not social) contacts between corporate personnel and government decision makers.

Under the New York law, a "lobbyist" must register

even if he does not receive compensation for his lobbying activities. He is covered by the Act if his expenditures or fees related to lobbying activities exceed $1,000 per year. The statement of registration, which must be filed with The New York Lobbying Commission, requires disclosure of information regarding the lobbyist, the interest represented, the governmental matters concerned, and the entities to be lobbied. Lobbyists must also file quarterly reports disclosing committees and agencies lobbied, expenses, reimbursements, and fees.

Most states regulate lobbying activities and impose registration and disclosure requirements similar to those of New York and the Federal Act. The statutes of a number of states define lobbying as broadly as does the New York Act, and several expand their coverage to include activities before municipal officials.

Foreign Boycotts

The President is authorized by the Export Administration Amendments of 1979,[147] to issue rules and regulations prohibiting any United States person or corporation from participating in any boycott by a foreign country against a country which is friendly to the United States and which is not itself subject to any form of boycott by the United States.[148] The antiboycott legislation occurred primarily in response to the Arab countries' boycott of Israel, with its concomitant impact on domestic business relations with both Israel and the Arab nations.[149]

The antiboycott law specifically directs that the President's regulations prohibit American corporations—including exporters, manufacturers, banks, insurers, shipping companies or freight forwarders and their foreign subsidiaries and affiliates—from participating in boycotts against friendly countries pursuant to an agreement with a foreign country.[150] These regulations must also prohibit American businesses from aiding a foreign boycott through discrimination or by providing information which would encourage discrimination.[151] The statute requires any domestic business which receives a request for information or a request to enter into an agreement which would further or support a foreign boycott to report such facts to the Secretary of Commerce.[152] These reporting requirements have a number of functions. First, because information reported to the Commerce Department, including the corporation's compliance 'intentions, must be made available for public inspection, they are relied upon to deter corporate compliance with boycott requests. Moreover, they are designed to permit close monitoring by Congress of boycott requests and to provide the Commerce Department with the information necessary to enforce the statute. Penalties for violation of the Act include fines up to $50,000 and imprisonment up to five years.[153]

Trading with the Enemy Act and Related Controls

Anyone who has missed Havana cigars has felt the impact of the Trading with the Enemy Act of 1917,[154] which prohibits or restricts imports from, exports to, and financial transactions with, countries whose interest are considered inimical to those of the United States. These controls are administered primarily by the Office of Foreign Assets Control (FAC) of the United States Treasury Department.

In recent years, the FAC has imposed almost total trade embargoes on Cuba, North and South Vietnam, North Korea, Cambodia, Rhodesia, and Uganda. Before the improvement in relations with the People's Republic of China, similar controls were exercised with regard to that country, but have been substantially relaxed since 1972.

Basically, FAC's regulations prohibit, except as specifically authorized by the Secretary of the Treasury or his designee, all payments, transactions in foreign exchange, and transfers of credit with respect to any property subject to the jurisdiction of the United States or any person subject to its jurisdiction, if the transaction is by, or on behalf of, one of the banned foreign countries or a national thereof, or involves property in which a banned country or one of its nationals has an interest.

Related regulations administered by FAC prohibit corporations within the United States from buying certain commodities abroad or facilitating the purchase of these commodities for the purpose of shipment to certain designated Communist countries. In addition, the export of the following items is prohibited: certain merchandise included in the Commodity Control List of the Department of Commerce;[155] and merchandise whose unauthorized exportation is prohibited by regulations relating to arms, ammunition, and implements of war, or relating to atomic energy facilities or to materials for use for non-military purposes.

Foreign Payments

The Foreign Corrupt Practices Act became law on December 19, 1977. It establishes requirements concerning recordkeeping and accounting controls for certain corporations. It makes it a crime for any person to authorize or promise payment of anything of value to any foreign government, agency or official or to any foreign political party, party official or candidate in order to obtain or retain business. Any transfer of value to any person where the transferor knows or should know that the transfer will be passed on to any of the foregoing persons is similarly made a crime.

Each violation of the FCPA by a business subjects it to a criminal fine of up to $1 million. Each violation of the act by an individual subjects him to a fine of up to $10,000 and/or imprisonment for up to five years. The FCPA is administered by the Justice Department and, with respect to reporting companies, by the Securities and Exchange Commission. Pursuant to FCPA, the SEC has proposed extensive rules that directly constrain companies to develop internal systems to ensure that "foreign payments" are not made and that specific reports to that effect are made directly to the board of directors.

5. Energy Regulation

Since the oil embargo of 1973, four Congresses and three Administrations have generated a monumental amount of legislative and regulatory activity in the area generally referred to as "energy." Between 1973 and October, 1978, when the six statutes comprising the National Energy Act[156] were enacted, Congress passed at least fifteen different laws[157] relating to energy. The most visible result is a huge new bureaucracy to regulate energy production and consumption. In theory, this effort seeks to implement a two-pronged policy: to ensure that the country can withstand another oil embargo and to ensure the long-term viability of the American economy by lowering the consumption of energy, especially oil, and by increasing all forms of domestic energy resources.

To be sure, not all companies are directly engaged in

the energy business. Nevertheless, a discussion of energy regulation seems useful here for two reasons: First, energy is a fundamental resource for most all economic pursuits. Consequently, as our discussion below will demonstrate, the regulation of energy substantially affects all types of corporate activities. Second, energy regulation does not consist of a single regulatory response to a particular form of market shortcoming—such as imposing standards to cure an externality. Instead it encompasses a series of different types of regulation each addressing a separate aspect of the energy field. In itself, then, a description of energy regulation demonstrates how several regulatory tools and theories can be used simultaneously to deal with different parts of a politically perceived problem. The tools and theories in this case include economic regulation, allocations, licenses, standards, disclosures, and financial incentives.

Pre-1973 Regulation

To put the current regulatory system relating to energy in a proper perspective, brief mention should be made of the regulatory system which was in place prior to the 1973 embargo.

The first major legislation to address energy issues specifically was the Hepburn Act of 1906,[158] which subjected oil, but not natural gas, pipelines to regulation as "common carriers" under the Interstate Commerce Act. The "transmission sector" of the oil industry business was thus (and still is) subject to "economic regulation" as a "public utility," in recognition of its "natural monopoly" attributes.

The next regulatory step was attendant upon the huge oil discoveries in the eastern Texas oil fields in the early

1930's, which resulted in allegedly ruinous price competition. Congress reacted with economic regulation—the Connally "Hot Oil" Act[159]—which banned the interstate shipment of oil produced in excess of the amounts permitted under state laws or regulations. In 1938 Congress enacted a comprehensive scheme of economic regulation for interstate natural gas pipelines, subjecting them to the jurisdiction of the Federal Power Commission.

The Reciprocal Trade Agreements Act of 1955[160] and its successor, the Trade Expansion Act of 1962,[161] provided statutory authority for the President to limit imports of oil by imposing fees on them. The 1962 Act was used after the 1973 embargo to limit imports,[162] but the entire import fee system was suspended because of serious questions about its efficacy as a method of restraining imports.

Natural gas prices have been regulated for a number of years both at the wellhead and at the end user level. Prices at the wellhead have been controlled under the Natural Gas Act[163] since 1954, when the Supreme Court determined that the Federal Power Commission had jurisdiction over the wellhead price of gas produced for shipment in interstate commerce. The decision was limited, however, to gas produced for interstate commerce, and a separate, generally unregulated, market was thereby created for intrastate natural gas. (The Natural Gas Policy Act of 1978[164] has completely, and with much complexity, rewritten the way in which natural gas is priced at the wellhead.)

With respect to retail natural gas prices—those paid by the ultimate user of the natural gas—they have historically been regulated by state public service and public utility commissions. Typically, those commissions have granted a particular company a market area monopoly, and then have set the prices based on a cost plus percentage profit system. That same system of economic regulation has been used in the area of electricity regulation at the retail level.

Post-1973 Regulation

The story of post-1973 energy regulation is best told by discussing the various functions now performed by the Department of Energy ("DOE"): information gathering; price regulation; conservation; and technology advancement.

1. Information Gathering

It has been asserted that a major reason for the lack of consensus on policy in the energy area has been the absence of solid information upon which to base policy decisions. The case of the dwindling and then expanding supply of natural gas is illustrative. In the winter of 1977, much of the Midwest suffered severe shortages of natural gas. As a result, the elimination of virtually all commercial use of natural gas became a major objective of the National Energy Plan announced on April 20, 1977. Even in mid-1978, when Congress passed the Powerplant and Industrial Fuel Use Act,[165] natural gas was viewed by the Administration as a rapidly dwindling fuel. Yet, in the fall and winter of 1978–79, the Administration shifted its view of how much natural gas was available, and industry was encouraged to switch from oil to natural gas.

As a result of such flip-flops in energy policy making, the problem of information gathering has been given considerable attention and has been addressed in a series of statutes, culminating in the establishment of a comprehensive system of federal energy information gathering and reporting. In particular, the Administrator of the Energy Information Administration of DOE is required to identify and designate "major energy producing companies" and to develop an annual energy-producer financial report which must yield data permitting comparison, evaluation, segregation, and determination of, among other matters, company revenues, profits, cash flow, and investments in total energy-related lines of commerce. The Department is further directed to develop a reliable data base concerning the competitive structure of sectors and functional groupings within the energy industry.

The DOE's information collection and reporting powers also have a policing function, in that many of the corporate filings may be disclosed publicly or to Congressional committees, and may be employed for law enforcement purposes.

2. Price Regulation

The price regulation system for energy and energy products has varied depending on the type of energy source involved, the nature of the sale, and the historical context when the regulation was initiated. As noted above, the federal government has regulated the interstate sale of natural gas since 1938; and regulation in that area was recently—albeit temporarily—extended to intrastate sales of natural gas as well. Oil price regulation, on the other hand, is quite recent and has largely been related to the problems of OPEC rather than domestic producers.

Oil. General oil price regulation was initiated as part of the overall wage and price freeze imposed in August, 1971, by President Nixon. This freeze, and the subsequent phased changes in the policy, applied to wellhead prices and to prices of products at the different levels of production. Before this program was phased out for the remainder of the economy, the oil embargo and subsequent OPEC quadrupling of the world price of oil caused Congress to impose specific controls on oil and oil products in the Emergency Petroleum Allocation Act of 1973 ("EPAA").[166]

The structure of the price regulations established either in the EPAA itself or by regulations promulgated pursuant to it set prices in tiers, with "old oil"—defined as oil produced from wells which were in commercial production on or before November 1, 1975—receiving a lower price than new oil. The theory was that this provided an incentive for new exploration and production, while preventing windfalls to oil companies merely because of the action of a foreign cartel. This structure was preserved in the Energy Policy and Conservation Act of 1975 ("EPCA"),[167] which extended the price regulations through May 31, 1979, with the President given the authority to extend controls through September 30, 1981. President Carter exercised his discretion in this regard by ordering the phase-out of these price controls; but he called at the same time for passage of a windfall profits tax.

The EPAA also established, and EPCA extended, the authority for price regulation of specific oil products, including gasoline, heating oil, and other specific refined products. Controls on gasoline have remained in effect. Price controls on other oil products have been converted to standby status, subject to reinvocation by the President.

The EPAA also established a complex system of allocation priorities and quotas, which has had a significant effect on the price to the user of the product. The regulations for this program have become among the most complex of any regulatory programs anywhere, with the resultant side effects of increased costs of compliance, confusion as to what constitutes compliance, and distortions in the marketplace. For example, during the gasoline shortages in the summer of 1979, reports were common of surpluses of gasoline in some areas when in other localities long gas lines prevailed. This allocation system is also being phased out for most oil and oil products.

Coal. Coal prices are not regulated at either the state or federal level. As a result, coal is the only major fuel whose price can vary with demand. Hence, customers are free to negotiate the best deal they can for a supply of coal. For all other major fuels, the price is established by regulation or by a foreign cartel.

Electricity. Electricity prices are regulated on both the state and federal levels. The distinction between the two regulatory systems lies in whether the transactions are wholesale or retail. The federal government, now through the Federal Energy Regulatory Commission ("FERC"), regulates wholesale transactions, primarily between electric utilities. The extent to which this authority extends beyond simple price setting for voluntary sales between two companies with government created monopolies in their own service areas has been a matter of some controversy. The major issue has been whether the federal government may order sales between utilities where at least one is an unwilling partner to the transaction. This has arisen during shortage situations when one utility is serving as a common carrier for a sale between utilities on either side of its service area. As the on-site generation of power through units powered by coal and oil as well as from solar and other exotic sources has become more popular, the federal government has been asked to set rates for the sale of electricity from utilities to these nonutility power producers and *vice versa*—primarily to avoid utility rates which would discourage this "competition."

States regulate the sale of electricity to end users, the "retail" sale of electricity. Traditionally, the structure of these rates has been the sole prerogative of the state commissions, which have generally based prices on a combination of factors, but principally the cost of serving those to whom power is provided. As long as the marginal cost of increased production was lower than the average cost of production, this was a popular approach—those who consumed higher amounts paid less per unit of energy but everyone received decreases in their rates on a fairly regular basis. However, a turnaround in construction costs, which occurred in the late 1960's and early 1970's, combined with the huge increase in fuel costs associated with the oil embargo, have essentially rendered this system of ratemaking obsolete. The Public Utility Regulatory Policies Act of 1978,[168] a federal law which is part of the National Energy Act, established guidelines for states to follow in responding to this problem. In general, states are directed to re-examine the relationship between their existing rate structures and the costs to the utilities of providing service to their customers. Special encouragement is given to adopting time-of-day, seasonal, interruptible and other rates which are not now part of most utilities' rate structures. State commissions must consider these guidelines within the next two to three years.

3. Conservation

Planning a More Energy-Efficient, Less Oil-Dependent Economy: Mandated Programs in Lieu of Markets. Three major statutes mandate programs or actions to achieve a more efficient use of energy in the economy. As the outline below indicates, these regulatory systems have had a basic impact on major sections of the economy.

1. ENERGY EFFICIENCY STANDARDS FOR CONSUMER PRODUCTS. DOE has, pursuant to provisions of EPCA, prescribed minimum energy efficiency standards for a long list of consumer appliances in order to improve their energy efficiency by at least 20 percent over the performance of 1972 models.

These programs obviously force companies and consumers to take actions they would not otherwise take. For example, consumers would normally select "energy-efficient" appliances only if the value of the fuel savings exceeded the increase in the price of the product. DOE's regulations, however, reflect an overriding policy objective. They force corporations to achieve specified energy efficiency levels in connection with consumer appliances even if it means a higher life-cycle cost to the consumer.

2. ENERGY EFFICIENCY STANDARDS FOR AUTOMOBILES. The automobile industry provides the most striking example of the impact of this type of regulation. The EPCA established mandatory corporate average fuel economy ("CAFE") standards for passenger cars of at least 27.5 miles per gallon by the year 1985, with the interim standards for the years 1981 through 1984 to be established by the National Highway Traffic Safety Administration ("NHTSA").[169] The ambitious targets for fuel economy set by CAFE will require General Motors, for example, to effectuate a 129 percent improvement in its EPA mileage ratings between 1974 and 1985, and the industry as a whole to improve its efficiency by 113.2 percent during the 1973–1985 period. Ironically, this task will be encumbered at each step by the regulatory requirements in the pollution control area, which are frequently inconsistent and conflicting with those in the energy area,[170] and by

the inability of the domestic manufacturers, after 1979, to include the domestic sale of cars that are manufactured by their foreign affiliates in calculating their compliance with CAFE standards.[171]

These regulatory constraints have also had the effect of assisting foreign automobile competitors. While the domestic companies must devote a substantial portion of their resources to improving their fuel efficiency by 63.4 percent during the period 1980–1985 (in accordance with CAFE standards), major importers will, on average, only have to improve their efficiency rating by 5.7 percent during this period.

3. ENERGY-EFFICIENT PERFORMANCE STANDARDS FOR NEW BUILDINGS. This program requires the development of "energy budget" standards for new buildings. They were to be in effect in all states by 1981, but have been delayed for at least one year. They aim to reduce average energy consumption substantially below the levels of pre-1973 buildings.

4. COAL CONVERSION: PROHIBITIONS ON POWER PLANT USE OF NATURAL GAS AND OIL. Since 1974, public utilities have been subjected to a coal conversion program designed to switch them from natural gas and oil to coal. The Power Plant and Industrial Fuel Use Act of 1978 expands this program by directly prohibiting the burning of oil and gas, unless an exemption is authorized. In existing plants, natural gas is limited to 1974–76 proportions and all natural gas use must end by 1990. Currently, however, DOE is allowing switches from oil to natural gas because of plentiful gas supplies and the need to reduce oil imports. Here again, this regulation directly substitutes government policy criteria for market criteria. It also brings the national energy policy and national environmental protection policies into their sharpest point of conflict. The requirement that utilities switch to burning

coal raises severe impediments to meeting national air quality standards or very substantially increases the cost of achieving those standards.

Using Disclosures and Economic Incentives to Improve Energy Efficiency and Lower Oil Use. The EPCA requires that basic consumer appliances, including central heating and cooling systems, be labeled with operating energy cost information. It also requires DOE to conduct consumer energy education programs with respect to the significance of estimated annual operating costs and the way comparative shopping can save energy and hence money. DOE has further to identify the ten most energy-consuming industries in the economy, establish an energy-use reporting system for them, and coordinate policies on ways to reduce their energy use.

The National Energy Tax Act of 1978 has substantially increased tax incentives for corporations to develop energy conservation products. In particular, an additional 10 percent investment tax credit is provided to businesses for investment in:

(i) alternative energy property (boilers which use coal or alternative fuels—not gas or oil; equipment to produce alternate fuels; pollution control devices);
(ii) renewable energy to heat, cool or provide hot water or generate electricity;
(iii) equipment to improve heat efficiency of existing industrial processes (heat exchangers).

The National Energy Tax Act also imposes penalties—termed the "Gas Guzzler" tax—to induce purchases of more fuel efficient motor vehicles.

Emergency Contingency Planning and Other Measures to Manage "Severe Energy Supply Interruption": The Energy Policy and Conservation Act of 1975. Congress has moved on three fronts to attempt to meet the danger of another oil boycott or sudden energy disruption by providing options to: increase domestic oil supplies or use alternative energy resources; reduce public and private demand for energy; and distribute the available supplies equitably.

1. EMERGENCY OPTION TO INCREASE OIL SUPPLIES OR SWITCH TO ALTERNATE FUELS. The EPCA authorizes two important measures to increase immediately supplies or oil for consumption. The first permits the President to order maximum efficient rates of production from existing domestic oil and gas wells.[172] The second empowers him to tap the Strategic Petroleum Reserve established by EPCA in 1975. An EPCA amendment to the War Production Act of 1950[173] also gives the President authority to allocate, upon emergency findings, any materials under contract to maximize domestic energy supplies. Supplies of alternate fuels can also be increased under other new statutory authorities. For example, the Power Plant and Fuel Use Act of 1978 empowers the President in an emergency to prohibit the burning of either oil or natural gas in utility boilers or major fuel burning installations[174] to free up such fuel for other uses. This same Act gives the President authority to allocate coal[175] and waive air quality standards, actions which would permit increased use of that fuel in place of oil.

2. EMERGENCY OPTION TO REDUCE PUBLIC AND PRIVATE DEMAND FOR ENERGY. Title II of EPCA established a mechanism for attempting to reduce demand for energy in a shortage crisis. It directs the President to draft emergency conservation contingency plans, subject to Congressional approval. The President may then activate the plan if he finds it required by a "severe energy supply interruption" or to meet U.S. obligations under the International Energy Program. In March, 1979, three years after EPCA was enacted, the Administration submitted three Standby Conservation Plans to Congress:

Emergency Weekend Gasoline Restrictions (Plan No. 1); Emergency Building Temperature Restrictions (Plan No. 2); and Emergency Advertising Lighting Restrictions (Plan No. 3). Congress approved only Plan No. 2, which is now in effect.[176] The lawmakers disapproved the other two plans largely because of constituent protests from those sectors of the economy which would be most burdened by them.

Express statutory prohibitions of certain potentially effective measures limit the scope of the actions the President may propose. For example, no tax, surcharge or user fee may be imposed as a method of reducing demand for energy and each plan must deal with only one "logically consistent subject matter."[177]

3. EMERGENCY OPTION TO ALLOCATE AVAILABLE OIL SUPPLIES FAIRLY. The government's program to allocate scarce oil supplies is generally found in the EPAA's mandatory price and allocation rules. An important additional allocation measure—the rationing of gasoline—is also available. The President is authorized to develop a rationing plan, subject to Congressional approval, and he may activate the plan in a "severe supply interruption," but again he must have Congressional approval. On March 8, 1979, the President submitted such a rationing plan to Congress, but it was disapproved. A second rationing plan was approved in 1980.

4. Technology Advancement

Another major effort involves the subsidization of research and development of new energy sources. Congress has declared that the nation suffers from a shortage of environmentally acceptable forms of energy, a shortage compounded by the failure to develop large domestic energy reserves of fossil fuels, geothermal, and solar energy because the unconventional energy technologies involved were deemed economically noncompetitive with traditional energy technologies. Congress therefore has contemplated a federal investment of more than $20 billion, and it has directed the administration to develop, demonstrate, evaluate for economic performance and where feasible bring to commercialization: production of low-sulfur fuels for boiler use; magnetohydrodynamic generation of electricity; coal gasification; syncrude and liquid oil from coal; syncrude from oil shale *in situ;* tidal power; geothermal power; synthetic fuels like hydrogen and methanol; fuel cells for electricity generation. Significantly, this undertaking envisions the creation of joint federal-industry corporations to manage each separate program.

In a more modest effort to stimulate reliance on new or alternate energy sources to increase domestic energy supplies, Congress amended the Federal Power Act in 1978 and also passed the Small Hydroelectric Power Projects Act. The Federal Power Act amendments aim to foster the increase of generation facilities by large electric power users by requiring electric utilities to buy and sell power from them at economical rates. Previously, utilities had market incentives not to deal with these customers, a restraint the amendments overcome by direct mandate. In large part, the "new" energy captured by the amendments is waste industrial heat used to turn a small turbine to make electricity. Other amendments foster the reopening of small hydro plants on so-called "low head" streams or falling waters. By requiring utilities to hook up to these small power producers, the amendments removed a market restraint from full development of this plentiful, cheap source of electric power. Removal of this restraint is accompanied by direct promotional assistance under the Small Hydroelectric Power Projects Act which establishes a $100 million loan project to encourage reopening or development of small hydroelectric facilities in existing dams which are not being used to generate electric power.

Notes

1. This discussion focuses on the impact of these regulatory programs on corporations, recognizing nonetheless that they apply as well to individuals and other noncorporate entities.

2. For example, California imposes additional restrictions on auto emission.

3. Executive Order No. 12092, Office of Management and Budget, "Anti-Inflation Measures Affecting Federal Contracts," 44 Fed. Reg. 1229 (1979).

4. 41 U.S.C. §35.

5. *See* pp. 155–57 *supra.*

6. Report of the Comptroller General of the United States, *Federal Regulatory Programs and Activities* (B-180224) (1978).

7. Professor Stephen Breyer of the Harvard Law School has used a taxonomy of regulation similar to that which follows to analyze whether existing regulatory programs are in fact responsive to the market failures which they are supposed to cure. *See* Breyer, *Analyzing Regulatory Failure: Mismatches, Less Restrictive Alternatives and Reform,* 92 Harv. L. Rev. 549 (1979) (hereinafter "Breyer"). *See also Report of the Commission on Law and the Economy,* American Bar Association, *Federal Regulation: Road to Reform,* chs. 3 & 4 (1979); and Committee on Governmental Affairs, U.S. Senate, 95 Cong., 2d Sess., *Framework for Regulation,* Vol. VI of the Study of Federal Regulation prepared pursuant to S. Res. 71 (1978) (hereinafter "*Framework for Regulation*").

8. *Framework for Regulation, supra* at 14.

9. Breyer, *supra* at 554.

10. *See* Executive Order No. 12092, Office of Management and Budget, "Anti-Inflation Measures Affecting Federal Contracts," 44 Fed. Reg. 1229 (1979).

11. Breyer, *supra* at 565–569.

12. Note that, in this instance, we are not referring to a license to engage in a line of business but rather to the regulation of the product in question.

13. *Framework for Regulation, supra* at 21–22.

14. *Id.*

15. 10 C.F.R. §211 (1979).

16. *Id.*

17. 16 U.S.C. §476.

18. *See* pp. 167–72 *supra.*

19. 29 U.S.C. §655(b)(7); *see, e.g.,* 29 C.F.R. §1910. 1017(e) (1979).

20. 29 C.F.R. §1904 (1979).

21. *Id.*

22. Federal Register, *Guide to Record Retention Requirements* (1978).

23. Office of Management and Budget, *Paperwork and Red Tape* (1978).

24. The Wagner Act, 29 U.S.C. §151 *et seq.*, was amended in 1947 by the Labor Management Relations Act (the "Taft-Hartley Act"), 29 U.S.C. §141 *et seq.*, which served to restrain certain union excesses in employing economic coercion. The final major addition to our labor laws was the Labor Management Reporting and Disclosure Act (the "LMRDA"), 29 U.S.C. §401 *et seq.* (which was aimed primarily at internal union abuses).

25. *See, e.g., Dal-Tex Optical Co.*, 137 NLRB 1782 (1962); *Dominican Santa Cruz Hospital*, 242 NLRB 153 (1979); and *Peerless Plywood Co.*, 107 NLRB 427 (1953).

26. *See, e.g., General Electric Co.*, 150 NLRB 192 (1964), *enforced, NLRB* v. *General Electric Co.*, 418 F.2d 736 (2d Cir. 1969), *cert. denied*, 397 U.S. 965 (1970).

27. *See, e.g., NLRB* v. *Erie Resistor Corp.*, 373 U.S. 221 (1963); *NLRB* v. *Great Dane Trailers, Inc.*, 388 U.S. 26 (1967); and *NLRB* v. *Washington Aluminum Co.*, 370 U.S. 9 (1962).

28. *Int'l Ladies' Garment Workers' Union* v. *NLRB*, 366 U.S. 731 (1961).

29. *See, e.g., Lehigh Portland Cement Co.*, 101 NLRB 529 (1952), *enforced*, 205 F.2d 821 (4th Cir. 1953); *Gulf Power Co.*, 156 NLRB 622 (1966), *enforced*, 384 F.2d 822 (5th Cir. 1967); and *Fibreboard Paper Prods. Corp.*, 138 NLRB 550 (1962), *enforced*, 322 F.2d 411 (D.C. Cir. 1963), *aff'd*, 379 U.S. 203 (1964).

30. *Griggs* v. *Duke Power Co.*, 401 U.S. 424 (1971).

31. 29 C.F.R. §1600 *et seq.* (1979).

32. *See, e.g., Albemarle Paper Co.*, v. *Moody*, 422 U.S. 405 (1975); *Griggs* v. *Duke Power Co., supra.*

33. 29 C.F.R. §1607 (1979).

34. 29 C.F.R. §1601 (1979).

35. 41 C.F.R. §60 (1979).

36. *Schultz* v. *Wheaton Glass Co.*, 421 F.2d 259 (3d Cir.), *cert. denied*, 398 U.S. 905 (1970); *Usery* v. *Columbia University*, 568 F.2d 953 (2d Cir. 1977).

37. *Hodgson* v. *Robert Hall Clothes, Inc.*, 473 F.2d 589 (3d Cir.), *cert. denied*, 414 U.S. 866 (1973).

38. 29 C.F.R. §800 (1979).

39. M. Ashford, *Crisis in the Workplace* 47 (1976).

40. 29 U.S.C. §655, 657, 658, 659.

41. 29 U.S.C. §661.

42. 29 U.S.C. §669–671.

43. 29 U.S.C. §656(a).

44. 29 U.S.C. §654(a).

45. 29 U.S.C. §652(8).

46. 29 U.S.C. §655(a).

47. 29 C.F.R. §1910.212(a) (1979).

48. 43 Fed. Reg. 49726 (1978).

49. 29 U.S.C. §655(b) (5).

50. *Industrial Union Dep't, AFL-CIO* v. *API*, 100 S.Ct. 2844 (1980).

51. *Marshall* v. *Barlow's, Inc.*, 436 U.S. 307 (1978).

52. 436 U.S. at 321.

53. 29 C.F.R. §1904 (1979).

54. Envir. Rep. (BNA), *Current Developments*, at 1378–79 (Dec. 1, 1978).

55. *Id.* at 1311.

56. The Business Roundtable, *Cost of Government Regulations Study*, Executive Summary, at 25–26 (March 1979). This study reflected the experiences of only a small sample of large firms; thus, the total expenditures were undoubtedly much higher.

57. 42 U.S.C. §4321 *et seq.*

58. 35 Fed. Reg. 15623 (1970).

59. 42 U.S.C. §6901 *et seq.*

60. 42 U.S.C. §4901 *et seq.*

61. 7 U.S.C. §135 *et seq.*

62. 16 U.S.C. §1451 *et seq.*

63. 15 U.S.C. §2601 *et seq.*

64. 42 U.S.C. §7409.

65. 42 U.S.C. §7407.

66. 40 C.F.R. Part 50 (1979).

67. A State Implementation Plan (SIP) must be submitted within nine months of the promulgation of an NAAQS for a given pollutant. The first such plans, for the original six regulated pollutants, were due January 31, 1972. EPA has four months in which to review the plans and approve, partially approve, or disapprove each. If EPA partially approves or disapproves a plan, the state must resubmit an entirely approvable plan within two months. If that does not occur, EPA must itself promulgate a plan sufficient to attain and maintain the standards. Despite this careful system, no plan, state or EPA, has ever provided for attainment and maintenance of all the NAAQS.

68. *See* 42 U.S.C. §§7501–7508.

69. *See* 41 Fed. Reg. 55524 (1976), *modified*, 44 Fed. Reg. 3274 (1979).

70. 42 U.S.C. §§7470–7479.

71. 42 U.S.C. §7411.

72. 42 U.S.C. §7420.

73. 33 U.S.C. §1251 *et seq.*

74. 33 U.S.C. §1251.

75. 33 U.S.C. §1311.

76. 33 U.S.C. §§1311 and 1342.

77. 33 U.S.C. §1316(a) (1).

78. 33 U.S.C. §§1317(a) (1) and (2).

79. 33 U.S.C. §§1317(b) (1) and 1284(b).

80. 33 U.S.C. §1288.

81. 33 U.S.C. §1344.

82. Federal Trade Commission Act, 15 U.S.C. §41 *et seq.*

83. *See* E. W. Kintner, *A Primer of the Laws of Deceptive Practices* 407–408 (1971); Federal Trade Commission Office of Policy and Planning, *Compliance and Enforcement Manual* 101–105 (1979).

84. Federal Trade Commission Act, 15 U.S.C. §41 *et seq.*

85. 15 U.S.C. §45.

86. Pub. Law 93-637, 88 Stat. 2183.

87. 15 U.S.C. §45.

88. *Pfizer, Inc.*, 81 F.T.C. 23 (1972).

89. 43 Fed. Reg. 17967 (1978).

90. In this regard the Commission also has under consideration rules dealing with the advertising of food, antacids, and over-the-counter drugs. It already has consummated rules in-

volving advertisements for ophthalmic goods and services and vocational schools.

91. 15 U.S.C. §45.

92. 16 C.F.R. 239 (1979).

93. Pub. Law 93-637, 88 Stat. 2183.

94. Federal Fair Packaging and Labeling Act, 15 U.S.C. §1451 *et seq.*

95. Wool Products Labeling Act, 15 U.S.C. §68.

96. Textile Fiber Products Identification Act, 15 U.S.C. §70.

97. Hobby Protection Act, 15 U.S.C. §2101 note.

98. Energy Policy and Conservation Act, 42 U.S.C. §6201 *et seq.*

99. Product Safety Letter No. 18, at 4 (April 30, 1979).

100. Consumer Product Safety Act, 15 U.S.C. §2056.

101. *See* 16 C.F.R. §§1201-02, 1205, 1207, 1209 (1979).

102. Standards for bicycles, children's sleepwear, electrically operated toys and upholstered furniture are either completed or are in process under other statutes administered by the Commission.

103. *See* 16 C.F.R. §§1301–1302, 1305 (1979).

104. 42 Fed. Reg. 30296 (1977).

105. Consumer Product Safety Act, 15 U.S.C. §2064.

106. *Id.* at §2064(d).

107. Consumer Product Safety Act, 15 U.S.C. §2061.

108. Federal Hazardous Substances Act, 15 U.S.C. §1261.

109. Poison Prevention Packaging Act, 15 U.S.C. §1471.

110. Lead-Based Paint Poisoning Prevention Act, 42 U.S.C. §4821.

111. Equal Credit Opportunity Act, 15 U.S.C. §1691.

112. Fair Credit Reporting Act, 15 U.S.C. §§1681–1681t.

113. Truth in Lending Act, 15 U.S.C. §1601.

114. Fair Debt Collection Practices Act, 15 U.S.C. §1692.

115. Fair Credit Billing Act, 15 U.S.C. §§1666–1666j.

116. National Banks Act, 12 U.S.C. §21.

117. *See, e.g.,* Fair Credit Billing Act, 15 U.S.C. §1666, which provides:

(a) This part does not annul, alter, or affect, or exempt any person subject to the provisions of this part from complying with, the laws of any State with respect to credit billing practices, *except to the extent that those laws are inconsistent with any provision of this part, and then only to the extent of the inconsistency.* The [Federal Reserve] Board is authorized to determine whether such inconsistencies exist. The Board may not determine that any State law is inconsistent with any provision of this part if the Board determines that such law gives greater protection to the consumer. (Emphasis added.)

118.   Equal Credit Opportunity Act, 15 U.S.C. §§1691–1691f.

119.   Federal Home Loan Mortgage Disclosure Act, 12 U.S.C. §2801.

120.   Fair Housing Act, 42 U.S.C. §§3601–3619.

121.   Fair Credit Reporting Act, *supra*.

122.   Truth in Lending Act, *supra*.

123.   Fair Credit Billing Act, *supra*.

124.   The retail installment sales acts of some states, which govern the sale of consumer goods and services, permit delinquency charges as well as the recovery of costs incurred in regaining the security for the debt. Such charges include repossession, reconditioning, and storage. In some states, Motor Vehicle Finance Acts permit a charge for the collection of delinquent payments and for the repossession of a motor vehicle to be included in the finance charges, or to be imposed as an alternative to the delinquency charge.

125.   16 C.F.R. §429.1(b) (1979).

126.   *See, e.g.*, N.Y. Pers. Prop. Law §426 *et seq.* (McKinney 1979).

127.   The "holder-in-due-course" doctrine, recognized by common law and the Uniform Commercial Code, provided that a third-party purchaser or holder of a negotiable instrument is entitled to payment by the signer regardless of any claims or defenses the signer may have against the seller of the goods. Thus, even if goods delivered turned out to be defective or other than those actually purchased, the buyer who signed the negotiable instrument (*e.g.*, an installment contract) would nonetheless be bound to pay a third party who obtained the instrument from the original seller in the ordinary course of business.

128.   *See* Preservation of Consumers' Claims and Defenses, 16 C.F.R. §433 (1979).

129.   *See, e.g.*, Connecticut Retail Installment Sales Financing Act, Conn. Gen. Stat. §42-83 *et seq.*

130. *See, e.g.*, Mass. Gen. Laws, ch. 93, §24.

131. *See generally* 15 U.S.C. §1692.

132. *See, e.g.*, N.Y. Gen. Bus. Law §600 *et seq.* (McKinney 1979).

133. *See First National Bank of Boston* v. *Bellotti,* 435 U.S. 765 (1977).

134. Federal Election Campaign Act, 2 U.S.C. §§431–456.

135. *Id.* §441b(b) (4). The new restrictions were enacted by Congress in response to the Federal Election Commission's Advisory Opinion No. 1975-23, 40 Fed. Reg. 56584 (1975), which had permitted the Sun Oil Company to use its general funds to administer its political action committee, to solicit contributions from stockholders and *all* employees, and to establish multiple PAC's each with separate contributions and expenditure limits.

136. *See* Federal Election Campaign Act, 2 U.S.C. §§437g(a) (7), 441j(a).

137. *See, e.g.*, Mass. Gen. Laws, ch. 55 §8 (corporate campaign contributions prohibited); Ga. Code §40.3808.2 (contributions from agents of public utility corporations prohibited).

138. *See, e.g.*, Iowa Code §56.29.3.

139. *See, e.g.*, Del. Code Ann., tit. 15 §8004.

140. 2 U.S.C. §§261–270.

141. *United States* v. *Harris,* 347 U.S. 612 (1954).

142. 2 U.S.C. §266(a).

143. *Id.* §264(a).

144. *Id.*

145. *Id.*

146. *See, e.g.*, N.Y. Leg. Law §1 (McKinney 1979).

147. 50 U.S.C. App. §§2401–2413.

148. *Id.* at §2407(a).

149. *See* 1977 U.S. Code Cong. & Adm. News, at 362, 365–367.

150. 50 U.S.C. App. §2407(a) (1) (A)–(F).

151. *Id.*

152. *Id.* at §2407(b).

153. *Id.* at §2410.

154. *Id.* §1 *et seq.*

155. 15 C.F.R. §399 (1979).

156. National Energy Conservation Policy Act, 42 U.S.C. §8201 *et seq.;* Power Plant and Industrial Fuel Use Act of 1978, 42 U.S.C. §8301 *et seq.;* Natural Gas Policy Act of 1978, 15 U.S.C. §3301 *et seq.;* Public Utility Regulatory Policies Act

of 1978, 16 U.S.C. §2601; Small Hydroelectric Power Projects Act of 1978, 16 U.S.C. §2701; National Energy Tax Act of 1978, 26 U.S.C. §§46, 4483.

157. Trans-Alaska Pipeline Act, 43 U.S.C. §1651 *et seq.;* Federal Energy Administration Act of 1974, 15 U.S.C. §761 *et seq.;* Energy Supply and Environmental Act of Coordination 1974, 15 U.S.C. §791 *et seq.;* Geothermal Energy Research, Development, and Demonstration Act of 1974, 30 U.S.C. §1121; Solar Energy Research, Development, and Demonstration Act of 1974, 42 U.S.C. §§5553, 57, 58; Non-Nuclear Energy Research and Development Act of 1974, 42 U.S.C. §5901 *et seq.;* Energy Reorganization Act of 1974, 42 U.S.C. §5801 *et seq.* (creating the Energy Research and Development Administration and the Nuclear Regulatory Commission); Energy Policy and Conservation Act of 1975, 42 U.S.C. §6201 *et seq.;* Energy Conservation and Production Act of 1976, 42 U.S.C. §§6211, 6219, 6325–27, 6801–17, 6831–40, 6861–72, 6881, 6861, 6892; Department of Energy Organization Act of 1977, 42 U.S.C. §7201 *et seq.;* Solar Photovoltaic Energy Research Development and Demonstration Act of 1978, 42 U.S.C. §5501 *et seq.;* Electric & Hybrid Vehicle Research Development and Demonstration Act, 15 U.S.C. §2501; Alaska Natural Gas Transportation, 15 U.S.C. §719 *et seq.;* Energy Extension Service in Energy Research and Development Administration, 42 U.S.C. §7001 *et seq.;* Non-Nuclear Energy Research and Development, 42 U.S.C. §5901 *et seq.*

158. 49 U.S.C. §1 *et seq.* The constitutionality of the Hepburn Act was upheld in *The Pipeline Cases,* 234 U.S. 548 (1914).

159. 15 U.S.C. §715. Implementing regulations appear at 30 C.F.R. §222 (1979).

160. 19 U.S.C. §1352a, repealed by Pub. L. 87-794 (1962).

161. 19 U.S.C. §1862.

162. Pres. Proc. No. 4341, Jan. 23, 1975, 40 Fed. Reg. 3965 (1975); Pres. Proc. No. 4355, Mar. 4, 1975, 40 Fed. Reg. 10437 (1975). Presidential Authority under the Trade Expansion Act of 1962 to "adjust imports" by imposing fees was upheld in *Federal Energy Administration* v. *Algonquin SNG, Inc.,* 426 U.S. 548 (1976).

163. 15 U.S.C. §§717–717w.

164. 15 U.S.C. §3301 *et seq.*

165. 42 U.S.C. §8301 *et seq.*

166. 15 U.S.C. §751 *et seq.*

167. 42 U.S.C. §6383.

168. 16 U.S.C. §2601 *et seq.*

169. 15 U.S.C. §2001 *et seq.* 49 C.F.R. §531 (1979).

170. *See, e.g., Automotive Fuel Economy and Emissions Experimental Data* (DOT 1979); *Fuel Economy and Emission Control* (EPA 1972).

171. 15 U.S.C. §2002.

172. 42 U.S.C. §6214.

173. 42 U.S.C. §§6240–41.

174. 50 U.S.C. App. §2071(c).

175. 42 U.S.C. §8374(b).

176. 42 U.S.C. §8374(a).

177. 42 U.S.C. §6262(a) (2).

5

The Constraining Influence of Social Values on Corporate Decision Making

Economic and legal forces do not constitute the only constraints on corporations, and this book would be incomplete without a discussion of the pressures which increasingly are being brought to bear on the large corporation by its various constituencies to act in ways not necessarily mandated as an economic or legal matter.[1] By "constituencies," we mean those elements in society which have (or assert they have) a proximate stake in what the corporation does, including, in addition to shareholders, such organizations as church groups; trade associations; consumers; consultants; employees; the news media; environmental, energy and other special interest groups; the "intellectual community," etc.[2]

Corporations obviously cannot accommodate every interest of every constituency. As discussed in Chapter 1, the role of corporate officers (consistent with their own moral and ethical values) is to manage the corporation in the best interest of the company's shareholders, to whom they are legally accountable as fiduciaries. But it is also clear that corporate managers are and must be attuned to social concerns, and that they have increasingly construed their fiduciary responsibilities as including the recognition of changing public attitudes concerning the social impact and role of the large corporation.[3]

Corporations will be attentive to social concerns for a variety of reasons. For one thing, as members of society themselves, a corporation's managers will frequently share in social values espoused by a constituency and, indeed, may be leaders in promoting national and local interests espoused by constituencies. Secondly, in many situations it will be important as a business matter for the corporation to demonstrate voluntary responsiveness to social concerns (this would appear to be particularly true for corporations heavily engaged in consumer product fields as well as for government contractors). Moreover, even with respect to issues which on their face may be antithetical to the interests of the corporation, its managers may go a great distance toward meeting constituency pressures in order to avoid the possibility of adverse public opinion or of more far-reaching government intervention if the matter is a likely candidate for legislation or administrative rulemaking.

Thus, as the following discussion of some of the more important corporate constituencies will illustrate, corporations are in fact subject to many constraining pressures which cannot readily be classified as economic or legal, but which derive from its important role in society generally.

Public Opinion and News and Broadcast Media

Public opinion exercises a constraining force upon the large corporation in three basic ways. It establishes the intellectual and moral environment within which corporate managers formulate their own views of corporate responsibility; it establishes in the mind of corporate managers the likely expectations of shareholders with respect to the corporation's economic and social performance; and it defines the public will to which government officials must be responsive if they want to remain in office.

The strength of public opinion will, of course, vary with each corporate policy issue. Sometimes a controversial issue will split the public into near equally-divided camps (e.g., affirmative action). Other times, however, a public consensus will emerge and this consensus will be influential in shaping corporate decision making (e.g., pollution control).

The sources of public opinion relied upon by the corporation are varied in scope—ranging from detailed opinion research and polling to subjective evaluations contained in news magazines and other popular commentary. Together, these diverse signals provide management with a reading on public opinion that is factored into the corporate decision making process.

Closely aligned with public opinion in its influence upon the corporation are the diverse pressures that emanate from news and broadcast media coverage. The principal means by which the media constrain corporate power is through their coverage of national and local corporate policy issues. Both their selection of particular events to cover and the consequent public exposure given to pressure groups can have an important impact on public opinion and, hence, corporate decision making.

231

Television, for example, provides an almost instant exposure of ideas and events which might otherwise remain obscure; so does investigative reporting, which is another significant source of media influence. Such media focus upon areas of corporate behavior can help contribute (as it did in the case of revelations of foreign bribery) to a public consensus for new statutes and regulations prohibiting such conduct. Here, much the same "disclosure policy" operates as in the area of securities law discussed in Chapter 2 above.

The media can also have a significant influence on public opinion and corporate behavior through editorial policies. Strong editorial concern over a particular corporate policy can help turn the tide of public opinion against it and give added attention to significant issues.

There is a longstanding opposition of interests between business and the news and broadcast media. From the corporate viewpoint, the media are often charged with biased reporting. The remarks of Louis Banks illustrate this perception:

> The news industry—television, radio, magazine, newspaper —stands as the principal arbiter of social attitudes toward business (and all institutions). Broadly speaking, mass media news selection and interpretation feeds the public's suspicions about corporate practice (with a certain amount of help from corporate malefactors), and interprets corporate affairs with a negative bias. This situation has prompted the choruses of antimedia hates that dominate many business panel sessions and conversations. . . .
>
> There is . . . a longstanding bias against corporate business in the general media. . . . The reasons are complicated and range from simple ignorance of corporate practice to a mindless pursuit of the kinetic or sensational.[4]

Another view is expressed by those, like Thomas Griffith, who believe that much of what businessmen perceive as bias:

. . . involves nothing more than a conscientious reporter trying to deal with some large and sensitive issues. Certainly the press mirrors, and at times tends to magnify, a number of broad American concerns about business—concerns about the durability of products and the trustworthiness and availability of service; worries about what business does to the environment; feelings about the unreachable impersonality of corporations as they become larger and computerized.[5]

Some of the perceptions that media are antibusiness may also be due to the inherent limitations on the ability of a mass news medium to deal accurately with complex problems in a short space. Business reporters on smaller newspapers, for instance, generally have little business savvy and often would rather be doing more "exciting" reporting. This same sort of observation has also been applied to television's coverage of business.[6]

Whatever the reason, however, it is clear that media coverage of corporate policy issues is often highly critical and that, given the wide dissemination of a media report, the prospect of hostile press reports must be taken into account by corporate management in the decision-making process. In this connection, moreover, many managers have concluded that they must try to respond in an active and systematic way to both general and specific media criticism by their own issue-oriented publicity —in the form of advertisements and other devices— which attempts to refute alleged factual and interpretive inaccuracies and to present the business viewpoint to the public on specific issues.[7]

Industry Associations

Within the category of industry associations are several distinct groups, each having varying degrees of influence on the activities of the business community. The influence these groups command stems from a number of sources, including the peer pressures which one executive can place upon another and the wide variety of informal and formal self-regulatory systems that have been established within these organizations.

One of the primary sources of industry association influence is the role which many of these organizations fulfill as standard-setting bodies. Several types of industry standard-setting bodies can be identified. One is the general industry self-regulatory group, in which rules of corporate behavior are established by members of the industry. Such groups[8] are frequently formed in response to the pressure of government officials and/or other corporate constituencies, and they often promulgate standards designed to make corporate behavior more socially responsible.

A second type of standard-setting group consists of industry organizations or professional associations which set professional or product standards that directly affect the industries in which their members are involved. The emphasis here is normally on product quality and safety —with standard-setting or certification programs (consistent with overriding antitrust strictures) generally establishing appropriate criteria of minimum acceptability and providing a basis for consumers intelligently to compare product performance (i.e., by being able to identify products which do and do not meet established standards). Examples of groups which fall into this category include: the Technical Association of the Pulp and Paper Industry, the American Institute of Aeronautics and Astronautics, the American Boilers' Manufacturing Association, the Public Relations Society of America, the American Society of Testing Materials, the American Society of Mechanical Engineers, the Financial Accounting

Standards Board, the Laser Institute of America, the Society for Industrial and Applied Mathematics, and the National Society of Professional Engineers. Thus, the Technical Association of the Pulp and Paper Industry does research and testing and develops quality criteria for a variety of products associated with its industry. Similarly, as discussed in Chapter 2, the Financial Accounting Standards Board, by establishing generally accepted accounting principles binding on all certified public accountants, significantly limits the accounting practices which may be used by publicly-held corporations (which must use CPA's to audit their operations).

In some cases, government regulation will enhance the influence of a private standard-setting group by either specifically sanctioning its existence (as the Securities Exchange Act does for associations regulating over-the-counter stockbrokers)[9] or adopting rules which enhance its power (as the SEC's Accounting Series Release No. 150 does for the FASB by stating that accounting principles inconsistent with those promulgated by the FASB are deemed to lack authoritative support).[10]

Other forms of influence upon corporate behavior are provided by general business organizations, such as the U.S. Chamber of Commerce, The Business Roundtable, The National Association of Manufacturers, and trade associations such as the American Petroleum Institute, the American Tobacco Institute, the Atomic Industrial Forum and the American Paper Institute. Although the primary objective of these groups is generally to serve as informational conduits between industry and government, they frequently serve as important focal points for the development of a response to constituency demands. Thus, the Council of the International Chamber of Commerce in 1972, adopted "Guidelines for International Investment" which appear to have led a number of multinational corporations to formulate policy statements and adopt regulations concerning the ethics of business conduct abroad. In a similar vein, The Business Roundtable has responded to SEC proposals for new corporate governance regulations with a set of recommendations of its own for voluntary corporate action to increase the independence of boards of directors.[11]

Employees

The power of unions to constrain corporate behavior is widely acknowledged, and the legal basis for these restrictions is described in the previous chapter. Union organization, however, is not the only source of employee influence upon corporate policy.

To begin with, a corporation is run by people—people who possess attitudes and ethical norms which influence their daily activities. While individual managers are not likely to keep their jobs if social policies become their exclusive concern, corporate policy still reflects the changing expectations which managers have about the proper role of their business in society. If action is proposed which offends the norms and values of top management (a proposal, for example, to market a patently unsafe product), such managers are likely to argue for an alternative course of conduct. For example, the chief executive of Eberhard Faber, Inc. was overruled by his board of directors on ethical grounds when on behalf of management he advocated a business relationship with a foreign company which was bribing officials of its government (even though such activity would not have subjected Eberhard to any legal exposure).[12]

Further, although top management will normally set the ethical tone for the corporation as a whole, the ethical norms of lower level employees also serve to constrain corporate behavior. Thus, if upper management ignores its employees' values and engages in conduct which they question on ethical (or legal) grounds, they risk being confronted by "whistle blowers" seeking the attention of the media as well as government officials.

The influence of employees' ethical norms on corporate decision making is further enhanced by the increasing number of professionals hired by large corporations to engage in "public affairs" or "social responsibility" work. Since their job is to identify and interpret changing constituency demands upon business, and to work with organizations in the community, they devote much of their time to examining changing public expectations about corporate behavior, and they will frequently recommend alterations in corporate practices to satisfy these expectations.

Employees also exercise appreciable influence upon corporate activity with respect to their daily working conditions. Aside from traditional union activity, employees are able to assert such constraints through both their individual demands in the job market and the activities of new organizations—such as "Nine to Five" in Boston, "Women Employed" in Chicago, "Women Working" in Cleveland, and "Women Office Workers" in New York—which represent women clerical workers and seek improvements in their working conditions.[13] With respect to professionals and management employees, an increasing number of qualified executives are willing to change jobs frequently in response to competitive offers, and thereby create pressure for desirable working conditions which a corporation must offer if it is to attract top-level personnel. In general, a major change appears to be taking place in the American work ethic which will undoubtedly influence corporate behavior. Today, many if not most employees are looking for more than salary and advancement from their jobs—expanding their expectations to include a greater hand in decision making, job sharing, "pleasant" working conditions, more time off, "no smoking" areas, and other quality-of-life factors.[14] Corporations will have no choice but to take account of these changing values as more workers make them important employment criteria.

Shareholders and Institutional Investors

The primary constituency of the corporation is, of course, its shareholders. As discussed in Chapter 1, organic corporate law mandates that a corporation's board of directors be elected by the company's shareholders, that these directors be responsive to shareholder interests, and that corporate decisions altering the basic structure of the corporation be subjected to shareholder vote.[15]

Moreover, as previously described in Chapter 2, shareholder decisions to buy and sell in the capital markets provide a significant constraint upon corporate power. These decisions reflect a judgment on the comparative financial performance of individual corporations and other investment opportunities—with the price of a company's stock and its ability to raise capital at a reasonable cost directly dependent upon the market's (i.e., investor's) evaluation of its prospects for success or failure. Shareholders thus wield considerable influence over corporate behavior which they are able to exercise by selling their shares when they are dissatisfied with managerial performance.

In recent years, many nonprofit institutional investors, such as churches, independent foundations, universities and employee pension funds, have extended the traditional financial criteria for determining when to buy or sell shares to include an evaluation of a company's social policies (e.g., environmental, employment, etc.). Several universities, for example, have recently sold their holdings in companies with investments in South Africa because of that country's policy of apartheid. This inclusion of nonfinancial criteria in the decision to buy or sell shares could, if followed widely, "internalize" the achievement of social and political objectives into the operation of the capital markets and bring to bear the discipline of the market to lower the stock price of companies which do not behave in a manner deemed by such investors to be socially responsible.

Similarly, many labor unions which control their members' pension funds have become increasingly active in using their stock interests to influence corporate behavior. Some unions, for example, have developed lists of companies whose labor policies are not approved of and whose stock they will not own. In the case of the J. P. Stevens Company, the Amalgamated Clothing and Textile Workers (ACTW) used a more indirect form of pressure—threatening the withdrawal of their pension funds from the Manufacturers Hanover Trust Company if that institution did not sever its directorial ties with J. P. Stevens. Similar pressure was applied by ACTW—by threatening adverse publicity and hostile nominations to the board of directors—to Avon and New York Life, with the result that the CEO's of both these companies resigned from the J. P. Stevens board.[16]

Another source of investor pressure upon large corporations is provided by banks, insurance companies, and other financial institutions. Increasingly, such institutions are asking for the disclosure of not only financial information, but "social responsibility" information as well (and thus indirectly for improved social performance). Moreover, as indicated in Chapter 2, the kind of "social responsibility" information that is considered by the SEC to be legally material to investment decisions is expanding, largely because regulatory and other social policy limits on corporate behavior have multiplied in number and significance—increasing the potential liability of corporations which do not perform in a socially responsible fashion.[17]

A number of insurance and investment companies, such as Equitable Life Assurance, Aetna Life and Casualty, Prudential, Travelers, St. Paul Companies, Connecticut Mutual Life, Bank of America, Citibank, Chemical Bank, and Rainier National Bank, have recently started to use social impact criteria in determining where to invest their funds. Some have set aside special categories of investment that the company is willing to undertake at lower return (or greater risk) than it would normally be willing to undertake, on the grounds of positive social return and the consequent long-term financial benefits that are likely to be derived from a positive social performance.

Similarly, several mutual funds have been established which have the express purpose of investing only in companies which provide some "social return." The best-known example is the Dreyfus Third Century Fund, which selects investments on the basis of their "leadership in, or . . . concern for, improving the quality of life in America."[18] Although many of these funds have not done well in the prevailing "bear market" over the last few years, Dreyfus Third Century is still in operation, and its performance has surpassed that of the "average" Dow Jones stock.

Investors can further constrain corporate behavior through the introduction of shareholder resolutions. Although these resolutions rarely pass, they can influence corporate decision making by publicly calling an issue to the corporation's attention, and providing a forum for the expression of constituency concerns. Thus, many times the introduction of a resolution will induce management to negotiate with the shareholder proponents, even though the resolution has little chance of being passed.[19] "Public interest proxy tactics" originated in 1967 with the efforts of a group named FIGHT, in Rochester, New York, to use proxy votes to compel Eastman Kodak Company to change certain employee policies which were regarded as discriminatory. "Campaign GM" in 1970 was one of the better-known subsequent shareholder fights.[20]

In recent years, the introduction of shareholder resolutions on both financial and social policy issues has become much more frequent and effective.[21] Such resolutions have covered a wide variety of issues—including corporate investment policies in South Africa, equal employment opportunity, compliance with the Arab boycott of Israel, the manufacture of antipersonnel weapons, the sponsorship of TV violence, TV advertising to children, corporate environmental practices, and corporate policies with respect to dividends, pensions, executive salaries, and other financial matters. Many large corporations have found that it is in their best interest to respond to such resolutions whenever possible, and to endorse their enactment when they believe they embody worthwhile suggestions.[22]

The influence and power of activist shareholders have been enhanced by the receptive attitude of many nonprofit institutional investors which own sizeable blocks of corporate stock. Responding sometimes to activist shareholders and sometimes to pressures within their own organizations, these groups, as noted above, are able to influence corporate policies and practices through their decision to buy and sell stocks, the leverage of the proxy vote, and related communications on proxy resolutions. Indeed, the Wall Street Rule—"vote with management or sell"—no longer holds firm for many nonprofit institutional investors with regard to proxy voting. The Investor Responsibility Research Center, an organization which monitors and reports on social policy issues for investment institutions, reports that most institutions responding to its surveys indicate that they now consider social policy resolutions on a case by case basis, rather than automatically supporting the position of management.[23] Indeed, some institutional investors, such as certain church groups, are inclined to initiate social policy resolutions of their own—further enhancing the importance of these investors as an influence upon corporate policy.

The "Intellectual Community"

One of the more amorphous groups that has a constraining influence on corporate behavior is what some have called the "intellectual community." As usually defined, this constituency consists of academics, students, authors, professionals, artists, and other well-educated citizenry who, through the generation and dissemination of ideas, have a substantial influence on what many members of society in general say and do. Characterized as "intellectuals" by Joseph Schumpeter[24] and the "new class" by Irving Kristol,[25] this group has articulated economic and social precepts which often diverge from those which motivated and are reflected in organic corporate chartering legislation.

Although this group usually lacks direct political power, it often provides staff members for political par-

ties, Congressional committees, and government agencies—positions distinguished in their ability to influence
how public policy is shaped. Another way the "intellectual community" can make its influence felt is through
commentary on corporate policy issues. Books such as
The Greening of America[26] by Charles Reich and John
Kenneth Galbraith's *The New Industrial State*,[27] for example, raised broad issues concerning the nature and direction of the capitalist system and the cultural values
assertedly surrounding it. In a similar vein, Barry Commoner's *The Closing Circle*,[28] Rachel Carson's empirical
study—*Silent Spring*[29]—and other such studies have focused public attention on more narrow corporate policy
issues. In each case, the ideas presented have stimulated
the interest and concern of other corporate constituencies.

Recent theories about the "intellectual community"
argue for a broad interpretation of its power. Irving Kristol has asserted that his "new class" concept extends
well outside the universities (e.g., student protests, as in
the Vietnam period) and political parties to government
and the nonprofit sector—and has, accordingly, much
more power to affect events directly:

> We are talking about scientists, teachers and educational
> administrators, journalists and others in the communication
> industries, psychologists, social workers, those lawyers and
> doctors who make their careers in the expanding public sec-
> tor, city planners, the staffs of the larger foundations, the
> upper levels of the government bureaucracy, and so on. . . .[30]

Paul Weaver links the attitudes of this class with the ex-
plosive growth in government regulatory powers over the
last two decades:

> The New Regulation . . . is the social policy of the new class
> . . . the new class is, among other things, bringing about

what Murray Weidenbaum has described as the "second managerial revolution. . . ." [That revolution is] transforming power from the managerial class to the new class, and from the quasi-public institutions to fully public ones—*i.e.*, to the government.[31]

And Kristol and others have argued that this "new class" is on the way to becoming entrenched in the regulatory functions of government, making the governmental atmosphere for regulation of business more stringent than ever before. Under this notion of a highly influential, antibusiness, "new class," the constraints the "intellectual community" imposes upon business are claimed to be enormous, amounting to nearly everything imposed through the regulatory process.

The idea of the "intellectual community" imposing such a pervasive constraint upon corporate behavior is, at a minimum, subject to some important limitations, including a basic but conceptually important "which came first—the chicken or the egg" question. Daniel Bell, for example (who is credited by some with first articulating the idea of the "new class"), has argued that the growth of government regulation is a response to "the 'systemic' impact of the structural changes in the capitalist society" rather than the activities or influences of any particular group.[32] And, in another vein, Andrew Hacker points out that whatever objective criteria one uses to describe any "new class" (of "intellectuals" or otherwise), its members will invariably consist of those who are both critical and supportive of business.[33] Thus, the number of academics who hold "free enterprise" chairs, or who are advocates of business viewpoints, to some extent offsets the impact of those who are hostile to business.

While the debate is bound to continue for some time, it does seem possible to draw some general conclusions about the impact and influence of the "intellectual community" on corporate accountability. First, ideas and the production and dissemination of information have assumed greater importance in society than ever before. Second, there has been a rise in the importance of the professions, which means a corresponding rise in the importance of the college-educated. And third, many people who may loosely be described as "intellectuals"—those who develop and disseminate ideas—do align themselves in varying degrees of opposition to traditional free enterprise values. That this is more true now than it was twenty years ago may not signal the arrival of a new antibusiness class, but it does indicate that the "intellectual community," both by dint of its ideas and the impact of those ideas on policy making, is likely to continue as an important direct and indirect influence on the corporation.

Public Interest Groups

The United States is a nation of organizations, associations, and clubs. Generally, each represents a particular —or "special"—interest. Recently, however, many organizations representing business constituencies have claimed to represent the citizenry in general (i.e., the "public interest").[34]

These self-styled "public interest" groups share several common characteristics. They generally embody a concern that the public welfare is inadequately protected and adopt for themselves a mandate to protect that welfare. They are often headed by a "charismatic" leader and are staffed by young, well-educated people (members of the intellectual "new class") dedicated to effecting change within the system. While their financing is generally modest, many receive significant support from foundations and from affluent individuals. Further, in recent years, many of these groups have become highly sophisticated in the use of experts, such as lawyers, scientists and economists, and in the use of the political process, including the media, politicians, the courts and the regulatory agencies.

Public interest groups are often advocates of different special interests (e.g., minorities, women, individuals with a special interest in the environment), and they basically seek a realignment of the power structure in favor of those interests. Frequently, different public interest groups will advocate goals which call for contradictory actions—as in the case of those who oppose nuclear power and those who support restrictive pollution control standards on the mining and burning of coal (one of the primary alternatives to nuclear power). Thus, the objectives of one public interest group will often impose substantial costs on other segments of society. Corporate managers confronted by the demands of these groups, therefore, must weigh not only the reasonableness of the proposed actions in the abstract, but also how the particular group's objectives fit within the overall fabric of economic, legal and social constraints facing the corporation.

One way to categorize public interest groups is by the subject area of their principal concern. Looking at them in this manner, four general categories can be identified.

1. Environmental and Energy Interest Groups

These groups are concerned with pollution, natural environments, conservation of natural resources, and the provision, consumption and pricing of energy. Originally, the older groups, such as the Audubon Society, Sierra Club and the National Wildlife Federation, were primarily concerned with traditional conservationist issues such as the protection of the wilderness. Recently, however, most of the older groups have broadened their agendas to include new energy-oriented issues and urban environmental concerns, and they have been joined in these causes by a multitude of new groups, such as the Clamshell Alliance and Abalone Alliance (nuclear power opposition); Environmental Action and INFORM (a range of environmental and worker health issues); the Environmental Defense Fund (lobbying and litigation on environmental issues); and the Union of Concerned Scientists.

2. Consumer Interest Groups

These groups are concerned with protecting the public from what they consider to be potentially hazardous products or fraudulent or deceptive business practices, protecting buyers from products or services which they believe do not meet reasonable quality standards, prosecuting damage suits on behalf of consumers, and demanding that more product information be made available to consumers. Ralph Nader and his affiliated group of organizations are usually credited with developing and guiding the modern consumer movement. Other major consumer groups today include: the Consumer Federation of America (CFA), the Consumers Union, Consumer Action, National Public Interest Research Group Clearinghouse, ACORN (Association for Community Organizations for Reform Now) and a variety of special issue consumer groups, such as Nutrition Action, Action for Children's Television, Action on

Smoking and Health, and Accuracy in Media, which focus upon areas of special concern to particular types of consumers (i.e., smokers, TV viewers, parents).

3. Civil Rights Groups

These organizations are concerned with all forms of civil rights issues, such as hiring, promotion, purchasing, accessibility of products and services, and community relations.

As the cause of minorities' rights has progressed in the United States, the work of the civil rights movement has expanded from the traditional, antidiscrimination activities of long-established organizations, such as the NAACP, the Urban League, and the American Civil Liberties Union, to the special interest advocacy activities of organizations like the Americans for Indian Opportunity and the National Congress of Hispanic American Citizens—whose goals are similar to, but often competitive with, those of the older groups. Other organizations have given special emphasis to particular issues, such as the pressure applied by some Jewish rights groups against corporations who have complied with the Arab boycott of Israel.

The women's movement has also accounted for a whole new set of civil rights organizations, such as the National Organization for Women (NOW), Women's Action Alliance, Catalyst, Association of Women Business Owners, and Women's Work, which focus on issues of gender discrimination. Some of the more recent Women's groups—notably the "Nine to Five" group in Boston and "Women Employed" in Chicago—have gone beyond the issue of equal access to job opportunities and lobbied for improvements in working conditions for women in cleri-

248

cal jobs, focusing particularly on banks and insurance companies.

Senior citizens have also become an important organized civil rights pressure group, represented by such entities as the National Council of Senior Citizens, the American Association of Retired Persons, and the Gray Panthers. Corporations face demands from these groups chiefly in the areas of pension rights and retirement benefits.

The areas of corporate activity which concern civil rights groups extend far beyond employment issues. Many of these groups concern themselves with such varied aspects of corporate behavior as marketing and advertising, plant site location, open housing, consumer education, credit, purchasing, insurance, banking, and opportunities for minority businesses.

In addition to such traditional tactics as public exposure, lobbying and litigation, civil rights groups often attempt to pressure individual corporations through demonstrations and other forms of activist confrontation. One prominent example is provided by the activities of PUSH (People United to Save Humanity), which obtained agreements from a number of major corporations to establish "targets" for minority hiring, promotion, purchasing, franchising, and professional services. While not all of the goals which have been set forth in these and similar agreements have been achieved, the very *process* of confrontation, negotiation, and compromise engaged in by PUSH has caused the target companies—and others who were watching the process—to consider whether changes in their policies with respect to minority hiring may be warranted in light of changing social expectations.

4. General Public Interest Organizations

These groups have diverse interests and purport to be concerned with all aspects of the public weal. Though originally associated with law firms, law schools and students who engaged in *pro bono publico* activities, general public interest organizations now include other professionals such as economists, scientists, accountants and engineers, and encompass a variety of diversified organizations, some of which specialize in particular areas and some of which do not—for example: a number of the divisions of the Nader organization (such as Congress Watch and Public Citizen, Inc.); Common Cause; the Council on Economic Priorities; Businessmen for the Public Interest; the Public Information Center; the Center for Law and the Public Interest; and Citizens Action.

Three types of general public interest organizations which are particularly active should be noted:

- *Church-related Organizations:* Over the past few years, several denominations have created organizations to study, and where necessary challenge, corporate practices in such areas as equal employment opportunity, investment decisions, and TV advertising. The leader in this area is the Interfaith Center on Corporate Responsibility, which conducts research and coordinates public interest proxy fights for a variety of church sponsored organizations.
- *"Alternative Economics" Organizations:* These organizations are suggesting alternative ways of solving political and economic problems. They include: the National Center for Economic Democracy (citizen challenges and community organizing); the Movement for Economic Justice (research); and the Exploratory Project on Economic Alternatives.
- *Public Policy Research:* Many public interest groups do research; recently, more organizations which specialize in high-quality research and analysis ("think tanks") have appeared, on both sides of the political spectrum.

Public interest group tactics range from the low-key (a private meeting with corporate executives) to the thoroughly theatrical (a demonstration in which litter is dumped on the chief executive officer's lawn to protest corporate environmental practices). Most of their strategies, however, fall within five principal categories: publicity and research; litigation; lobbying; citizen action/ community organization; and shareholder action. Many groups develop particular expertise in one tactic and concentrate their efforts there. The Council on Economic Priorities, for example, is a research-oriented group, while National People's Action (the major organization behind "redlining" challenges to banks and insurance companies) is a classic citizen action group. Of course, many groups make use of several strategies and tactics, and some, like the Association for Community Organizations for Reform Now (ACORN) and the Nader network, skillfully employ them all.[35]

Government Threats and Persuasion

While government's principal role in the area of corporate accountability is in the adoption of direct legal constraints, government officials can also apply more subtle pressures on corporations to alter their behavior in desired ways. Such informal governmental constraints, which fall short of outright regulations, can be broken down into two general categories.

1. Executive Branch "Jawboning"

The fight against inflation, and the federal government's role therein, provides the most prominent recent example of governmental "jawboning"—public and private dialogues between government officials and corporate executives in which business is "asked" to conduct its operations in a certain fashion (in the case of inflation, to hold down price increases to certain levels).[36] Such jawboning is commonly used by Executive Branch officials to seek the "voluntary" achievement of public policy objectives (e.g., energy conservation, the support of minority businesses, affirmative action in hiring) through alterations in corporate activities that are not strictly mandated by law.

The pressure for business to comply with such governmental "requests" is derived from a number of sources. First, there is the threat of new, direct, and generally more intrusive government regulation if business does not voluntarily comply. For example, former Secretary of Health, Education and Welfare Joseph Califano made it very clear that if hospitals did not "voluntarily" reduce price increases, he would propose stringent cost containment legislation; and such legislation, based on the failure of voluntary efforts at cost control, was indeed introduced in 1979.[37] Second, there is the likelihood of public disclosure of those companies that resist governmental jawboning and the adverse publicity that will accompany such disclosure. Finally, on the borderline of direct regulation, the Executive Branch may, as in the case of the current wage-price guidelines, attempt to condition the award of government contracts on business compliance with certain public policy objectives.[38]

Government jawboning is often most effective against large corporations. The reasons include the fact that it is the larger companies which usually bear the greatest brunt of new government regulation, and they also provide the most visible targets for adverse publicity (and constituency reaction). Also, precisely because of their size and visibility, noncompliance by the large corporation with well-publicized government "requests" is also more likely to arouse the interest of the media.

2. Legislative and Regulatory "Posturing"

In addition to legislative proposals which actually become law, many bills which would constrain corporate decision making are not enacted. However, in many situations the mere threat of such legislation can cause corporations to alter their behavior—through the identification of the concerns motivating those advocating the legislation and the examination of the corporation's current policies relating to the proposals. For example, even though the proposed legislation establishing a consumer protection agency was not enacted, the debate which went on around it for several years helped convince many companies to improve their "consumer response mechanisms." Similarly, recent debate over proposals for labor law reform appear to have prompted some companies to improve their employee relations. And legislative proposals to limit conglomerate mergers stimulated a wide-ranging debate and new research into the causes, costs, and benefits of such merger activity.

Moreover, legislators and other government officials can put pressure on corporations even without expressly proposing new legislation. The threat of government action, for example, is implicit every time Congressional hearings are held on corporate policy issues or a Presidential commission is created to study them. In each case, corporations are forced to analyze anew the issues raised at these hearings. Similarly, regulatory officials at many levels of government can propose rules or hold hearings on issues of direct importance to the business community. The threat of such agencies acting within their broad delegation of quasi-legislative authority can be as effective a constraint upon corporate decision making as the threat of new legislation.

Legal Counsel, Auditors, and Other Professionals

Attorneys, auditors, and other professionals have traditionally had to balance their role as their client's representative with a responsibility to counsel against unlawful (or otherwise questionable) behavior. Because of their close relationship to the corporation, these professionals are often able to win acceptance of their positions without confrontation and with substantially less resistance and delay than might accompany others advocating the same positions.

Professional influence upon the corporation stems from many sources. In the case of attorneys, it is their role as legal counsel and advisor. Many large corporations specifically look to their outside law firm to function as a sounding board and critic of their operations and, as a result, it is frequently said that the nation's business laws are more often enforced in the lawyer's office, where proposed transactions are reviewed, than in the courtroom, as a result of litigation. Outside auditors similarly constrain corporate behavior while performing their professional service—analyzing and confirming the accuracy of corporate accounts.

Other outside consultants—from general management consultants who provide advice in basic business areas, like marketing, finance, and strategic planning, to more specialized consultants, in areas like engineering, pollution control, public relations, communications, and social performance—influence corporate behavior by providing management with fresh viewpoints. Unwedded to previous corporate policies and practices, these consultants can substantially assist management in modifying outdated notions of corporate performance.

To an increasing degree, the SEC appears to view professionals as one of the front lines in the battle against securities law violations, and is looking to such persons to police corporate conduct, as well as to investigate and take affirmative corrective action. In this connection, an SEC administrative law judge has ruled that where management failed to heed an attorney's advice with respect to disclosure of the company's financial circumstances, the attorney should have so informed the board of directors;[39] and a federal district court has held that a lawyer has a special duty to insure compliance with federal and state registration requirements and to ascertain the truth of all promotional material given to investors.[40]

Notes

1. *See generally* D. Vogel, *Lobbying the Corporation: Citizen Challenges to Business Authority* (1978); Burck, *The Intricate "Politics" of the Corporation*, Fortune, at 109 (April 1975); G. Molitor, *Process of Political Innovation . . . A Corporate Response to Planning and Implementing Policy* (presented to the Industrial Management Center, Jan. 13–18, 1976).

2. Two of the corporation's most important constituencies —consumers and unions—are discussed elsewhere in this book. *See* pp. 179–97, 147–62 *supra*.

3. *See, e.g.,* Statement of The Business Roundtable, *The Role and Composition of the Board of Directors of the Large Publicly Owned Corporations* (Jan. 23, 1978) (hereinafter "Roundtable Statement"); Address by Bryan F. Smith at the Business Week Conference For Corporate Directors, *What Society Expects, and What Directors Owe to Society*, at 3-8 (New York, June 7, 1979); *Final Report of the Fifty-Fourth American Assembly* (Columbia University: April 13–16, 1978).

4. Banks, *Taking on the Hostile Media*, Harv. Bus. Rev. 125, 129 (March/April, 1978).

5. Griffith, *Must Business Fight the Press?* Fortune, at 204 (June 1974).

6. *Id.*

7. *See, e.g., Banks, supra* at 125; Menzies, *Union Carbide Raises Its Voice*, Fortune, at 86 (Sept. 25, 1978).

8. Examples of groups which fit into this category include: the National Association of Broadcasters (limitations on commercial minutes per hour; products advertised, etc.); the American Council of Life Insurers; the National Retail Merchants Association; the American Banking Association; and the Automobile Manufacturers Association.

9. *See* 15 U.S.C. §78o–3.

10. *See* SEC Accounting Release No. 150, 39 Fed. Reg. 1260 (1973).

11. *See Roundtable Statement, supra;* BNA Daily Report for Executives, at M-1 (Jan. 20, 1978).

12. Faber, *How I Lost a Great Debate About Corporate Ethics*, Fortune, at 180 (Nov. 1976).

13. *See Female Office Workers Form Groups to Fight Sex Bias, Petty Chores*, Wall Street Journal, at 1, col. 1 (Feb. 24, 1978).

14. The May 1978 issue of Psychology Today carried a series of articles entitled *Special Report: The New Job Values*, which provides a good overview of these changing employee attitudes.

15. *See* pp. 1–6 *supra*.

16. *See generally The New Strategies Unions are Trying*, Business Week, at 63 (Dec. 4, 1978).

17. See pp. 50–57 *supra*.

18. *See* B. Longstreth and H. D. Rosenbloom, *Corporate Social Responsibility and the Institutional Investor: A Report to the Ford Foundation* 20 (1973).

19. *See* D. Vogel, *supra*.

20. *See* B. Longstreth and H. D. Rosenbloom, *supra* at 1-11.

21. *See, e.g.,* N.Y. Times, Apr. 9, 1978, §F, at 1, col. 3, at 8, col. 4; *id.,* May 16, 1977, at 43, col. 2; *id.,* Jan. 23, 1977, §F, at 15, col. 3; *id.,* Aug. 31, 1976, at 41, col. 7; *id.,* Aug. 22, 1976, §F, at 13, col. 6; *id.,* Apr. 12, 1976, at 45, col. 5; *id.,* Jan. 4, 1976, §3, Part II, at 47, col.1.

22. For example, a number of managements have negotiated for the withdrawal of shareholder resolutions urging the adoption of so-called "Sullivan principles"—guidelines devel-

oped by the Rev. Leon Sullivan, founder of the National Opportunities Industrialization Center, which require a company to pledge to implement fair employment practices in South Africa, including equal pay for equal work, training for management and other skilled positions, and general improvement in the employees' quality of life. Rather than contest these resolutions, many managements have voluntarily adopted them. *See* N.Y. Times, May 16, 1977, at 43, col. 2.

23. M. O'Connor, *The 1978 Proxy Season: How Institutions Voted on Shareholder Resolutions and Management Proposals*, at 7 (Investor Responsibility Research Center, Sept. 1978).

24. J. Schumpeter, *Can Capitalism Survive?* 85 (Harper Colophon ed. 1978).

25. I. Kristol, *Two Cheers For Capitalism* (1978).

26. C. Reich, *The Greening of America* (1970).

27. J. K. Galbraith, *The New Industrial State* (3d ed. 1978).

28. B. Commoner, *The Closing Circle* (1971).

29. R. Carson, *Silent Spring* (1962).

30. I. Kristol, *supra* at 27, 28.

31. Weaver, *Regulation, Social Policy and Class Conflict*, The Public Interest, at 59 (Winter 1978).

32. Bell, *The New Class: A Muddled Concept*, Society, at 23 (Jan./Feb. 1979).

33. Hacker, *Two "New Classes" or None?*, Society, at 54 (Jan./Feb. 1979).

34. For a discussion of the origins of the public interest movement, *see generally* J. M. Berry, *Lobbying for the People* (1977).

35. *See generally*, Vogel, *supra*.

36. For a description of the "jawboning process," *see* Meadows, *The Jawboners' Earnest Exercise in Futility*, Fortune, at 48 (June 19, 1978).

37. *See* S.570, H.2626, 96th Cong., 1st Sess. (1979).

38. *See, e.g.*, 2 *Views on How Business Has Handled Carter Guidelines*, Chicago Tribune, §5, at 3 (April 29, 1979).

39. *In re Carter*, [1979 Transfer Binder] Fed. Sec. L. Rep. (CCH) ¶82,175.

40. *Felts* v. *National Account Systems Ass'n, Inc.*, 469 F.Supp. 54 (N.D. Miss. 1978).

Index

PROGRAM FOR STUDIES OF
THE MODERN CORPORATION
Graduate School of Business, Columbia University

PUBLICATIONS

FRANCIS JOSEPH AGUILAR
Scanning the Business Environment

MELVIN ANSHEN
Corporate Strategies for Social Performance

MELVIN ANSHEN, *editor*
Managing the Socially Responsible Corporation

HERMAN W. BEVIS
Corporate Financial Reporting in a Competitive Economy

COURTNEY C. BROWN
Beyond the Bottom Line

COURTNEY C. BROWN
Putting the Corporate Board to Work

COURTNEY C. BROWN, *editor*
World Business: Promise and Problems

CHARLES DE HOGHTON, *editor*
The Company: Law, Structure, and Reform

RICHARD EELLS
The Corporation and the Arts

RICHARD EELLS
The Political Crisis of the Enterprise System

RICHARD EELLS, *editor*
International Business Philanthropy

RICHARD EELLS and CLARENCE WALTON, *editors*
Man in the City of the Future

JAMES C. EMERY
Organizational Planning and Control Systems: Theory and Technology